DESCRIPTIVE LIST OF PERSIAN CORRESPONDENCE

Volume V (1805)

OTHER VOLUMES IN THE SERIES

1. Descriptive List of Persian Correspondence, Vol. I (1801) (Delhi, 1974)
2. Descriptive List of Persian Correspondence, Vol. II (1802) (Delhi, 1984)
3. Descriptive List of Persian Correspondence, Vol. III (1803) (Delhi, 1995)
4. Descriptive List of Persian Correspondence, Vol. IV (1804) (Delhi, 2004)

Descriptive List of Persian Correspondence

Volume V (1805)

Edited by

MIRZA MUMTAZ BAIG

NATIONAL ARCHIVES OF INDIA
NEW DELHI

MANOHAR
2014

First published 2014

ISBN 978-81-7304-988-0

Published by
Ajay Kumar Jain *for*
Manohar Publishers & Distributors
4753/23 Ansari Road, Daryaganj
New Delhi 110 002

Typeset by
Ajay Arts
New Delhi-110002

Printed by
Salasar Imaging Systems
Delhi-110035

Contents

Preface

The National Archives of India has a rich collection of Persian records of the East India Company, which date back to 1759. With a view to making this valuable source of information more accessible to the scholar community, it had been our endeavour to bring out its suitable reference media. In the present series of 'Descriptive List of Persian Correspondence' four volumes covering the years 1801, 1802, 1803 (in cyclostyle) and 1804 (computer generated) have already been published, and I am extremely happy to place before you the present volume, which is fifth in the series.

This volume contains 1275 rare and unpublished letters of the year 1805. These letters mainly in Persian Shikesta (cursive) throw significant light not only on diplomatic and political relations of East India Company as well as its other administrative affairs but also furnish first hand information on various small but important matters that may have not found mention in the historical studies of the period covered in this volume. These letters were exchanged between the Governor-General, the Residents, Agents, Secretary, the Commander-in-Chief and other high officials of the East India Company and the titular Mughal Emperor Shah Alam II, rulers of various Indian Princely States, Nawwabs and petty chiefs of small principalities, etc.

The correspondences also include a number of letters to and from the rulers and high officials of the neighbouring countries such as Pasha of Baghdad (56, 63, 116, 119-26, 299-303, 1077-78), King of Persia (1159-62) regarding Perso-Russian battle and Raja of Nepal, etc. Besides, a sizeable number of newsletters/intelligence reports from Patiala, Multan and Kabul are of special interest which throws light on Jaswant Rao Holkar's efforts to placate the ruler of Afghanistan to fight against the Company and restore the crumbling power of Marathas (271, 272, 291, 292, 733, 965, 975, 978, 979, 981, 983).

The opening years of nineteenth century was marked by political turmoil in India, and witnessed the concentration of power in the hands of East India Company, the campaigns of Lord Lake and Arthur Wellesley in 1803-04 had almost established the British paramountcy over a large part of north India, Deccan and Orissa and the year 1805 was destined to see the culmination of the total breakdown of the crumbling Maratha power. Consequently a number of letters incorporated in this volume contain congratulatory messages addressed by various Indian rulers, Chiefs and Dignitaries on the victory of the Company over the Marathas (52, 53,

251, 252). The year 1805 covered in this volume also saw the relentless efforts of Jaswant Rao Holkar to reorganize an anti-Company alliance of Indian rulers. Besides, intelligence reports received from various quarters of India, correspondences relating to strategic alliances, peace negotiations and treaty agreements, etc., shed significant light on the nature of contemporary statecraft, diplomacy and military affairs. I am sure that the researchers and students of history will find these documents as an authentic and first hand source to advance their studies and understanding of the course of the establishment of British paramountcy.

Before concluding, a few words about the format of this volume may be added. The format adopted in the previous volumes of this series has been retained. Illustrations of a few selected documents have been provided at the end of the volume. These, as well as other features such as highlighted references in each entry, running footnotes, page headers, etc., will certainly assist the users in consulting this volume.

Lastly, I would like to place on record my appreciation for the efforts of Shri Mirza Mumtaz Baig, Assistant Archivist (OR), who has provided a gist of each letter with suitable annotation and diligently checked and compared the text, prepared glossary of the technical terms and the nominal index. Shri Anil Kumar, UDC, typed out the manuscript diligently. I am thankful to each one of them.

This work has been carried out under the able supervision of Shri S. M. R. Baqar, Deputy Director of Archives (now retired), and Dr. Sanjay Garg, Deputy Director of Archives. I extend my complements to both of them.

MUSHIRUL HASAN
Director General of Archives,
Government of India

New Delhi

Note on Listing

1. The margin contain the date on which the letter was received/issued, while the one shown in the text appears in the documents.
2. Dates in bold type denote copy of issue (CI).
3. Personal titles, viz., Mr., Shri, etc., whether or not included in the document, have been dropped. Regal/Military titles are, however, retained.
4. Abbreviations

   AI – Abstract of Issue
   AR – Abstract of Receipt
   CI – Copy of Issue
   CR – Copy of Receipt
   OR – Original Receipt
   SI – Secretary's Issue
   TI – Translation of Issue
   TR – Translation of Receipt
   WC – With Cover
   WS – With Seal

Descriptive List of Persian Correspondence

1805

Jan. 1 1. From Nawwab Nusrat Jang of Dacca.[1] Acknowledges receipt of his (addressee) letter containing instructions regarding Nawwab Shams al-Daulah and Muhammad Taqi Khan. Refers to his (writer) letter of apology and again requests for forgiveness for not following his instructions. Dated 11 December 1804.[2]

OR 1, f 1; CR 22, pp. 1-4, no. 1; TR 51, pp. 7-9; AR 20, p. 26.

Jan. 1 2. From Nawwab Nusrat Jang of Dacca. Referring to his (writer) previous letter and solicits his (addressee) instructions for, what treatment should be given to Nawwab Shams al-Daulah when he arrives in Dacca. Also assures of his (writer) loyalty. Dated on 27 December 1804.[3]

OR 2;[4] WS, WC, f 1; CR 22, pp. 5-7, no. 2.

Jan. 1 3. From Maharaja Sundar Singh. Congratulatory with *nazr* on the occasion of *Roz-e-Kalan* (Christmas).

OR 3;[5] WS, WC, f 1; TR 51, p. 9, no. 2; AR 20, p. 31.

Jan. 2 4. Seton at Bareilly to Hastdil Shah. Acknowledging receipt of his letter informs about the defeat of Holkar near Farrukhabad

[1]Name of the writer does not appear from the OR, however, CR and TR bears the name as follows: Intazam al-Daulah Nasir al-Mulk Saiyid Ali Khan Bahadur Nusrat Jang.

[2]The date of drafting of letter appears on Copy of Receipt (CR).

[3]The date of drafting comes from CR.

[4]Enclosed with a letter from the Senior Judge at Dacca to the Persian Secretary, dated 28 December 1804. The document bears the seal of the writer on its cover.

[5]The document bears the seal of the sender on cover and also date of receipt as 1 January 1805.

and his subsequent flight to the fort of Deig and its siege by General Lake. Dated 17 December 1804.

OR 4,[1] *f 1; CR 22, pp. 7-9, no. 3(i).*

Jan. 2 5. Seton to Amar Singh Thapa.[2] Refers to the intimate friendly relation of Lord Wellesley and Raja of Nepal. Complains that Lal Singh, a *jagirdar* is supporting the Raja of Srinagar and other refractory elements in the hilly region of Srinagar. Dated 17 December 1804.

OR 5,[3] *f 1; CR 22, pp. 9-11, no. 3(2).*

Jan. 2 6. Seton to Thapa Ranchor Singh, *subahadar* (governor) of Kumaon on the part of Raja of Nepal. To the same effect as the foregoing. Dated 17 December 1804.

OR 6,[4] *f 1, CR 22, pp. 12-14, no. 3(3).*

Jan. 2 7. Seton to Chautra Hastdial Shah *naib* of Maharaja Nepal in Srinagar. To the same effect as the foregoing. Dated 17 December 1804.

OR 7,[5] *f 1, CR 22, pp. 14-16, no. 3(4).*

Jan. 2 8. Seton to Randhir Singh Kaji, an officer of Raja of Nepal, posted in Srinagar. To the same effect as the foregoing. Dated 21[6] December 1804.

OR[7] *8, f 1; CR 22, pp. 16-21, no. 3(5).*

Jan. 4 9. Intelligence report dated 10[8] *Ramazan* AH 1219 (13 December 1804) from Amritsar, regarding following matters:

(i) Death of the mother of Maharaja Saheb Singh of Patiala and his subsequent movement.

(ii) Occupation of the fort of Sahgawara by Ranjit Singh of Lahore.

(iii) Occupation of the territory of Sansar Singh of Nagarkot by Raja of Nepal.

(iv) Movement of Shah Shuja al-Mulk in Afghanistan.

[1]Copy received as enclosure to a letter from Seton.

[2]An Executive officer of the Raja of Nepal posted in Srinagar.

[3]The copy of the letter is an enclosure to a letter from Seton.

[4]Copy enclosed with a letter from Seton, dated 17 December 1804.

[5]Ibid.

[6]This date seems to be wrong as the date of drafting of the letter to which this letter is enclosed according to endorsement in English in upper part of the document is 17 December. It may be the mistake of the copier.

[7]Copy enclosed with a letter from Seton, dated 17 December 1804.

[8]TR bears 18 *Ramazan* AH 1219.

(v) Copy of the letter of Raja Saheb Singh to Col. Ochterlony for help.

(vi) Copy of letter of Kale Khan the *naib mutawassil* of the Rani of Raja Ilyas to Col. Ochterlony.

OR 9,[1] f 1; TR 51, pp. 9-14, no. 3; AR 20, p. 10.

Jan. 4 10. Intelligence report from Amritsar dated 4 *Ramazan* 1219 AH (13 December 1804). To the same effect as the foregoing.

OR 10, f 1.

Jan. 5 11. Persian Secretary to Bishambhar Pandit. Acknowledges addressee's letter regarding the writer's safe arrival at Calcutta; the gifts (elephants and jewels) along with a letter from Venkoji Bhonsla; regrets for not being able to present them to the Governor-General because of the latter's preoccupations.

SI 1, pp. 3-4, no. 2.

Jan. 5 12. Persian Secretary to Nawwab Nusrat Jang of Dacca. Complementary reply in return of the writer's safe arrival at the presidency.

SI 1, p. 4, no. 3.

Jan. 5 13. Persian Secretary to Maharaja Sunder Singh. Acknowledges the addressee's complementary letter along with *nazr* on the occasion of Christmas.

SI 1, pp. 4-5, no. 4.

Jan. 7 14. From Shams al-Nisa Begam of Awadh, widow of Asaf al-Daulah, to Col. John Collins, the Resident at Lucknow. Explains her financial difficulties, however, offers forty thousand rupees as *dastgardan* (loan) to the addressee. Also expresses her desire to visit Mecca. Dated 30 December 1804.[2]

OR,[3] ff 2; CR 22; pp. 35-38, no. 4.

Jan. 7 15. From Col. John Collins, the Resident at Lucknow to Shams al-Nisa Begam, the widow of Nawwab Asaf al-Daulah of Awadh. Acknowledges her letter and gratefully declines to accept her offer of loan. Dated 30 December 1804.[4]

OR 12, f 1; CR 22, pp. 38-39, no. 5.

[1]Copy enclosed with a letter from the Resident at Delhi to the Secretary to the Government, dated 20 December 1804.

[2]Date appearing in CR is the date of its receipt in the Resident's office.

[3]Copy (in duplicate) received with a letter from the Resident at Lucknow, dated 30 December 1804.

[4]CR bears the date 26 *Ramazan* 1219 AH (30 December 1804).

Jan. 7 16. Edmonston, the Persian Secretary to Raja of Coojan (Cuttak). Referring to his letter addressed to Governor-General points out some irregularity in its transmission and directs him (the addressee) to make all representation to Governor-General only through the Commissioner.

TI 51, p. 7, no. 1; CI 41, pp. 1-2, no. 1; AI 20, p. 61.

Jan. 8 17. From Raja Bikram Shah of Nepal. Refering to his (writer) previous letter informs that Pandit Raj Krishna has been appointed his (writer's) *wakil* at the court of Governor-General, Wellesley. Also attaches a list of goods sent as gift.

OR 13; WS, WC, ff 2; TR 51, pp. 14-16, no. 4; AR 20, p. 31.

Jan. 9 18. From Raja Mitrajit Singh of Tekari. Complementary on the eve of *Roz-e-Kalan* (Christmas day) with a *nazr* of five gold *muhrs.*

OR 14; WS, ff 2; TR 51, p. 16, no. 5; AR 20, p. 32.

Jan. 9 19. Persian Secretary to Rai Rajib Lochan. Expresses concern at the intelligence of the addressee will forward it to Jahangirnagar.

SI 1, p. 5, no. 5.

Jan. 10 20. From Saiyid Ali Khan Nusrat Jang. To the same effect as the foregoing OR 14.

OR 15,[1] WS, WC, ff 2.

Jan. 10 21. From Elphinstone, Resident at Nagpur to Raja Ganga Ram Pandit. Informs that *Pindaris* have plundered the region of Sewti Chhapra and now intend to attack addressee's area as they have moved towards west. Also assures that further information regarding their movement will be sent accordingly. Dated 29 *Shaban* 1219 AH (2 December 1804).

OR 16,[2] f 1; CR 22, pp. 100-01, no. 28(1).

Jan. 10 22. From Raja Ganga Ram Pandit to Elphinstone. Informs about the movement of a force of *Pindaris* and that of the Raja of Nagpur around Bhusdahi, Thana Borgaon and Ainikota. Also says that any information in this regard will be sent accordingly. Dated 8 December 1804.

OR 17,[3] f 1; CR 22, pp. 101-02, no. 28(2).

[1]The Original letter is accompanied by a *yaddasht* of it.

[2]Copy received with a letter from Elphinstone, the President at Nagpur.

[3]Copy received to a letter from Raja Ganga Ram Pandit to Elphinstone.

Jan. 10 23. From Elphinstone to Ganga Ram Pandit. Acknowledges receipt of his letter with the news of devastation of the villages of the addressee's territory by Raghuji Bhonsla's force. Referring to their previous talk says that instructions have been sent to Sakha Ram Bakhshi regarding placement of forces in village Chhapra and Sankora, etc. Also says that if Raghuji Bhonsla sticks to his words he would travel tornorrow to visit that side. Dated 7 December 1804.

OR 18, f 1; CR 22, pp. 102-03, no. 28(3).

Jan. 10 24. Elphinstone to Ganga Ram Pandit. Acknowledges his letter. Referring to the presence of *Pindaris* in village Bhusdahi. Says that responsibility of that area lies with the Raja (of Nagpur, Bhonsla). Also informs about the movement of *Pindaris* from addressee's territory to Berar and suggest arranging for the safety of his area. Dated 9 December 1804.

OR 19,[1] f 1; CR 22, p. 103, no. 28(4).

Jan. 10 25. From Raja Ganga Ram Pandit to Elphinstone. Acknowledging his letters informs that the two letters addressed to Amrit Rao is being sent to him at Amrawati and the reply, as soon as it is received will be dispatched. Also describes the devastation of Ainikota and Ranigaon, etc., by the forces of Raghuji Bhonsla. Dated 10 December 1804.

OR[2] 20, f 1; CR 22, p. 103, no. 28(5).

Jan. 10 26. From Raja Ganga Ram Pandit to Elphinstone. Encloses reply from Amrit Rao. Says that his intention is not known so far. Assures of dispatching the report about current situation regularly. Also informs about the arrival of the forces of Raghuji Bhonsla at Manikgarh. Dated 12 December 1804.

OR 21,[3] f 1; CR 22, pp. 104-05, no. 28(6).

Jan. 10 27. From Elphinstone to Ganga Ram Pandit. Acknowledging his letter advises not to be anxious of troublemakers as they will be dealt shortly. Also says that Raghuji Bhonsla would either keep to his promise or suffer. Dated 10 December 1804.

OR 22,[4] f 1; CR 22, p. 105, no. 28(7).

Jan. 10 28. From Elphinstone to Ganga Ram Pandit. Acknowledging receipt of his letter informs about the arrival of *topkhana* of

[1]Copy enclosed with a letter from Elphinstone to Ganga Ram Pandit.
[2]Copy received with a letter from Ganga Ram Pandit to Elphinstone.
[3]Ibid.
[4]Copy enclosed with a letter from Elphinstone to Ganga Ram Pandit.

Bakhshi Sakha Ram to Nagpur. Also informs that 1,000 men of Raghuji have crossed the Wardha River and killed one Gosain who was going from Nagpur. Also informs about the security arrangements of frontier and other *thanas*. Dated 11 December 1804.

OR 23,[1] *f 1; CR 22, pp. 105-06, no. 28(8).*

Jan. 10 29. From Elphinstone to Ganga Ram Pandit. Acknowledging receipt of his letter says that he (addressee) would not be a looser if peace continues but warns him to be ready for any eventuality. Dated 13 December 1804.

OR[2] *24, f 1; CR 22, p. 106, no. 28(9).*

Jan. 10 30. From Ganga Ram Pandit to Elphinstone. Acknowledging his letter informs that after strengthening his garrison he has dispatched a small party under the Command of Dada Madho Raoji to Amaravati. Adds that due to presence of troops at Amaravati, the villagers are panicky. Dated 15 December 1804.

OR 25,[3] *f 1; CR 22, pp. 107-08, no. 28(10).*

Jan. 10 31. Raja Ganga Ram Pandit to Elphinstone. Acknowledging his letter along with two letters addressed to Col. Bernad (?) and Amrit Rao informs about the devastation of Bham and Amner by the forces of Raghuji Bhonsla. Also says that Madho Rao has been sent to Amaravati who will be joined by a garrison under the command of Mahipat Ram from Nalkapur (?). Further informs about the fortification of the fort. Dated 16 December 1804.

OR 26,[4] *f 1; CR 22, pp. 108-09, no. 28(11).*

Jan. 10 32. From Ganga Ram Pandit to Elphinstone. Acknowledging his letter assures about the strengthening of the garrison and administration of *thanas* and fortresses, etc. Informs about receipt of a letter from Raja Mahipat Ram offering to surrender his area of Ankut and Argaon against war indemnity. Dated 17 December 1804.

OR 27,[5] *f 1; CR 22, pp. 109-10, no. 28(12).*

[1]Copy received as enclosure with a letter from Elphinstone to Raja Ganga Ram Pandit.

[2]Ibid.

[3]Copy received with a letter from Raja Ganga Ram Pandit to Elphinstone.

[4]Ibid.

[5]Ibid.

Jan. 10 33. From Elphinstone to Raja Ganga Ram Pandit. Says that in accordance with the terms of the treaty between the government of *Bandagan-e-Aali* (the Nizam) and the Company, the former is not allowed to declare war and sieze territory of the Raja of Nagpur without a bilateral talk. Dated 17 December 1804.

OR 28,[1] *f 1; CR 22, pp. 110-11, no. 28(13).*

Jan. 10 34. Persian Secretary to Munni Begam. Acknowledges receipt of the gifts sent by the addressee and requests her not to send such expensive gifts in future.

SI 1, pp. 5-6, no. 6.

Jan. 12 35. From Jagat Singh of Jaipur to General Gerard Lake (the Commander-in-Chief). Acknowledging his letter refers to the friendly relation between them and says that Hakim Sober De Silva and Capt. William Astrick (?) would apprise him of the details of the alliance recommended against the enemy.

OR 29,[2] *f 1; CR 22, pp. 40-41, no. 6(1).*

Jan. 12 36. Maharaja Jagat Singh of Jaipur to General Gerard Lake. Offers heartiest congratulations on the success of the British forces under the command of the addressee over the enemy (Jaswant Rao).

OR 30,[3] *f 1; CR 22, pp. 41-43, no. 6(2).*

Jan. 12 37. From Gajraj Misr[4] of Nepal. Referring to the failure of the government of Nepal to adhere to the treaty and his loyalty, seeks permission to stay in Benares under the British protection. Assures of his loyalty to the Company till death. Also says that he will regularly inform about the day-to-day happenings of this region and Tibet to Capt. William Duglus Nixon.

OR 31;[5] *WS, WC, f 1).*

Jan. 12 38. Rana Kirat Singh of Gohad to General Gerard Lake. Referring to the rebellions and disturbances created by the enemy of the Company, assures his strong loyalty and attachment to the Company.

OR 32,[6] *f 1; CR 22, pp. 43-44, no. 7.*

Jan. 12 39. Rana Kirat Singh of Gohad to G. Mercer. Explains his

[1]Copy received with a letter from Elphinstone to Raja Ganga Ram Pandit.
[2]Copy received with a letter from Mercer, dated 30 December 1804.
[3]Ibid.
[4]Name of the writer does not appear in the text of letter but on cover.
[5]Received along with a letter from Capt. Knox, dated 12 January 1805.
[6]Copy received along a letter from Mercer, dated 24 December 1804.

misery due to drought and hostile attitude of neighbouring states, particularly Ambaji, who has collected a large number of troops at Raipur to molest and devastate the areas of British Dependencies. However, he assures of all possible efforts to defy the enemy. Also requests to send Jawala Parsad for consultation on the present situations.

OR 33,[1] *f 1; CR 22, pp. 44-49, no. 8.*

Jan. 12 40. General (Lake) to Rana Kirat Singh of Gohad. Acknowledges receipt of his letter regarding his misery due to disturbances created by enemies. Says that the responsibility of the security of that region was given to the forces of Bundelkhand and General Mury (posted in Deccan). However, assures that the reinforcement will be sent shortly to check the menace. Also says about the presence of Jaswant Rao Holkar in the fort of Deig with his forces. Dated 18 December 1804.

OR 34,[2] *f 1; CR 22, pp. 49-51, no. 9.*

Jan. 14 41. Collector of Agra to the Secretary. Revenue statement of *parganas* Dholpur, Bari and Rajakhera for the year 1211 *fasli*.

OR 35,[3] *f 1; CR 22, pp. 51-56, no. 10.*

Jan. 14 42. From Shiv Narayan Singh. Complementary with *nazr* on the occasion of *Roz-e-Kalan* (Christmas).

OR 36, f.1; WS, WC, TR 51, p. 17, no. 6, AR 20, p. 37.

Jan. 14 43. Raja Ranjit Singh of Bharatpur to Mercer. Informs that a confident person has been deputed to attend to General Lake and explain the matters which find no place in the letter. Dated 22 *Ramazan* (AH 1219) (25 December 1804).

OR 37,[4] *f 1; CR 22, pp. 89-90, no. 24.*

Jan. 14 44. Mercer to Raja Ranjit Singh of Bharatpur. Says that the matters referred to do not require to be explained by sending a confident person. Also expresses that there is no further need to correspond in this regard. Dated 28 December 1804.

OR 38,[5] *f 1; CR 22, pp. 90-91, no. 25.*

[1]Copy received along a letter from Mercer, dated 24 December 1804.

[2]Ibid.

[3]Enclosed with a letter from the Collector of Agra.

[4]Copy enclosed with a letter from the Agent to Governor-General, dated 31 December 1804.

[5]Ibid.

Jan. 16 45. From Jhau Lal,[1] a subordinate officer of Nawwab Wazir at Patna. Complementary with the *nazr* on the eve of *Roz-e-Kalan* (Christmas).

OR 39,[2] f 1; TR 51, p. 17, no. 7; AR 20, p. 32.

Jan. 16 46. Abul Hasan, the Agent at Sindh to Governor-General. Referring to the receipt of a letter from Mir Sahib, informs about the movement of prince Kamran with his forces from Herat to Qandhar and that of Zaman Shah's from Qandhar to expel the former. Also informs about the movement of French and Arab vessels and the capture of many ships by them. Further expresses his willingness to attend to the addressee through land route. Dated 11 *Shaban* 1219 AH (15 November 1804).

OR 40, f 1; CR 22, pp. 56-59, no. 11; TR 51, pp. 17-19, no. 8; AR 20, p. 10.

Jan. 16 47. Abul Hasan, Agent to the Governor at Sindh. Copy of OR 40.

OR 41,[3] f 1; CR 22, pp. 56-59, no. 11; TR 51, pp. 17-19, no. 8.

Jan. 16 48. From Nizam al-Mulk Asaf Jah of Hyderabad. Congratulates on the success of British forces over the Marathas.

OR 42,[4] WS, WC, ff 2; CR 22, pp. 60-63, no. 13; TR 51, pp. 19-21, no. 9; AR 20, p. 27.

Jan. 16 49. From Mir Alam.[5] To the same effect as the foregoing OR 42.

OR 43,[6] WS, WC, f 1; CR 22, pp. 59-60, no. 12; TR 51, p. 22, no. 10; AR 20, p. 21.

Jan. 17 50. From Jagat Singh[7] of Jaipur. Requests for the exemption of

[1]Name of the writer does not appear in the letter but comes from TR 51, and AR 20.

[2]Received with a letter from the Magistrate of Patna to the Persian Secretary, dated 7 January 1805.

[3]Copy enclosed with a letter from the Acting Secretary and translator at Bombay, dated 24 January 1805.

[4]Received as enclosure to a letter of the Resident at Hyderabad to the Persian Secretary, dated 31 December 1804.

[5]*Wakil* and minister of the Nizam of Hyderabad since 1804; His full name was Saiyid Abul Qasim Khan and was son of Mir Saiyid Raza (Foreign Deptt. Misc. vol. 129, pp. 55-56) quoted in *Index to Titles* (1798-1885), p. 4.

[6]Enclosed with a letter from the Resident at Hyderabad to the Persian Secretary, dated 31 December 1804.

[7]Name of the writer comes out only from the seal and TR.

rahdari (road tax) to some of his men who have been sent to Gaya to perform some rites for the consolation of the soul of late Maharaja.

OR 44, WS, f 1; TR 51, p. 22, no. 11, AR 20, p. 32.

Jan. 18 51. From Amat al-Zahra Bahu Begam[1] of Murshidabad. Referring to the loan of three lakh rupees to Col. Collins as an assistance to fight against the Marathas, assures her deep confidence in the Company government. Requests to direct Collins to issue and transmit *tamassukat* (public securities) of three lakh rupees as per established rule of the Company. Dated 6 Shawwal 1219 AH. (8 January 1805).

OR 45,[2] f 1; CR 22, pp. 95-98, no. 27; TR 51, pp. 23-25, no. 12; AR 20, p. 5.

Jan. 18 52. From Raghuji Bhonsla of Nagpur. Expresses pleasure on the victory of the Company over Jaswant Rao Holkar under the command of Lord Lake and Major General Frazer on 13 January 1805.

OR 46,[3] WS, WC, f 1; TR 51, pp. 26-27, no. 13; CR 20, pp. 63-64, no. 14(i).

Jan 18 53. From Bahu Begam. Same as OR 45.

OR 47,[4] ff 2, WS; CR 22, pp. 95-98, no. 27; TR 51, pp. 23-25, no. 12; AR 20, p. 5.

Jan. 18 54. From Nawwab Nusrat Jang of Dacca. Informs about the safe arrival of Muhammad Taqi Khan on 29 *Ramazan* 1219 AH (2 January 1805). Dated 14 January 1805.

OR 48,[5] f 1, WS; TR 51, p. 27, no. 14; AR 20, p. 26.

Jan. 19 55. Guman Singh, the newswriter of Bhao Sahib. Referring to correspondence made with Amir Khan says that he has sent 100 rupees out of a total of 500 rupees.

OR 49,[6] f 1; CR 22, pp. 64-65, no. 14(2).

[1]Name of the writer does not come forth from the document but from TR as Bahu Begam for full name see *Index to Titles*, p. 22.

[2]Enclosed with a letter from the Resident at Lucknow, dated 10 January 1805.

[3]Received along with a letter from the Resident at Nagpur.

[4]Original letter enclosed with a letter from the Resident at Lucknow, dated 10 January 1805.

[5]For reference of sequence please see OR 1 and 2.

[6]Copy enclosed with a letter from Capt. Baillie, dated 8 January 1805.

Jan. 21 56. Refers to the memorandum presented by Sulaiman Agha, the envoy of the Wazir, Asaf Nazir Ali, *Pasha* of Baghdad and orders to extend all hospitality to the said envoy wherever he goes as he has come to further strengthen the friendship of the two states.

OR 50,[1] *f 1.*

Jan. 21 57. Persian Secretary to Nawwab Nasir al-Mulk. Thanks the addressee on receiving presents of Oranges from him.

SI. 1, pp. 6-7, no. 7.

Jan. 22 58. From Maharaja Jhau Lal of Awadh. Requests for the recovery of his *amwal-o-ajnas* (property) from Fath Singh, son of Jaswant Singh with whom the writer had deposited the said property sometimes back. Also requests for a *dastak-e-rahdari* for his family to travel from Lucknow to Azimabad (Patna).

OR 51,[2] *WS, WC, f 1; TR 51, pp. 28-29, no. 15; AR 20, p. 32.*

Jan. 22 59. Muhammad Ali, Agent at Mandvi on behalf of Major Walker, the Resident at Baroda, to Jonathan Duncan the Governor of Bombay. Informs about the suppression of *Utabis* an Arabs by the Sultan of Muscat and later his death at the hands of *Wahabis*. Also says about the existing peace in Mandvee and Bhuj as Fath Muhammad *jamadar* and Hansraj are supposed to meet shortly and settle the terms of peace. Dated 3 *Ramazan* 1219 AH. (6 December 1804).

OR 52,[3] *f 1; CR 22, pp. 67-69, no. 16; TR 51, pp. 29-31, no. 16; AR 20, p. 10.*

Jan. 22 60. From Qasim Ali Khan of Lucknow. Referring to the receipt of the letter of Governor expresses his extreme loyalty to the Company and assures of his everlasting loyalty.

OR 53,[4] *WS, WC, f 1; CR 22, pp. 65-67, no. 15; TR 51, p. 32, no. 17; AR 20, p. 7.*

Jan. 23 61. From Sharaf Ali Khan[5] of Lucknow. Acknowledging receipt

[1]A free translation of the Persian OR is also given.

[2]Enclosed with a letter from the Magistrate at Patna to the Persian Secretary, dated 15 January 1805.

[3]Enclosed with a letter from the Acting Agent to Persian Secretary at Bombay, dated 29 December 1804.

[4]Enclosed with a letter from the Resident at Lucknow to the Persian Secretary, dated 13 January 1805.

[5]Ashraf Ali Khan, see *Index to Titles*.

of his letter congratulates on the success of the Company in capturing the fortress of Deig.

OR 54,[1] WS, WC, f 1; CR 22, pp. 69-70, no. 17; TR 51, p. 32, no. 18; AR 20, p. 1.

Jan. 23 62. Muhammad Najm al-Din Khan, *Qazi al-Quzat* (the Chief Qazi) to the Secretary to the Government. Forwards the *sanads* pertaining to the appointment of *qazis* in various *parganas* of Itawah district. Adds that the *sanad* in respect of Zain al-Abedin is held up. Seeks orders in this regard.

OR 55, WS, f 1.

Jan. 23 63. To Ali Pasha of Baghdad. Acknowledges the delivery of Egyptian horses through his envoy Sulaiman Agha. Referring to the dispute between the people of Basra and Captain of an English vessel regarding an Egyptian woman requests for a free discussion and assures that the matter will be judiciously investigated. Adds that due to sickness of the envoy a ship along with a physician has been provided for his departure. Also enlists the gifts sent with the envoy.

TI, 51,[2] pp. 7-14, no. 2; CI 41, pp. 2-13, no. 2; AI 20, p. 60.

Jan. 25. 64. To Nawwab Wazir. Expresses satisfaction on the recovery of the addressee from severe indisposition.

TI, 51, p.14, no. 3; AI 20, p. 68.

Jan. 27. 65. From Imdad Husain Khan of Farrukhabad. Elucidating the good qualities of Cloud Russel[3] welcomes the arrival of Cuthbert to replace the former and hopes the latter would also maintain the friendship in the same fashion as the former did.

OR 56,[4] WS, WC, f 1; CR 22, pp. 70-71, no. 18; TR 51, pp. 32-33, no. 19, AR 20, p. 11.

Jan. 28 66. From Muhammad Najm al-Din Khan, *Qazi al-Quzat*. Referring to the *Aimma* and *Al Tamgha* grants allotted to him and his relatives by the previous rulers even at a time when these grants were seized from other people; Complains that Saadat

[1]Enclosed with a letter from the Resident at Lucknow, dated 14 January 1805.

[2]For previous reference please see OR 50 vide slip no. 56.

[3]TR gives "Lloyd" while OR and CR bear "Claud Russel"; he was Assistant Persian Secretary. [DLPC, Vol. III (1803), letter no. 648.]

[4]Enclosed with a letter from the Acting Agent at Farrukhabad to the Persian Secretary, dated 10 January 1805.

Ali Khan has seized these grants from him and his relatives. Requests for the restoration of these grants or assignment of some new ones as compensation, around Kanpur. Also assures of his loyalty to the Company.

OR 57, WS, f 1; CR 22, pp. 77 82, no. 21(1); TR 51, pp. 33-38, no. 20; AR 20, p. 8.

Jan. 28 67. From Muhammad Najam al-Din Khan, *Qazi al-Quzat*. *Yaddasht* of the grants in possession of the *Qazi al-Quzat* and his relatives.

OR 58, WS, f 1; TR 51, pp. 38-40, no. 20; AR 20, p. 8; CR 22, pp. 82-83, no. 21(2).

Jan. 28 68. From Harak Chand Jagat Seth of Murhsidabad. Expresses gratitude for the permission to go for a pilgrimage to Jagannath and an introductory letter to Col. Harcourt with a *dastak-e-rahdari*. Informs that he has sent the letter through his agent and he will set out for Jagannath on 5 *Magh* (16 January).

OR 59, WS, WC, f 1; TR 51, pp. 40-41, No. 21; AR 20, p. 17.

Jan. 28 69. From Nawwab Wazir Muhammad Khan of Bhopal. Elucidating the friendship existing between the Company and Bhopal and refers to the treaty of friendship. Hopes that this friendship may be honoured by the officers of the Company.

OR 60,[1] *WS, f 1; CR 22, pp. 71-73, no. 19; TR 51, pp. 41-43, no. 22, AR 20, p. 5.*

Jan. 28. 70. From Saiyid Ali Khan Nawwab Nusrat Jang of Dacca. Recommends the continuance of the pension of 15 rupees, 6 *annas* and 10 *gandas* to Durga Prasad Misr following the death of his father Bindraban Misr.[2]

OR 61, WS, WC, f 1; TR 51, pp. 43-44, no. 23, AR 20, p. 26.

Jan. 28 71. From Durga Prasad Misr. Requests for the continuance of the pension of 15 rupees, 6 *annas* and 10 *gandas* in his name that had previously been granted to and drawn by his deceased father Bindraban Misr.

OR 62,[3] *f 1; TR 51, pp. 44-45, no. 23, AR 20, p. 26.*

[1]Enclosed with a letter from Jankins, dated 17 December 1804.
[2]See OR 62, application of Durga Prasad Misr.
[3]Sent with a letter from Nawwab Wazir of Dacca (see OR 61).

Jan. 28 72. From Raja Udit Narayan Singh at Benares. Offers greeting on the eve of Christmas.

OR 63, WS, f 1; TR 51, p. 45, no. 24; AR 20, p. 33.

Jan. 28 73. From Natha Gobind Rao. Referring to the devastation of Sangor by Mir Khan Afghan and also due to famine informs that Daulat Rao Sindhia has set out for the said place. Requests for some aid against him.

OR 64,[1] *f 1; CR 22, pp. 73-77, no. 20.*

Jan. 31 74. From Ilahi Khanam, w/o Wazir Ali Khan of Lucknow. Complains that the elder Begam of Wazir Ali Khan pays them only Rs. 43 for the maintenance of herself and her household, out of a total of Rs. 600 that is being paid by the Company every month. Requests to issue an order to the Resident at Lucknow to pay her part of pension separately.

OR 65, WS, f 1; TR 51, pp. 45-47, no. 65; AR 20, p. 40.

Jan. 31 75. From Shah Alam II. Referring to his letter regarding appointment of Muizz al-Mulk Nasir al-Daulah Bahadur (Sir David Ochterlony) to the royal court, says that no reply has so far been received.

OR 66, WS, WC, f 1; CR 22, pp. 87-89, no. 23; TR 51, pp. 47-48, no. 26; AR 20, p. 19.

Jan. 31 76. Nawwab Qasim Ali Khan[2] of Lucknow to Edmonston. Acknowledging the receipt of his letter, anticipates a letter regarding the welfare and disposition of the addressee and Governor-General.

OR 67,[3] *WS, WC, f 1.*

Jan. 31 77. From Nawwab Qasim Ali Khan of Lucknow. Complementary, requesting the Governor-General to Communicate, occasionally, account of his health.

OR 68,[4] *WS, WC, f 1; CR 22, pp. 65-67, no. 15; TR 51, pp. 32, no. 17; AR 20, p. 7.*

[1]Enclosed with a letter from Commander-in-Chief, dated 17 January 1805.

[2]Name of the writer appears on the seal only for details see *Index to Titles*, p. 164.

[3]Enclosed with a letter from the Resident at Lucknow to the Persian Secretary, dated 13 January 1805.

[4]Ibid.

Jan. 31 78. From Ashraf Ali Khan of Lucknow. Complementary, expresses happiness on the Company's victory and capture of the fortress of Deig.

OR 69,[1] *WS, WC, f 1.*

Jan. 31 79. From Mirza Munim Bakht, son of Shah Alam II, to Col. Ochtertony. Expressing his brotherly relation with the addressee requests for some more monetary help as Rs. 40 is quite a meager amount to maintain his expenses and of his dependents.

OR 70,[2] *f 1; CR 22, pp. 82-87, no. 22.*

Jan. -- 80. Chautria Hastdil Shah to Seton. Commends the British victory over Jaswant Rao Holkar and informs that Garhwal is in possession of Nepal and that Gurkhas would occupy Dehra Doon and Sirmaur after *Dussehra.* Dated 3 October 1804.

OR 75, WS, f 1; CR 22, pp. 33-35, no. 3(5).

Jan. -- 81. Col. J. Kirkpatrick to Mir Alam Bahadur, the *wakil* of Nizam Hyderabad. Informs that the amount due from the *talluqas* of Gavilgarh according to the treaty with Raghuji Bhonsla has not yet been collected. Asks the addressee to arrange for the collection of the same amount and also sent a reasonable number of contingents for the security of Berar. Dated 31 December 1804.

OR 76,[3] *f 1.*

Jan. -- 82. Mir Alam, *wakil* of the Nizam of Hyderabad to James Kirkpatrick. Responding to the addressee's letter regarding collection of money from Raghuji Bhonsla and security of Berar, says that Keshav Rao, *wakil* of Raghuji Bhonsla has submitted Rs. 49,000. Further says that a sizeable number of *sawars* and *piyadahs* (cavalry and foot soldiers) have been sent for the security of Berar.

OR[4] *77, f 1.*

Jan. -- 83. Mir Alam Bahadur to James Kirkpatrick. Referring to his previous letter regarding the case of Raghuji Bhonsla says that

[1]Enclosed with a letter from the Resident at Lucknow to the Persian Secretary, dated 13 January 1805.

[2]Ibid.

[3]Copy enclosed with a letter from the Resident at Hyderabad, dated 13 January 1805.

[4]Enclosed with a letter from the Resident, dated 13 January 1805.

the Bhonsla has written to his *wakil* that excess money should not be collected. Also says that details in this regard may be sent later.

OR 78,[1] *f 1.*

Jan. -- 84. From Nawwab Madar al-Daulah of Lucknow. Congratulating the addressee on the capture of the fortress of Deig. Requests for some assignment under the government.

OR 79,[2] *f 1; CR 22, pp. 99-100, no. 27(2).*

Jan. -- 85. Nawwab Madar al-Daulah of Lucknow to Edmonston, the Persian Secretary. Referring to his previous congratulatory letter to the Governor-General, congratulates the addressee on the capture of Deig.

OR 80,[3] *f 1.*

Feb. 1 86. Thakur Mulchand *Jamadar-e-topkhana* of Daulat Rao Sindhia to Kunwar (?). Referring to the recommendation of Himmat Bahadur requests the addressee to visit the writer's place as the situation is very favourable. Dated 6 *Shawwal* (1219 AH) (8 January 1805).

OR 81,[4] *f 1.*

Feb. 2 87. Muhammad Najm al-din Khan, *Qazi al-Quzat*. Says that two *sanads* in favour of Ata Allah and Mazhar Ali are being submitted. Dated 29 January 1805.

OR 82,[5] *WS, f 1.*

Feb. 3 88. Shambhu Nath to Maulavi Riayat Ali Khan. Gives information about geo-political situations of Doon. Says that Raja of Srinagar has occupied and established his rule over Doon.

OR 83, f 1; CR 22, pp. 160-62, no. 2;
TR 51, pp. 48-52, no. 28.

Feb. 4 89. From Bishambhar Pandit, *wakil* of Raghuji Bhonsla. Anticipates that the Governor-General will honour the presents being sent through his agent Venkoji Bhonsla on the happy

[1]Enclosed with a letter from the Resident, dated 13 January 1805.

[2]Enclosed with a letter from the Resident at Lucknow to the Persian Secretary, dated 20 January 1805.

[3]Ibid.

[4]Copy of Persian letter along with its Marathi version from Capt. Bailie, Agent to Commander-in-Chief, dated 22 January 1805.

[5]Despatched from the Department of the ceded Province, dated 2 February 1805.

occasion of the marriage of writer's son.

OR 84,[1] *WS, f 1; TR 51, pp. 52-53, no. 30; AR 20, p. 5.*

Feb. 4 90. Munshi Mir Aziz Allah to Mir Alam, *wakil* of Nizam Hyderabad. States that the amount of *zar-e-tahsil* (revenue) from the districts of Gavilgarh be kept ready. Dated 13 January 1805.

OR 85,[2] *fl; CR 22, pp. 249-50, no. 25.*

Feb. 4 91. From Bishambhar Pandit. Complementary. Informs about the gifts sent through Venkoji Bhonsla.

TR 51,[3] *p. 52, no. 29; AR 20, p. 5.*

Feb. 7 92. Lord Lake to *chaudhuris*, *qanungos, zamindars,* etc. Notifies the grant of the *mahal* of Kaman to Sawai Bakhtawar Singh as *amani* w.e.f. the beginning of 1212 *fasli kharif.* Asks them to obey and cooperate with him in all matters and make all efforts to promote agriculture.

OR 87, f 1; CR 22, pp. 162-63, no. 3.

Feb. 7 93. General G. Lake, Commander-in-Chief to Raja Sawai Jagat Singh of Jaipur. Referring to the favours and friendliness of the Company for its dependents and their subjects informs about the misdeeds of Maharaja Ranjit Singh, who in spite of all favours and friendly treatment joined hands with the enemy (Jaswant Rao Holkar) of the Company and her friends. Further says about the success of Company's forces over them and capture of the fort of Deig. Adds that now they are besieged in the fort of Bharatpur and hopefully they will soon be captured and suppressed so that other ill wishers may learn a lesson. Dated 5 January 1805.

OR 88,[4] *f 1; CR 22, pp. 163-65, no. 4.*

Feb. 7 94. General G. Lake to Zaib al-Nisa Begam. Warns her to beware of the baseless rumors and asks to be at alert to check any intrigue fabricated by her own men. Dated 16 December 1804.

OR 89,[5] *f 1; CR 22, pp. 179-81, no. 10(1).*

[1]See also , TR 51, p. 52, no. 29.

[2]Enclosed with a letter from the Resident at Hyderabad, dated 21 January 1805.

[3]See also OR 84.

[4]Copy enclosed with a letter from Mercer, dated 10 January 1805.

[5]Copy enclosed with a letter from Mercer, dated 6 January 1805.

Feb. 7 95. Zaib al-Nisa Begam to General G. Lake. Explains her misery due to transfer of her properties and plight of 55 villages belonging to *parganas* Ludhiana and Sardhana, etc., at the hands of Sikhs. Says that due to these difficulties she decided to stay in Niel (?) district. Also expresses her astonishment on the addressee paying heed to the rumors.

OR 90,[1] *f 1; CR 22, pp. 181-82, no. 10(2).*

Feb. 8. 96. Nana Gobind Rao to Capt. Baillie. Acknowledging receipt of his letter assures of his loyalty to the Company. Also says that he would not follow the path of Raja Ranjit Singh who in spite of all favours became defiant and joined Holkar. Further informs about the disturbances created by Daulat Rao Sindhia in Sang and urges that the security of the people rests on the government. Hopes for a prompt action in this regard.

OR 91,[2] *f 1; CR 22, pp. 166-69, no. 5.*

Feb.10. 97. Mir Abd Allah to the Acting Collector at Muradabad. Requests the addressee to induce the Governor-General to issue an order in regard to the payment of thirty thousand Lucknawi rupees to the writer from the treasury of Patna or Murshidabad or elsewhere as per convenience, instead of Muradabad which the writer had advanced as loan to the Company one year back at the behest of General G. Lake to meet out the expenses of the administration of Rohilkhand. Argues that if he receives this amount from Muradabad treasury as wished by the Company it will cost him Rs. 2,000 more in transferring it to Patna (his residence). Dated 12 January 1805.

OR 92,[3] *f 1; CR 22, pp. 169-73, no. 6; TR 51, pp. 54-58, no. 31; AR 20, p. 11.*

Feb. 10 98. Nawwab Begam (Munni Begam) to Pattle, the Superintendent of *nizamat* affairs. Requests the addressee to represent her case before the Governor-General for a deduction of Rs. 300 per month from the pension of the deceased Nawwab Mahdi Ali Khan against the loan and other debts and continue the rest Rs. 500 as a pension in the name of his daughter

[1]Copy enclosed with a letter from Mercer, dated 6 January 1805.

[2]Copy enclosed with a letter from Capt. Baillie, dated 29 January 1805.

[3]Copy enclosed with a letter from the acting collector at Moradabad, dated 26 January 1805.

Gauhar al-Nisa Begam. Hopes for a favourable response.

OR 93,[1] *f 1; CR 22, pp. 173-74, no. 7; TR 51, pp. 59-60, no. 32; p. 11; AR 20, p. 11.*

Feb. 14 99. From Nawwab Nasir al-Daulah of Murshidabad. Complementary, with a present of Kanaula (Oranges). Dated 5 *Shawwal*, 47 *Julus* (of Shah Alam II).

OR 94, WS, WC, f 1; TR 51, p. 60, no. 33; AR 20, p. 28.

Feb. 15 100. From Nawwab Zia al-Daulah Tahawwur Jang of Patna.[2] Complementary on the eve of *Roz-e-Kalan* (Christmas).

OR 99, WS, WC, f 1; TR 51, p. 60, no. 34; AR 20, p. 19.

Feb. 15 101. From Nawwab Saadat Ali Khan.[3] Acknowledging his letter says about his recovery from the sickness. Thanks for the addressee's affectionate care. Dated 5 *Zulqada* 1219 AH (4 February 1805).

OR 100,[4] *WS, WC, f 1; CR 22, pp. 174-76, no. 8; TR 51, pp. 61-62, no. 35; AR 20, p. 41.*

Feb. 15 102. From Nawwab Wazir (Saadat Ali Khan) of Awadh. To the same effect as the previous letter (OR no. 100). Dated 5 *Zulqada* 1219 AH (6 February 1805).

OR 101,[5] *f 1; CR 22, pp. 174-76, no. 8; TR 51, pp. 61-62, no. 35; AR 20, p. 41.*

Feb. 15 103. From Nawwab Shams al-Daulah of Murshidabad. Expiating his disobediences and misdeeds seeks the favour of

[1]Copy enclosed with a letter from the Superintendent of *nizamat* affairs, dated 6 February 1805.

[2]Karim Quli Khan, Zia al-Daulah Zia al-Mulk, Muqarrab al-Khaqani, Farzand Khan Bahadur Tahawwur Jang (Son of Mumin al-Daulah I and brother of Abbas Quli Khan; held *jagirs* in suburbs of Patna, attended on Shuja al-Daulah of Awadh. (*Index to Titles*, p. 95; C PC, VIII, 957-59.)

[3]Yamin al-Daulah, Nizam al-Mulk Bahadur, Mubariz Jang, Wazir al-Mumalik-e-Hindustan (raised to the *Masnad* of Awadh by Sir John Shore on 21 January 1789; died 10 July 1814, remembered "Jannat Aramghah" after death. (*Index to Titles*, p. 180, *Tarikh-e-Awadh* by Najm al-Ghani, Lucknow, 1919, pp. 6, 96.)

[4]Enclosed with a letter from the Resident at Lucknow, dated 7 February 1805.

[5]Copy enclosed with a letter from the Resident at Lucknow, dated 7 February 1805.

the addressee and beg pardon for all his sins committed against the Company's government.

OR 102, WC, f 1; CR 22, pp. 176-79, no. 9; TR 51, pp. 62-66, no. 36, AR 20, p. 38.

Feb. 17[1] 104. Intelligence report from the court of Zaib al-Nisa Begam. Referring to the incoming news from Shahjahanabad (Delhi) says that an engagement took place with the enemy and Mir Khan Afghan has consequently been injured. Also reports about a severe battle with the Marathas and the subsequent preparation of battalions by the Begam. But it is not clear as yet to which quarter these battalions will be mobilized. Dated 29 Shawwal 1219 AH (31 January 1805).

OR 103,[2] f 1; TR 51, pp. 66-67, no. 37; AR 20, p. 10.

Feb. 17 105. Akbarabadi Begam to King Shah Alam II. Represents that the *amils* of *pargana* Patodahi (Pataudi) have collected Rs. 425 from village Pahari (?) as a part of a contribution of Rs. 2,500 intended for the support of Narayan Rao's troops and have further made a demand of Rs. 120 on them. Requests to direct Nasir al-Daulah (Ochterlony) not to inflict such sufferings on the *zamindars* of this village which are granted to her as *tayul*, and restore the said amont. Also requests to order Faiz Talab Khan to save the villages of Jatauli and Pahari from similar grievances.

The document also bears the order of Shah Alam II in his own handwriting commanding Colonel Ochterlony to direct the *amils* to refrain from disturbing the aforesaid villages in future.

OR 104,[3] f 1; CR 22, pp. 182-83, no. 12(1); TR 51, pp. 67-69, no. 38; AR 20, p. 10.

Feb. 17 106. *Parwana* issued by General Perron addressed to *chaudhuris, qanungos, zamindars, muzarians,* etc., of *pargana* Pataudi notifying the assignment of the villages of Sherpur and Jatauli to Hafiz al-Nisa Khanam. Dated 23, *Rabi I*, 45 *Julus* of Shah Alam II (18 July 1803).

OR 105,[4] f 1; CR 22, pp. 183-84, no. 12; TR 51, pp. 69-70, no. 39; AR 20, p. 10.

[1]The date of receipt comes forth from AR 20, p. 10, only.

[2]Enclosed with a letter from the Resident at Delhi.

[3]Enclosed with a letter from the Resident at Delhi to the Secretary to the Government, dated 3 February 1805.

[4]Attested copy bearing seal of Qazi Inayat Khan, enclosed with a letter from the Resident at Delhi, dated 3 February 1805.

Feb. 18 107. From Raja Mahanand Rai of Murshidabad. Requests to direct Pattle to help him recover a debt of Rs. 40,000 from the Nawwab of Bengal for the proposed pilgrimage to Jagannathji on the eve of Holi.

OR 106, WS, WC, f 1; CR 22, pp. 184-85, no. 13; TR 51, pp. 70-71; no. 40; AR 20, p. 33.

Feb. 18. 108. From Daulat Rao Sindhia. Complains against the negligence of Webbe, the Resident at his court in context of the treaty of friendship.

OR 107,[1] WS, WC, f 1; CR 22; TR 51, pp. 72, 74, no. 41; AR 20, p. 8.

Feb. 18 109. From Maharaja Daulat Rao Sindhia. Referring to the two treaties of peace and alliance concluded between the Company and the writer complains against Webbe who failed to execute the requisites of the terms of the treaty particularly in respect of pecuniary matters. Draws attention of the addressee to some unadjusted points of the said treaty. Dated 13 *Rajab* (1219 AH) (18 October 1804).

OR 108, WS, WC, ff 2; TR 51, pp. 74-102, no. 42; AR 20, p. 8.

Feb. 18 110. Mir Jafar to A. Seton. Says that the troops of the enemy have attacked and plundered Hapur after crossing over Phoolghat of Ganga. Offers his services to crush the enemy.

OR 135,[2] WS, f 1.

Feb. 20 111. Intelligence report from the newswriter at Jaipur to Col. Ochterlony, the Resident at Delhi. Gives an account of the day-to-day routine of the Raja of Jaipur and informs about the victory of Sindhia over the Raja of Sagaur and also about the rift between Sindhia and Holkar.

OR 109,[3] ff 2.

Feb. 20 112. Intelligence report from the newswriter at Amritsar to Col. Ochterlony, the Resident at Delhi. Informs about the arrival of Maharaja Sahib at *qasba* Moong (?); devastation of the forts of Phagwarah (?) and Shahadarah, etc., by Raja Ranjit Singh of Lahore and his movement from Lahore to

[1]Treaty of Sarji Arjangaon concluded between the Company and Daulat Rao Sindhia on 30 December 1803.

[2]Enclosed with a private letter from A. Seton, dated 18 February 1805.

[3]Enclosed with a letter from the Resident at Delhi, dated 6 February 1805.

Amritsar and the subsequent rallying of the Sikhs around him. Also informs about the stay of *shahanshah* (king) at Qandhar and arrest of Ismail Khan *subedar* of Qandhar and subsequent transfer of his *jagirs* to Bahawal Khan.

OR 110,[1] *f 1.*

Feb. 20 113. From Raja Sukhmi Rai. *Yaddasht*, containing list of men, animal and other provisions enlisted on *dastak-e-rahdari* to be taken along in the journey.

OR 111, WS, f 1.

Feb. 23[2] 114. To Daulat Rao Sindhia. Asks the addressee to enquire into the voilative acts of his servants committed over the British Resident at his court and bring the culprits to book otherwise he has to loose his credibility as the ally of Company's government. For further communications refers to Jenkins, the Acting Resident.

TI 51, pp. 15-21, no. 4; AI 20, p. 48;
CI 41, pp. 12-18, no. 3.

Feb. 24 115. Mir Alam to James Kirkpatrick, the Resident at Hyderabad. Says that he and his dependents are depositing Rs. 3 lakh in the Company's treasury so that each of them may get their proper share of interest annually. Also says that the papers of the share of each of them should be issued in his name.

OR 112,[3] *f 1; CR 22, pp. 185-86, no. 14.*

Feb. 25 116. From Pasha of Baghdad. Complains against the misconduct of Jones,[4] the British Resident in Baghdad, affecting the religion and government of the country. Requests to check his uncalled for activities. Solicits that Raymond may be sent to him for the purpose of instructing his government, etc.

OR 113,[5] *WS, f1; TR 51, pp. 102-50, no. 43;*
AR 20, p. 6; CR 22, pp. 186-218, no. 15.

Feb. 25 117. From Nawwab Nusrat Jang[6] (of Dacca). Requests for the

[1]Enclosed with a letter from the Resident at Delhi, dated 16 February 1805.

[2]Date of drafting.

[3]Copy enclosed with a letter from the Resident at Hyderabad, dated 11 February 1805.

[4]Harford Jones.

[5]Received with a private letter from Lumsden, dated 1 February 1805.

[6]Writer's name as appears in the seal on cover Intazam al-Daulah Nasir al-Mulk Saiyid Ali Khan Nusrat Jang Bahadur.

continuance and transfer of the pension granted to late Mirza Ghulam Haider in the names of his grandmother, mother and sister.

OR 114, WS, f 1; TR 51, pp. 151-53, no. 44; AR 20, p. 26.

Feb. 25 118. From Wali Khanam, Sakina Khanam and Noor al-Nisa Khanam (grandmother, mother and sister of late Mirza Ghulam Haider respectively). Request for the continuation of the pension of the late Mirza in their names, as they do not have any other source of subsistence.

OR 115,[1] WS, f 1: TR 51, p. 153, no. 44; AR 20, p. 26.

Feb. 26 119. Correspondence[2] between Muhammad Nabi Khan[3] and Harford Jones, regarding the corpse and the burial ceremony of late Haji Mohammad Khalil Khan for which the former had sent his son Nazar Ali.

OR 116,[4] f 1; CR 22, pp. 154-61, no. 45; TR 51, pp. 154-61; no. 45; AR 20, p. 13.

Feb. 26 120. Letter of Muhammad Nabi Khan to Harford Jones and its reply to the same effect as the foregoing document OR 116.

OR 117,[5] ff 2, WC; CR 22, pp. 221-26, no. 17; TR 51, pp. 154-61, no. 45; AR 20, p. 13.

Feb. 26 121. From Aqa Nabi Khan. Informs about his arrival at Busrah on his way to the port of Bushehr (Bushire) and expect an early visit to Bengal in order to see His Excellency the Governor-General.

OR 118, WS, f 1; CR 22, pp. 241-44, no. 22; TR 51, pp. 161-63, no. 46; AR 20, p. 1.

Feb. 26 122. From Aqa Nabi Khan. Informs that he has been appointed Ambassador of Persia to the British government in India. Also

[1]The document bears the seals of the applicants.

[2]The document bears the copies of the letters of both Muhammad Nabi Khan and Harford.

[3]Persian Ambassador to the British government in India. See TR 51, p. 161, no. 46; p. 163, no. 47.

[4]Enclosed with a letter from the Resident at Baghdad, dated 23 November 1804.

[5]Ibid.

informs that he will set out from Bushehr for Bengal in the month of *Muharram* (April).

OR 119,[1] f 1; CR 22, pp. 236-40, no. 20; TR 51, pp. 163-66, no. 47; AR 20, p. 1.

Feb. 26 123. From Muhammad Nabi Khan. Asks the addressee for a loan of Rs. 50,000 to be returned after his arrival in Bombay. Dated 17 *Shaban* 1219 AH (19 November 1804).

OR 120,[2] f 1; CR 22, pp. 226-27, no. 18.

Feb. 26 124. Correspondence[3] between Balyuz,[4] Mirza Buzurg and Muhammad Sayeed *daftardar* regarding victory of Persian troops over Russian forces.

OR 121, f 1; CR 22, pp. 227-36, no. 19.

Feb. 26 125. From Aqa Nabi Khan. Communicates his arrival at Kazemien on way to Fort William (*Baldah taiyibah*) and having had an interview with Harford Jones. Also expresses his intention of embarking from Bushehr in April for Bengal.

OR 122, f 1, WS; CR 22, pp. 218-20, no. 16; TR 51, pp. 163-66, no. 47; AR 20, p. 1.

Feb. 26 126. From Balyuz Beg to Khalid Kuhna (?) Beg. Requests the addressee to see into the circumstances under which the pockets supposed to be received by the writer from Halab and Istambul through Tataar but could not happen due to delay occurred in the way and make it convenient for the proper delivery of the said pockets to the writer.

OR 123[5] f 1; CR 22, pp. 240-41, no. 20(1).

Feb. 27 127. From wife of Mahr Ali Agha. Explains the causes for the delay occurred in the delivery of the pocket coming from Istambul en route to Baghdad.

OR 124,[6] f 1; CR 22, pp. 141-42, no. 20(2).

[1]Enclosed with a letter from the Resident at Baghdad, dated 28 September 1804.

[2]Ibid.

[3]The document bears three letters in Arabic and Persian: (*i*) from Balyuz (?) to Mohammad Sayeed Daftardar (in Arabic), (*ii*) from Mirza Buzurg to Balyuz (?) (in Persian) and (*iii*) from Mahammad Sayeed Daftardar to Jones, the Resident (in Arabic)

[4]Perhaps Harford Jones Balyuz, the British Resident at Baghdad.

[5]Enclosed with a letter from the Resident at Baghdad, dated 30 November 1804).

[6]Ibid.

Feb. 27 128. Intelligence report from the newswriter at Sindhia's court against the British agent with the help of *Pindaris,* and the destruction of villages by them. Further states about the serious fighting between Holkar and Mir Khan, etc.

OR[1] 125, f 1.

Feb. 28 129. Proclamation issued by General Lake, the Commander-in-Chief to the Sikh *sardars.* Commands all the Sikh Chiefs (except Gurudatta Singh) to severe their relation with Gurudatta Singh who has created disturbances in the British territory. Also asks them to settle peacefully within their respective territories. If any of them violated the spirit of the proclamation he would lose his credibility to be pardoned.

OR 126,[2] f 1; CR 22, pp. 244-45, no. 25; TR 51, pp. 166-67, no. 48; AR 20, p. 13.

Feb. 28. 130. From Shambhu Bharti. Complains against the mishandling and plundering of his house by Raghuji Bhonsla, consequent upon a false representation of Yashwant Rai Ramchandra that the writer had been purchased by the British officers. Requests to allow him to present before the addressee his followers to clarify his position. Waits for his commands in this regard. Dated 5 *Shaban* 1219 (9 November 1804).

OR 127, WS, WC, f 1; CR 28, pp. 245-47, no. 24; TR 51, pp. 168-70, no. 49; AR 20, p. 38.

Feb. 28 131. Shambhu Bharti to General Wellesley. Gives a detailed account of his destruction at the hands of Raghuji Bhonsla consequent upon the false information of Rai Ramchandra (see OR 127). Requests the addressee to direct Elphinstone to restore his properly. Also solicits service under the British government.

OR 128, WS, WC, f 1; TR 51, pp. 170-74, no. 49; AR 20, p. 38; CR 22, pp. 247-49, no. 24 (2).

Feb. 28 132. Intelligence from the newswriter at the *deorhi* of Nawwab Nasr Allah Khan Bahadur of Rampur. Informs about the arrival of General Smith along with his battalion and cavalrymen at Amroha. Also informs about the march of Amir Khan towards Kashipur. Dated 18 February 1805.

OR 129, f 1.

[1]Enclose to a letter from the Resident at Nagpur to the Secretary to Government, dated 27 February 1805.

[2]Enclosed with a letter from the Agent to Commander-in-Chief to Secretary to the Government, dated 17 February 1805.

Feb. 28 133. Nawwab Nasr Allah Khan to Nekchand *wakil* at Bareilly. Informs about the arrival of Amir Khan at a distance of 7 *kuroh* from Rampur at the head of more than 50,000 *sawars*. Also says that the said Khan has threatened to join him otherwise he will take action against him (the writer). Further says that he has dispatched the details of the present circumstances to the Governor-General and has solicited his help, etc., etc.

OR 130,[1] *f 1; CR 22, pp. 262-64.*

Feb. -- 134. James Kirkpatrick to Mir Alam. Expresses happiness on the addressee's becoming Prime Minister of Hyderabad. Assures of his help in solving the affairs of Surur Afza Begam and Raja Rajinder Bahadur. Dated 28 January 1805.

OR 95,[2] *f 1; CR 22, pp. 252-53, no. 27(d).*

Feb.[3] -- 135. Mir Alam to James Kirkpatrick, the Resident at Hyderabad. Expresses gratitude on being appointed as Prime Minister of Nizam Hyderabad on his behest and seeks his cooperation in solving the affairs of Surur Afza Begam and Raja Rajender Bahadur. Dated 23 January 1805.

OR 96,[4] *f 1; CR 22, pp. 252-53, no. 27(d).*

Feb. -- 136. Abul Hasan (Bahbani) from Hyderabad Sindh to Governor of Bombay. Informs about the attack of Firoz al-Din on Qandhar and his negotiation with Shuja al-Mulk of Kabul. Also informs about offer of Holkar to Shuja al-Mulk for help. Dated 14 *Ramazan* 1219 AH (16 December 1804).

OR 97,[5] *f 1.*

Feb. -- 137. Abul Hasan Bahbani to the Governor of Bombay. Informs about the mobilization of forces by Firoz al-Din against Qandhar and its counter by Shuja al-Mulk. Also expresses anxiety for not receiving any letter from the addressee.

OR 98,[6] *f 1.*

[1]Enclosed with a letter from Seton, dated 19 February 1805.

[2]Copy enclosed with a letter from the Resident at Hyderabad, dated 31 January 1805.

[3]Date of the receipt of letter is not coming forth. It may be somewhere in mid-February as the date of dispatch is 31 January 1805.

[4]Copy enclosed with a letter from the Resident at Hyderabad, dated 31 January 1805.

[5]Copy enclosed with a letter from the Acting Secretary at Bombay, dated 24 January 1805.

[6]Ibid.

Feb. -- 138. Proclamation issued by A. Seton to the people of Katehar. Asks the people of Katehar to be loyal and sincere to the Company's government as the object of this government is to provide all ease and comfort to its subjects.

OR 131,[1] *f 1; CR 22, pp. 255-58, no. 24.*

Feb. -- 139. Daulat Rao Sindhia to Raja Kanchangir Gosain (?) of Sikandra (Kanpur). Invites the addressee for a personal visit to the writer at Kotah.

OR 132, WS, WC, f 1; CR 22, pp 157-58, no. 1.

Feb. -- 140. Intelligence report from the newswriter at Muradabad to A. Seton. Informs that Amir Khan at the head of more than 10,000 *sawar* has surrounded the *kothi* of . . . [*sic*]. Also says that the said Khan has decided to attack the *kothi* in the night. Dated 16 *Zulqada* 1219 AH (15 February 1805).

OR 133, f 1, CR 22, pp. 264-66, no. 30.

Feb. -- 141. Intelligence report from the newswriter at Rampur to A. Seton. Informs about the arrival of fifty injured troops of Amir Khan at Rampur and their fight with the *zamindar*. Also says that they have thought to cross over Ganga. Further informs about the correspondence of Hasan Ali Khan and Amir Khan where in the latter has demanded Rs. 2,00,000 from the former, etc., etc.

OR 134, f 1.

Mar. 2 142. Chiragh Ali Khan, the Prime Minister of Persia to the Resident at Bushehr (Bushire). Informs that an order has been issued, to arrest Shaikh Rehma and bring him to punishment for the disturbances, he has created.

OR 136,[2] *f 1, CR 22, pp. 271-75, no. 1(1).*

Mar. 2 143. Shaikh Rehma of Nakhita to Haji Sulaiman at Bushehr (Bushire). Informs that he has heard about the issuance of an order for his (writer's) arrest. Expresses his willingness to leave

[1]The document is bilingual (Persian and Hindi) enclosed with a letter from the Agent at Bareilly, dated 20 February 1805.

[2]Enclosure to a letter from Mr. Parsley, the Resident (Incharge) at Bushehr, dated 11 January 1805.

Nakhita and take asylum somewhere on any island.

OR 137,[1] f 1; CR 22, pp. 275-77, no. 1(2).

Mar. 2 144. Munshi Muhammad Hasan at Shiraz to the Resident at Bushire. Informs about the where about of Shaikh Rehma and gives details of the property plundered at Nakhita.

OR 138,[2] f 1; CR 22, pp. 277-80, no. 1(3).

Mar. 3 145. From Raja Rajinder of Coorg. Acknowledges with thanks the bestowal of mark of honour and the sword by the Company's government. Assures of his loyalty and service to the Company.

OR 139, f 1; CR 22, pp. 282-83, no. 3. TR 51, pp. 174-75, no. 50; AR 20, p. 34.

Mar. 3 146. From Raja Rajinder of Coorg. Sends some gift items consisting of elephant, sandalwood and sword, etc.

OR 140,[3] WS, WC, f 1; CR 22, pp. 283-84, no. 4; TR 51, p. 175, no. 50.

Mar. 3 147. From Raja of Coorg. Acknowledges receipt of his letter wherein the addressee has desired to expand the territory of the writer. Thanks for this gracious offer and bestowal of a sword as a mark of honour and distinction on the writer.

OR 141,[4] WC, f 1; CR 22, pp. 280-81, no. 2; TR 51, pp. 175-76, no. 51; AR 20, p. 34.

Mar. 3 148. From Saiyid Abul Qasim Khan Tabatabai. Complementary on the eve of Christmas along with one gold *muhr*.

OR 142, WS, WC, f 1; TR 51, p. 176, no. 52; AR 20, p. 1.

Mar. 5 149. Intelligence report from the court of Daulat Rao Sindhia. Gives a brief description of the engagements of Daulat Rao Sindhia at Sangor, on 4 *Zulqada*, Tuesday (5 February 1805).

[1]Enclosed with a letter from Parsley, Resident (Incharge) at Bushehr, dated 12 January 1805.

[2]Enclosed with a letter from Parsley, Incharge of the Residency at Bushehr (Bushire), 12 January 1805.

[3]Enclosed with a letter from the Resident at Coorg to the Persian Secretary to the Government, dated 10 February 1805.

[4]Ibid.

Says that the Maharaja inspected the artillery pieces brought from Ujjain and appreciated. Also says about his check up by Hakim Mir Asad Ali; his taking lunch and listening to music, etc., etc. Dated 5 *Zulqada*, Wednesday (6 February 1805).

OR 143,[1] *f 1; TR 51, pp. 177-81, no. 53; AR 20, p. 13.*

Mar. 6 150. From Gajraj Misr of Nepal. Informs about the murder of Diwan Damodar Pande and his son by Raja Ran Bahadur of Nepal. Also says the Raja's tyranny against the sons of the deceased Diwan and also against Mirza Muhammad Wali. Further says that as the sons of late Diwan are unable to represent them physically hence their petition is carried on by Mirza Muhammad Wali who is going to present his own case. Requests to offer all possible protection to them keeping in view the old good relations.

OR 144,[2] *f 1; TR 51, pp. 181-85, no. 54; AR 20, p. 16.*

Mar. 6 151. From Ratan Sen, son of Raja Pirthipal Sen of Butwal. Complains against the oppression and tyranny of Raja of Nepal and capture of Palpa by him. Requests for help from the Company for the release of his father and other relatives and also to overthrow the Raja of Nepal from Palpa.

OR 145,[3] *f 1; TR 51, pp. 185-92, no. 55; AR 20, p. 34.*

Mar. 6 152. From Raja Pirthipal Sen of Butwal. Complains against the highhandedness of the Raja of Nepal. Requests to adopt some measures for the release of the writer from the prison of the Raja of Nepal. Also requests to provide some maintenance allowance to his son and family members who have taken asylum in Gorakhpur.

OR 146, f 1; TR 51, pp. 192-94, no. 56; AR 20, p. 34.

Mar. 6 153. From the *Peshwa*. Referring to the treaty of Bassien acknowledges the friendly relations between the two governments. Requests for a joint-venture for the annihilation of Jaswant Rao Holkar. Appreciates the administrative changes

[1]Copy enclosed with a letter from the Resident at Nagpur, dated 16 November 1805.

[2]Spiritual Guide to the ruler of Nepal. See *Index to Titles*, p. 60.

[3]OR 144 for reference.

carried out by the Company in his state and requests to send an instruction to General Henery Wellesley to implement them properly.

OR 147, WS, WC, f 1; CR 22, pp. 284-86, no. 5; TR 51, pp. 195-98, no. 57; AR 20, p. 30.

Mar. 6 154. From the Peshwa (Baji Rao II). Adverting to the appointment of Col. Close (as Resident) at the court of Daulat Rao Sindhia in place of late Webbe, expresses his feelings that the friendly relation between the two governments would find a regular strength during the Residency of Col. Close. Also acknowledges appointment of Capt. Sydenham as the representative of Col. Close during latter's absence.

OR 148,[1] WS, WC, f 1; CR 22, pp. 286-88, no. 9; TR 51, pp. 198-202, no. 58; AR 20, p. 30.

Mar. 6 155. From Ranbam Pandey and Karbir Pandey[2] of Nepal. Adverting to the long services of his predecessors for eighteen generations under the Residency of various Residents, explains the brutal atrocity of Raja Ran Bahadur of Nepal against the family of late Diwan Damodhar Pandey on a mare reason of latter's inclination towards the Company's government. Requests for the redressal of their difficulties and also beg for their subsistence.

OR 149,[3] f 1; TR 51, pp. 202-07, no. 59; AR 20, p. 34.

Mar. 6 156. To Nawwab Nasr Allah Khan of Rampur. Appreciates the addressee's courage and adventure in saving Rampur from the onslaught of Amir Khan and confers a *khilat* on him in appreciation. Expresses his hope that the addressee will show the same zeal and promptness in future. Also expresses hopes that all the accomplices of Amir Khan will be arrested and punished.

CI 41, pp. 18-26, no. 4; TI 51; pp. 21-23, no. 5; AI 20, p. 57.

Mar. 8 157. From Maharaja Ajit Singh of Rewa. Refers to the letter of his son to the addressee and writer's meeting with Augustus Brooke. Says that he has decided to establish a friendly relation

[1]Enclosed with a letter from the Resident at Poona to the Persian Secretary, dated 15 February 1805.

[2]Nephews of late Diwan Damodhar Pandey of Nepal (see TR 51).

[3]Represented to the Governor through Mirza Muhammad Wali.

with the British government. Asks the address to leave the territories of Sahawan, Harsinghpur, Pargana Bardawain, Amwa Kaleyanpur, Goethi, etc. contiguous to the boundary of Bundelkhand, now under British control as these have been the part of his dominion since the time of Emperor Akbar. Also proposes to send a letter in this regard under his (addressee's) seal and signature. Further proposes to sign an agreement of friendship and alliance for the defence.

OR 150,[1] *WS, f 1; CR 22, pp. 289-91, no. 7; TR 51, pp. 207-10, no. 60.*

Mar. 8 158. Tekchand, *wakil* of Nasr Allah Khan (Nawwab Rampur) to A. Seton. Informs that Amir Khan has moved from Hasanpur towards Alhad and also devastated Hasanpur.

OR 151,[2] *f 1; CR 22, p. 291, no. 8.*

Mar. 8 159. *Yaddasht* of an application for *dastak-e-rahdari* from Keshav Lochan requesting for *maafi-e-mahsulat* (exemption from toll taxes) who is to go to Orissa for *darshan*. Also gives detail of the belongings.

OR 152, f 1.

Mar. 8 160. Petition of Ram Singh for a *dastak-e-rahdari* for Raja Sardul Singh and Fateh Kishan Purohit who are to go to Gayaji and Kashiji for a pilgrimage.

OR 153, WS, f 1.

Mar. 8 161. From Daulat Rao Sindhia. Memorandum of points unadjusted by Webbe, in conformity to the treaty. Containing ten points the memorandum highlights the points regarding adjustment of revenue from some area, war tactics adopted by the Company and the arrangement of security for Sindhia's dominion, etc., etc.

OR 154,[3] *f 1; TR 51, pp. 210-17, no. 61; AR 20, p. 8.*

Mar. 12 162. To the Nizam. Complementary in reply to the addressee's letter of congratulation on the success of the British forces over the Maratha (Holkar).

CI 41, pp. 391-93, no. 136; TI 51, p. 24, no. 6; AI 20, p. 57.

[1]Enclosed with a letter from W.A. Brooke to Edmonston, dated 27 February 1805.

[2]Enclosed with a letter from Seton, dated 25 February 1805.

[3]Enclosed with a letter from Daulat Rao Sindhia to his *wakil* Bhagwant Rao.

Mar. 12 163. To Mir Alam. To the same effect as the TI 6 of 1805.

CI 41, pp. 394-95, no. 137; TI 51, p. 24, no. 7; AI 20, p. 54.

Mar. 12 164. From Nawwab Muin al-Mulk (Dilawar Jang) Bahadur (of Murshidabad). Complementary with the present of one *bahangi* ice.

OR 155,[1] WS,[2] WC, f 1; TR 51, pp. 217-18, no. 62; AR 20, p. 9.

Mar. 12 165. From Siraj al-Din Ali Khan.[3] Requests for the issuance of a *parwana-e-rahdari* to Moti Lal, one of his friends who wants to go to Lucknow, his native place.

OR 156, WS, f 1.

Mar. 12 166. From Muhammad Najm al-Din. Requests for the issuance of a *dastak-e-rahdari* for his son Muhammad Sayeed al-Din who has to go to Bareilly to take over the charge of *qazi* there.

OR 157, WS, f 1.

Mar. 12 167. Newsletter from the newswriter at Delhi to the Resident at Delhi. Informs about the encampment of *wazir-e-mamalik* at Shikarpur (Sindh) accompanied by Mir Mahmud at the head of about 40,000 troops and gunmen. Also informs about the kidnapping of the niece of Mir Mahmud by the Chief of Talpur and her consequent *nikah* with him. Further says about the offer of Rs. 22 lakh by the said Chief to the king to cover up his misdeeds, etc., etc.

OR 158(a), f 1.

Mar. 14 168. News writer from Rampur. Informs that Amir Khan has arrived near Muradabad and the order of Nawwab to Kalyan Rai Bakhshi to guard the city against the expected onslaught of the said Khan.

OR 159,[4] f 1; CR 22, pp. 294-95, no. 10.

Mar. 16 169. From Rao Shiv Rao of Jhansi. Acknowledges receipt of a *khilat* from the Governor-General through Captain Baillie. Also requests to always consider him among the faithful and loyal.

OR 160, WS, WC, f 1; TR 51, pp. 218-19, no. 63; AR 20, p. 35.

[1]The document is illuminated golden.

[2]Seal appears both on the letter and the cover.

[3]*Qazi al-Quzat* of Calcutta.

[4]Enclosed with a letter from Col. Collins to Edmonston, dated 6 February 1805.

Mar. 16 170. From Purnaiya.[1] Refers to his earlier letter. Informs about the departure of Col. Malcolm at the head of 3,000 troops torwards Poona along with General Wellesley. Also says about the rebellious acts of the *zamindars* of Chittor and Badarkonda and their subsequent suppression. Further informs about the arrangement made by the writer for the supply of food to these regions, etc. etc.

OR 161,[2] WS,[3] WC, f 1; CR 22, pp. 296-99, no. 12; TR 51, pp. 219-24, no. 64; AR 20, p. 31.

Mar. 16 171. From Nawwab of Carnatic.[4] Refers to the honour he received from the King of Great Britain in the shape of a letter. Encloses a copy of the said letter and informs that he has got permission from Lord William Bentick to send his letter to the king through Vice-Admiral Rainier who is supposed to leave for Great Britain. Also encloses a translation of this letter. Dated 28 February 1805.

OR 162,[5] WS, WC, f 1; CR 22, pp. 295-96, no. 11; TR 51, pp. 224-26, no. 65; AR 20, p. 2.

Mar. 17 172. To Raja Jagat Singh of Jainagar (Jaipur). Complying with his (addressee) request grants permission to remit the amount of duties in favour of two confidential servants of the addressee.

CI 41, pp. 396-97; TI 51, p. 24, no. 8; AI 20, p. 61.

Mar. 17 173. To Azim al-Daulah (of Carnatic). Complementary in reply to his letter congratulating the addressee for having received a letter from the King of the Great Britain congratulating him on his accession to the *masnad* of his ancestors.

CI 41, pp. 398-99, no. 141; TI 51, p. 25, no. 9; AI 20, p. 43.

Mar. 17 174. To Raja Raghuji Bhonsla. Acknowledges addressee's letter of congratulation for British victory over Jaswant Rao Holkar refers to the treachery of Raja of Bharatpur and also of its consequences with which he will suffer; emphasizes

[1]*Diwan* of Mysore (1799-1810). See *Index to Titles*, p. 164.

[2]Enclosed with a letter from the Resident at Mysore to the Persian Secretary, dated 26 February 1805.

[3]Rectangular wax seal on the cover.

[4]Azim al-Daulah ?

[5]Enclosed with a letter from the Secretary at Fort George to the Chief Secretary. Dated 2 March 1805.

the necessity of British support for the independence of Sambhalpur and Patna. Assures that the British government has no intention of interfering in the affairs of addressee's state lest he violates the treaty of Deogaon.

CI 41, pp. 21-26, no. 5, TI 51, pp. 25-30, no. 10; AI 20, p. 61.

Mar. 17 175. From Jaswant Rao Ramchandra (of Nagpur). Refers to the letter of General Wellesley to Lt. Colonel Kirkpatrick to satisfy the requests of the writer. Says that nothing could be done in this respect due to improper hassle created by the *talluqadars* of the Nizam. Requests to direct Col. Kirkpatrick to prevent the *talluqdaars* from creating obstruction in the fulfilment of the writer's request. Also informs about some gifts sent to the addressee. Dated 23 January 1805.

OR 163,[1] *WC, f 1; CR 22, pp. 299-300, no. 13; TR 51, pp. 231-32, no. 66; AR 20, p. 18.*

Mar. 17 176. From Raja Raghuji Bhonsla. Complementary with a present of sugar coated sesame on passing the sun into the Zodiac sign of Capricorn.

OR 164,[2] *WC, WC, f 1; CR 22, pp. 300, no. 14; TR 51, p. 232, no. 67; AR 20, p. 33.*

Mar. 18 177. From Nawwab Wazir of Awadh. Congratulatory on the occasion of the bestowal of the title of 'Sir' on Major General Wellesley (Governor-General's brother) by the king of Great Britain. Dated 11 March 1805.

OR 165, WS, WC, f 1; CR 22, pp. 301-02, no. 15; TR 51, pp. 232-33, no. 68; AR 20, p. 41.

Mar. 18 178. From Nawwab Wazir (of Awadh). To the same effect as the foregoing OR 165.

OR 166,[3] *f 1; CR 22, pp. 301-02, no. 15; TR 51, pp. 232-33, no. 68; AR 20, p. 41.*

Mar. 18 179. Copy of intelligence report from Col. Ochterloney, the Resident at Delhi to Col. Collins, Resident at Lucknow. Informs about the conspiracy being hatched between Mir

[1]Enclosed with a letter from the Resident at Nagpur, dated 25 February 1805.
[2]Enclosed with a letter from the Resident at Nagpur.
[3]Enclosed with a letter from the Resident at Lucknow.

Khan and Alamas Ali Khan to share the territories of Nawwab Safdar Jang.

OR 167,[1] *f 1; CR 22, pp. 292, no. 9.*

Mar. 18 180. Mirza Muhammad (newswriter at Peshawar) to the Resident at Delhi. States that Jaswant Rao Holkar is keen to invite the king of Kabul to India. He has also sent some presents to him through his *wakil*. Also informs about the offer of presents to the said king by the *amirs* of Sindh while the former encamped in Sindh.

OR 168 (a), f 1.

Mar. 18 181. Newsletter from the camp of General Smith. Informs about the encampment of Amir Khan near Tajpur and the devastation of the villages around by him. Also gives a short account of the clash of Amir Khan's troops with the Company's forces.

OR 168 9b), f 1.

Mar. 18 182. Ranjit Singh of Lahore to Shambhu Nath *tahsildar* of Saharanpur. Says that he has sent Lala Dhokul Singh to Begam Samru as per her desire for setting down the affairs. Desires that a *harkara* should be sent along with the Lala for his safe arrival. Adds that the writer will proceed to the addressee if the negotiation with Begam Sahiba (Begam Samru) turns favourable.

OR 168[2] *(c), f 1; TR 51 pp. 233-34, no. 60; AR 20, p. 10.*

Mar.19 183. Raja Ranjit Singh (of Lahore) to General Lake (Commander-in-Chief). Assures the addressee of his sincerity and attachment towards the Company government. Requests the addressee to ignore his past mistakes in order to revive the friendship between the two states.

OR 169,[3] *f 1; CR 22, pp. 302-04, no. 16(1).*

Mar. 19 184. From Raja Ranjit Singh (of Lahore). Informs about the departure of Kishan Singh who will give a detailed account of the writer to the addressee. Requests for the strengthening

[1]Copy enclosed with a letter from the Resident at Lucknow, dated 4 March 1805.

[2]Enclosed with a letter from the Resident at Delhi to the Secretary, dated 4 March 1805.

[3]Enclosed with a letter from Mercer, dated 9 March 1805.

of the friendly terms with the Company's government. Dated 5 March 1805.

OR 170,[1] *f 1; CR 2, pp. 304-05, no. 16(2).*

Mar. 19 185. General (Lake) to Raja Ranjit Singh of Lahore. Refers to the receipt if addressee's letter expressing regret for some untoward happenings on the part of the addressee. Says that all the mishappenings have occurred due to addressee. Asks him to personally come to relinquish these matters.

OR 171,[2] *f 1; CR 22, pp. 305-06, no. 16(3).*

Mar. 19 186. General Lake (Commander-in-Chief) to Raja Ranjit Singh (of Lahore). Refers to the weakening of their relation due to the interferences of selfish elements; asks him to pay compensation of the losses on the part of the Company and personally come to the writer if he (the addressee) wants to revive and strength the old friendly relation with the Company government. Dated 26 February 1805.

OR 172,[3] *f 1; CR 22, pp. 306-08, no. 16(4).*

Mar. 24 187. From Nawwab Wazir of Awadh. Complementary with a present of pomegranate and other fruits. Dated 5 *Zilhijja* 1219 (8 March 1805).

OR 173, WS, WC, f 1; CR 22, p. 9, no. 18;
TR 51, p. 234, no. 70; AR 20, p. 41.

Mar. 24. 188. Nawwab Wazir to Sir George Barlow. Complementary with present of pomegranate. Dated 5 *Zilhijja* 1219 AH (8 March 1805).

OR 174,[4] *f 1.*

Mar. 24 189. Nawwab Wazir to Graham. Complementary with present of pomegranates. Dated 5 *Zilhijja* 1219 AH (8 March 1805).

OR 175,[5] *f 1.*

Mar. 24 190. Nawwab Wazir to Edmonstone. Complementary with present of pomegranate. Requests to distribute other packets of fruits among the Governor-General and the concerned

[1]Enclosed with a letter from Mercer, dated 8 March 1805.

[2]Copy enclosed with a letter from Mercer, dated 9 March 1805.

[3]Ibid.

[4]Copy enclosed with a letter from the Resident at Lucknow, dated 18 March 1805.

[5]Ibid.

persons. Dated 5 *Zilhijja* 1219 (8 March 1805).

OR[1] *176, f 1.*

Mar. 24 191. Nawwab Wazir to Speke. Complementary with present of pomegranate, etc. Dated 5 *Zilhijja* 1219 AH (8 March 1805).

OR 177,[2] *f 1.*

Mar. 24 192. Nawwab Wazir to Edmonstone. Detailed list of fruits sent as gift to Governor-General and other notables for its proper distribution among them.

OR 176,[3] *f 1.*

Mar. 24 193. Intelligence report from Kabul. Informs about the arrival of Shuja al-Mulk at Multan along with band of troops to collect the revenue from the rulers of Multan and Sindh and also to punish them for their misbehaviours, etc., etc. Dated 7 February 1805.

OR 179,[4] *f 1.*

Mar. 27 194. Intelligence report from Lahore. Informs that letters have been dispatched to Bagh Singh, Saheb Singh, Nahar Singh etc. either to come in person or send their men for the construction around the fort. Also informs about the amputation of ear and nose of a *uchakka* (ruffian) as punishment; destruction of Ahyapur, Pulkari and Pulka, etc., by Sardar Fath Singh Ahluwalia; etc., etc.

OR[5] *180, f 1.*

Mar. 27 195. To Nawwab Wazir. Complementary in reply to the addressee's congratulatory letter on the honour and dignity conferred on Major General Sir Arthur Wellesley.

CI 41, pp. 399-401, no. 142;
TI 51, p. 30, no. 11; AI 20, p. 68.

Mar. 27 196. To Raja Raghuji Bhonsla of Nagpur. Acknowledges the presents of Sugar and sesame sent on the occasion of the sun's

[1]Copy enclosed with a letter from the Resident at Lucknow, dated 18 March 1805.
[2]Ibid.
[3]Ibid.
[4]Enclosed with a letter from the Resident at Delhi, dated 2 March 1805.
[5]Enclosed with a letter from the Resident at Delhi, dated 13 March 1805.

entering the orbit of Capricorn.

CI, 41, pp. 401-02, no. 143; TI 51, p. 31, no. 12; AI 20, p. 61.

Mar. 27 197. To Qutluq Sultan Begam. Complementary letter in reply to her *shuqqa*.

CI 41, pp. 402-03, no. 144; TI 51, p. 31, no. 13; AI 20, p. 53.

Mar. 27 198. To Munni Begam. Complementary in reply to her letter accompanying presents of Pickles and Preserves.

CI 41, pp. 403-04, no. 145; TI 51, pp. 31-32, no. 14; AI 20, p. 55.

Mar. 27 199. To Dilawar Jang of Bengal. Acknowledges the presents of Oranges.

CI 41, pp. 404-05, no. 146; TI 51, p. 32, no. 15; AI 20, p. 49.

Mar. 27 200. To Amrit Rao. Expresses pleasure over the addressee's loyalty to the Company. Has issued instruction to the Company's officers to provide him all facilities at Benares where he wants to reside. Hopes that the addressee will reduce the number of his retinues.

CI 41, pp. 26-29, no. 6; TI 51, pp. 32-35, no. 16; AI 20, p. 43.

Mar. 27 201. To Aqa Nabi Khan, Ambassador of the King of Persia (Iran). Expresses pleasure over his appointment as Ambassador at Fort William. Requests to come directly to Calcutta. States that instructions have been sent to the officers at Bombay to provide all essential assistance.

CI 41, pp. 29-33, no. 7; TI 51, pp. 35-37, no. 17; AI 20, p. 44.

Mar. 27 202. To Nawwab Yavar al-Daulah in reply to his petition for a *dastak-e-rahdari*. Grants the *dastak-e-rahdari* for a journey from Calcutta to Hyderabad along with his provisions. The list of goods is given.

CI 41, p. 404, no. 147.

Mar. 27 203. Petition of Nawwab Yavar al-Daulah for the grant of a *dastak-e-rahdari* for a journey from Calcutta to Hyderabad along with his men and provisions.

OR 181, f. 1.

Mar. 28 204. From Babbu Begam of Awadh. Notifies the marriage of a daughter of the late Nawwab al-Daulah Bahadur Firoz Jang with Mirza Muhammad Jalil s/o Sultan Muhammad Dawood Mirza. Dated 23 *Zilhijja* 1219 AH (26 March 1805).

OR 182, WS, WC, f 1; CR 22, pp. 309-10, no. 18; TR 51, p. 234, no. 71; AR 20, p. 60.

Mar. 28 205. Nawwab Nasir al-Mulk Azd al-Daulah of Bengal. Complains against the ill treatment meted out to the writer by Smith. Dated 17 *Zilhijja,* 1219 AH (20 March 1805).

OR 183,[1] *WS, WC, f 1; CR 22, pp. 310-12, no. 19; TR 51, pp. 235-36, no. 72; AR 20, p. 28.*

Mar. 28 206. Smith, Judge and Magistrate of Murshidabad to the Nawwab of Bengal. Encloses a complaint lodged by one Begam of Hasanpur against the conduct of one of his (addressee's) relations Nawwab Sharaf al-Din Ali Khan *alias* Walijan who has illegally kept her two daughters in his *mahalsara* (female apartments), and also detained the complainant for a week when she beg that her two daughters should be released. Asks the addressee to manage for the release of the said girls, as any legal action against the culprit would be against the honour and dignity of addressee's family.

OR 184, f 1; CR 22, pp. 312-15, no. 21; TR 51, pp. 237-39, no. 73 (a); AR 20, p. 12.

Mar. 28 207. Smith to Nawwab of Bengal. Refers to his previous letter regarding the complaint lodged against Walijan by one Begam of Hasanpur. Expresses surprise and anxiety over the addressee's indifference and carelessness and asks him to reply soon what action he is going to take in this case. If it is not done he (the writer) would be compelled to take legal action to execute justice as the complainant is regularly insisting for the justice.

OR 185, f 1; CR 22, pp. 315-17, no. 22(1); TR 51, pp. 239-41, no. 73 (b); AR 20, p. 12).

Mar. 28 208. Smith to Nawwab of Bengal. Acknowledges Nawwab Walijan's letter and expresses his displeasure over the violent language used by the said Nawwab. Requests the addressee to

[1]Enclosed with a letter from the Superintendent of Nizamat affairs, dated 28 March 1805.

convey his disappointment to Walijan in order to secure the respect and honour of the court.

OR 186, f 1; CR 22, pp. 321-23, no. 23(1); TR 51, pp. 241-43, no. 73(c), AR 20, p. 12.

Mar. 28 209. Smith to the Nawwab of Bengal. Informs about the case of Nawwab Walijan Khan that it has been forwarded to criminal court of Murshidabad from the court of Circuit.

OR 187, f 1; CR 22, pp. 323-24, no. 23 (2); TR 51, pp. 243-44, no. 73 (d); AR 20, p. 12.

Mar. 28 210. Smith to the Nawwab of Bengal. Refers to his earlier letters to the addressee for the redressal of the case of Walijan Khan. Informs that the court has ordered the said Khan to release the two girls from his *harem*. Requests to convey this decision to Walijan Khan and make him abide by the court order. Further says that if the court's order is not complied with, necessary legal action will be taken against Walijan. Dated 2 March 1805.

OR 188, f 1; CR 22, pp. 317-21, no. 22 (2); TR 51, pp. 244-48, no. 73 (c); AR 20, p. 12.

Mar. 28 211. Smith to the Nawwab of Bengal. Expresses his disappointment over the negligence shown to the writer. Says that he has also left the practice of asking after the addressee's health and welfare as he did not visit the writer in return of the writers visit.

OR 189, f 1; CR 22, pp. 324-27, no. 23 (3); TR 51, pp. 248-51, no. 73 (f); AR 20, p. 12.

Mar. 28 212. Smith to Saiyid Sharaf al-Din Ali Khan of Bengal *alias* Nawwab Walijan Khan. Sends court order to the addressee to release the two daughters of one Begam of Hasanpur, district Murshidabad who are kept in his *harem*. Warns the addressee to refrain from such acts in future. Dated 14 February 1805.

OR 190, f 1; CR 22, pp. 327-28, no. 23 (4); TR 51, pp. 251-52, no. 73 (g); AR 20, p. 12.

Mar. 28 213. Smith to Walijan Khan. Raises strong objections against the improper language used by the addressee in his letter to the writer. Expresses his disappointment on the addressee's disobedience in respect of the orders of district court of Murshidabad.

OR 191, f 1; CR 22, pp. 328-31, no. 23(5); TR 51, pp. 252-55, no. 73 (h); AR 20, p. 12.

Mar. 28 214. Nawwab Nasir al-Mulk to Edmonston. Explains in detail the ill-treatment meted out to the writer by Smith in regard to the complaint of one Begam of Hasanpur. Requests the addressee to bring Smith to book. Dated 17 *Zilhjja* 47 *Julus* (of Shah Alam II) = (20 March 1805).

OR 192, WS, WC, f 1; TR 51, pp. 255-63, no. 74; AR 20, p. 28.

Mar. 28 215. Amir al-Daulah Amir Khan to the *Sahus* and *Baqqals* of Anup Shahar. Orders them to deposit their *nazr* and military charges in time otherwise they will themselves be responsible for their destruction and unbecoming.

OR 193,[1] f 1; CR 22, pp. 331-32, no. 24.

Mar. 30 216. Raja of Nepal to A. Seton. Refers to the old friendly relation subsisting between the two states. Acknowledges his letter asking, there in, to send a letter to the Governor-General. Transmits his reply to the Governor-General along with the copy of Governor-General's letter. Congratulates the addressee on the rapid success of British forces.

OR 194,[2] f 1; CR 22, pp. 336-37, no. 26; TR 51, pp. 263-64, no. 75/76; AR 20, p. 13.

Mar. 30 217. From Raja of Nepal. Explains the causes of difference between the writer and Raja of Srinagar on the arbitration of British government.

OR 195,[3] WS, WC, f 1; CR 22, pp. 332-36, no. 25; TR 51, pp. 265-68, no. 25; AR 20, p. 32.

Mar. 30 218. Seton to Nawwab Muhammad Nasr Allah Khan of Rampur. Forwards a letter from the Governor-General to the addressee. Dated 17 March 1805.

OR 196,[4] f 2;[5] CR 22, pp. 337-39, no. 27.

Mar. 30 219. From A. Seton to Nasr Allah Khan of Rampur. Asks the addressee to apprehend and detain Munir Khan and interrogate him for his actions regarding arrival and flight of Rahmat

[1]The document is the copy of Original.

[2]Enclosed with a letter from the Agent to the Governor-General in the Ceded Provinces to the Secretary, dated 18 March 1805.

[3]Ibid.

[4]Copy enclosed with a letter from Seton, dated 17 March 1805.

[5]The Second folio has no connection with the main letter, folio I.

Khan, the accomplice of Amir Khan Afghan. Dated 30 March 1805.

OR 251[1] *(b), f 1.*

Mar. -- 220. Saiyid Abul Qasim Khan, *tahsildar* of Pilibhit to Seton. Expresses his anxiety over not getting the required help from the British government to fight against the *Pindaris*. Seeks permission to recruit 3,000-4,000 troops on a salary of Rs. 6-7 per month. Dated 9 March 1805.

OR 197,[2] *f 1; CR 22, pp. 339-44, no. 28(1).*

Mar. -- 221. Intelligence report from the newswriter at Badaun to Seton. Informs about the demand of money by Abd Allah Khan, *risaladar* of Amir Khan for the payment of troops. Also informs about Mir Hasan *tahsildar's* continuation of service and absence of *qanungo* and *navishtadar* from *kachehri*.

OR 198,[3] *f 1; CR 22, pp. 344-45, no. 28(2).*

Mar. -- 222. From Muhammad Aazam Khan, *chaudhary* of Badaun. Refers to his previous report of 5 *Zilhijja*. Gives details of the happening of 6 and 7 of the same month. Explains how Abd Allah Khan with the assistance of some other *sardars* attacked Badaun and taken it under possession. Also says about writer's own weakness due to lack of men, material and firearms, etc.

OR 199,[4] *f 1; CR 22, pp. 345-47, no. 28(3).*

Mar. -- 223. Newsletter giving details of the verbal statement of Parmanand and Chunni Lal who have come from Amir Khan's camp. Gives detailed picture of the men, arms and material in the camp of Amir Khan, etc.

OR 200,[5] *f 1; CR 22, pp. 347-49, no. 28(4).*

Mar. -- 224. Seton to Qazi Ghulam Nabi. Refers to Amir Khan's letter addressed to the write. Says that Amir Khan has collected men only for the plunder and destruction of the area. Although he cannot face the British forces, yet the safety of Bareilly is at

[1]Copy enclosed with a letter from Seton, dated 29 April 1805.

[2]Copy enclosed with a letter from Seton, dated 11 March 1805.

[3]Copy of original letter enclosed with a private letter of Seton, dated 10 March 1805.

[4]Enclosed with a letter from Seton, dated 10 March 1805.

[5]Ibid.

stake. Asks the addressee to make arrangement for the safety and security of the said area. Dated 7 March 1805.

OR 201,[1] f 1; CR 22, pp. 349-51, no. 29.

Mar. -- 225. Copy of OR 204. See also ORs 167 and 203.

OR 202 f 1, CR 22, p. 292, no. 9.

Mar. -- 226. Copy of OR 204. See also ORs 167 and 202.

OR 203, f 1; CR 22, p. 292, no. 9.

Mar. -- 227. Same as ORs 167, 202 and 203.

OR 204, f 1; CR 22, p. 292, no. 9.

Mar. -- 228. Shiv Rao Bhao of Jhansi to Capt. John Baillie. Expresses his deep sense of gratitude for the bestowal of a *khilat* on him by the addressee through Qamr al-Din Khan. Also expresses his hopes for further strengthening of their relations.

OR 205,[2] f 1; CR 22, pp. 354-56, no. 31.

Mar. -- 229. From Shiv Rao Bhao of Jhansi. Acknowledges the receipt of a *khilat* from Capt. Baillie. Expresses his gratitude for this *khilat*.

OR 206,[3] f 1; OR 22, pp. 356-68, no. 32.

Mar. -- 230. Intelligence report from the newswriter at the camp of Lord Lake (at Bharatpur). Informs that four cannons were dug out from the house of Samru. Also informs that differences persist between Raja Ranjit Singh of Bharatpur and Holkar but there is no any likelihood of war between them, etc., etc. Dated 26 March 1805.

OR 207, f 1.

Mar. -- 231. Intelligence report from the newswriter at the camp of General Smith (Ganeshpur). Informs about the movement of the said General from village Milk towards Ganeshpur; arrival of Amir Khan at Ahlad and meeting of Dawood Khan Mewati, Nawwab Ahmad Ali Khan and Nawwab Nasr Allah Khan of Rampur to him, etc., etc.

OR 108,[4] f 1.

[1]Copy enclosed with a letter from Seton, dated 9 March 1805.

[2]Enclosed with a letter from the Agent to the Comander-in-Chief, dated 27 February 1805.

[3]Enclosed with a letter from the Commander-in-Chief, dated 27 February 1805.

[4]Enclosed with a letter from the Resident at Lucknow, dated 2 March 1805.

April 2 232. To Daulat Rao Sindhia. Refers to his (Writer) previous letter expecting an apology from the addressee (Daulat Rao Sindhia) for the violation of the terms of the treaty by the *Pindaris*, serving under him by committing outrage against the British Representative. Further says that if the addressee does not intend to do so, the British government has resolved to withdraws its agent from the addressee's court and break all friendly relations.

CI 41, pp. 32-36, no. 8; TI 51, pp. 37-40, no. 18; AI 20, p. 48.

April 4 233. To Daulat Rao Sindhia. Acknowledges addressee's letter through his *wakil* wherein the address has refuted various allegations and charges levelled against him by the British government. Cites and explains various acts of violence and aggression committed by the addressee's officers and dependents against the British interests. Also condemns the addressee for inaccuracy and fallacy of his statements in his letter. Asks the addressee to satisfy the British representative regarding these matters otherwise the British government would be compelled to take measures against him.

CI 41, pp. 36-91; no. 9; TI 51, pp. 41-101, no. 19; AI 20, p. 48.

April 6 234. From Jagat Singh of Murshidabad. Informs about his return from the pilgrimage of Jagannathji to Murshidabad. Expresses his thanks to the addressee for providing facilities through his officers at various points of journey.

OR 209,[1] WS, WC, f 1; TR 51, p. 269, no. 78; AR 20, p. 17.

April 7 235. Raja Raghuji Bhonsla. Congratulatory on the success of General Fraser and Lord Lake along with some presents like cloths, jewels and an elephant. Encloses a list of the articles of gift.

OR 210, WS, WC, ff 2; TR 51, pp. 269-72, no. 79; AR 20, p. 33.

April 7 236. Mirza Ahmad Ali Khan to Col. Ochterlony. Refers to the petition of Nawwab Ghulam Muhammad Khan to the addressee to enter into the service of the Company. Recommends the

[1]Delivered by *wakil* of Jagat Seth.

case of the said Nawwab and stands surety for his conduct in future.

OR 211,[1] WS, WC, f 1; CR 22, pp. 379-80, no. 4; TR 51, pp. 273-74, no. 81; AR 20, p. 10.

April 7 237. Saiyid Shukr Allah to Col. Collins, Resident at Lucknow. Expresses his sincerity and integrity towards the Company's government and recounts his services towards the government. Advises the address not to believe the Marathas (Holkar). Also seeks permission for the passage of his army through Kanpur.

OR 213[2] (a), f 1; CR 22, pp. 383-85, no. 5.

April 8 238. Muhammad Nasr Allah Khan to A. Seton. Suggests sending Munir Khan along with Wali Khan to facilitate the enquiry into his conduct with regard to the escape of Rahmat Khan. Dated 3 *Muharram* 1220 AH (4 April 1805 AD).

OR 251[3] (c), f 1.

April 8 239. Statement of Nemat Allah, a surgeon and witness in the case of Munir Khan's involvement in Rahmat Khan's flight. States that he visited Munir Khan's *haveli* to give some treatment to Rahmat Khan who was wounded by a gunshot. Also clarifies that Munir Khan was not present in his *haveli* when he went to see Rahmat Khan; etc. Dated 8 April 1805.

OR 251[4] (e), ff 2.

April 8 240. Statement of Mulla Muhammad Beg, a trooper of Nasr Allah Khan. Records his statement that he saw Rahmat Khan twice in the *haveli* of Munir Khan. Also says that when Saiyid Ahmad Khan and others were making arrangement for the flight of Rahmat Khan, he was present there but fails to ascertain whether Munir Khan was present at that time, etc. Dated 8 April 1805.

OR 251[5] (f), ff 4.

April 9 241. Statement of Diler Khan, a servant of Nasr Allah Khan, in the case of Rahmat Khan's flight and the alleged involvement of Munir Khan. States that he has never seen Rahmat Khan but

[1]Enclosed with a letter from the Resident at Delhi to the Secretary, dated 25 March 1805.

[2]Copy enclosed with a letter from the Resident at Lucknow, dated 2 April 1805. Also see OR 246.

[3]Copy enclosed with a letter from A. Seton.

[4]Enclosed with a letter from A. Seton, dated 29 April 1805.

[5]Ibid.

has heared his name. Also states that he was sent by Nasr Allah Khan to inform Munir Khan to bring Rahmat Khan before him (Nasr Allah Khan); etc. Dated 9 April 1805.

OR 251[1] *(g), ff 2.*

April 10 242. Jaswant Rao Holkar to Nawwab Saadat Ali Khan Bahadur (of Awadh). Requests the addressee to get the property of Shukr Allah Chaudhry of *pargana* Bisoh from Mirza Mahdi who has siezed it sometimes back. Also requests to help Ehsan Ali, Raja of Muhammedi (?) and Lal Singh, Raja of Dholarah who are imprisoned there.

OR 213[2] *(b), f 1; CR 22, pp. 385-87, no. 6.*

April 11 243. Col. Close to Sukh Ram Shriji Rao Ghatke. Acknowledges receipt of the addressee's letter and intimates that it has been forwarded to the Governor-General. Dated 26 March 1805.

OR 214 (a), f 1; CR 22, pp. 387-90, no. 7 (i); TR 51, p. 275, no. 82 (a); AR 20, p. 14.

April 11 244. Col. Close to Jaswant Rao Ghorpade. Acknowledges the receipt of his (addressee) letter and intimates about its transmission to Governor-General. Dated 26 March 1805.

OR 214[3] *(b), f 1; CR 22, pp. 388-89, no. 7 (ii); TR 51, p. 275, no. 52 (b); AR 20, p. 14.*

April 11 245. To Nawwab Qasim Ali Khan. Acknowledges receipt of his letter along with the present of *itr* (perfume).

CI. 41,[4] *p. 406, no. 148; TI 51, p. 101, no. 20; AI 20, p. 47.*

April 11 246. To Nawwab Ashraf Ali Khan.[5] Acknowledges his letter along with a present of *itr* (perfume).

CI 41, pp. 408-9, no. 151; TI 51, p. 104, no. 21; AI 20, p. 45.

[1]Enclosed with a letter from A. Seton. Dated 29 April 1805.

[2]Copy enclosed with a letter from the Resident at Lucknow, dated 2 April 1805. Also see OR 246.

[3]Persian translation of the Marathi letter, enclosed with a letter from the Resident at Poona to the Secretary, dated 26 March 1805.

[4]Son of Nawwab Salar Jang and Nephew of the elder Begam of Lucknow; pensioner of the British government resided at Benares. (*Index to Titles*, p. 164.)

[5]Sharaf al-Daulah, Sharif al-Mulk, Bahadur Diler Jang, of Lucknow; had a liberal pension under British grantees; Probably died in 1811. (*Index to Titles*, p. 17.)

April 11 247. To Jahanabadi Begam.[1] Complementary in reply to her Congratulatory letter on the success of British troops (against the Marathas).

CI 41, pp. 406-7, no. 149; TI 51, p. 102, no. 22; AI 20, p. 51.

April 11 248. To Raja Raghuji Bhonsla.[2] Complementary in reply to addressee's invitation on the eve of his nephew's marriage.

CI 41, pp. 416-17, no. 160; TI 51, p. 102, no. 23, AI 20, p. 61.

April 11 249. To Nawwab Dilawar Jang (of Farrukhabad). Condolatory letter on the death of the addressee's grandson.

CI 41, pp. 417-18, no. 161; TI 51, p. 103, no. 24; AI 20, p. 49.

April 11 250. To Nawwab Dilawar Jang (of Farrukhabad). Complementary in reply to the addressee's congratulatory letter on the success of British troops.

CI 41, pp. 415-16, no. 159; TI 51, p. 103, no. 25; AI 20, p. 49.

April 11 251. To Raja of Jainagar (Jaipur). Complementary in reply to addressee's congratulatory letter on the conclusion of peace with Daulat Rao Sindhia and Raja of Berar.

CI 41, pp. 418-20, no. 162; TI 51, p. 103, no. 26; AI 20, p. 61.

April 11 252. To Nawwab Nusrat Jang. Complementary in reply to addressee's letters on the subject of Muhammad Taqi Khan's return to Dacca.

CI 41, pp. 423-25, no. 166; TI 51, p. 104, no. 27 AI 20, p. 58.

April 11 253. To Bahu Begam. Complementary reply to her letter lamenting the infrequency of the writer's correspondence.

CI 41, pp. 411-12, no. 154; TI 51, p. 104, no. 28; AI 20, p. 46.

April 11 254. To Nasir al-Mulk of Murshidabad. Complementary reply to addressee's letter accompanying a present of Oranges.

CI 41, pp. 410-11, no. 153; TI 51, p. 104, no. 29; AI 20, p. 58.

[1]Second wife of Jahandar Shah, the eldest son of Shah Alam II.

[2]Maharaja Raghuji Bhonsla II, son and successor of Madhoji Bhonsla in the government of Berar and Nagpur in May 1788; Brother of Venkoji Bhonsla, died on 22 March 1816 (*Index to Titles*, p. 166).

April 11 255. To Nawwab Madar al-Daulah of Lucknow. Praises the addressee's spirit for public service but declines his request for his appointment as ambassador at the court of Delhi on behalf of Company's government.

CI 41, pp. 420-21, no. 163; TI 51, p. 105, no. 30; AI 20, p. 55.

April 11 256. To Bishambhar Pandit (*wakil* of Raghuji Bhonsla). Complementary in reply to the addressee's letter of thanks for the writer's favour. Also congratulates him for being felicitated with a *khilat* by Raghuji Bhonsla.

CI 41, pp. 421-22, no. 164; TI 51, pp. 105-06, no. 31; AI 20, p. 46.

April 11 257. To Hari Bhadra Pandit. Complementary. To the same effect as previous one.

CI 41, pp. 422-23, no. 165; TI 51, pp. 105-06, no. 32; AI 20, p. 50.

April 11 258. To Saiyid Abul Qasim Khan. Complementary in reply to addressee's congratulatory letter on the eve of Christmas.

CI 41, p. 413, no. 156; TI 51, p. 106, no. 33. AI 20, p. 45.

April 11 259. To Harak Chand Jagat Seth of Murshidabad. Complementary in reply to his letter of congratulation on the eve of Christmas.

CI 41, pp. 412-13, no. 155; TI 51, p. 106, no. 34; AI 20, p. 51.

April 11 260. To Babu Shiv Narayan Singh, Raja of Benares, Complementary in reply to addressee's congratulatory letter on the eve of Christmas.

CI 41, p. 408, no. 150; TI 51, p. 107, no. 35; AI 20, p. 66.

April 11 261. To Raja Mitrajit Singh of Tekari. In reply to his complementary letter on the eve of Christmas.

CI 41, pp. 414-15, no. 158; TI 51, p. 107, no. 36; AI 20, p. 62.

April 11 262. To Jhau Lal. In reply to his complementary letter accompanying *nazr* on the occasion of Christmas.

CI 41, p. 414, no. 157; TI. 51, p. 107, no. 37; AI 20, p. 51.

April. 11 263. To Raja Sunder Singh (*diwan* of Mubarak al-Daulah). In reply to his complementary letter on the eve of Chritsmas.

CI 41, pp. 409-10, no. 152; TI 51, p. 108, no. 38; AI 20, p. 62.

April 12 264. Raja Ranjit Singh of Bharatpur to Col. Lake, Commender-in-Chief. Expresses his agreement to the terms of the peace treaty offered by the Company's government, however, explains his financial handicap to pay an amount of Rs. 50 lakh. Assures that he will neither have any connection with the enemies of the Company nor demolish the fortification of Bharatpur. Also requests to return the fortress of Deig.

OR 215,[1] *f 1; CR 22, pp. 392-95, no. 9(1).*

April 12[2] 265. General Lake to Raja Ranjit Singh of Bharatpur. Requests the addressee to dispatch the desired confidential person and assures him (the addressee) of the sincerity of the British government towards the writer. Dated 26 March 1805.

OR 216,[3] *f 1; CR 22, pp. 395-96, no. 9.*

April 13 266. From Thapa Amar Singh to A. Seton. Expresses his anxiety for not receiving any letter from the addressee and reassures the alliance of the two governments. Says that it is learnt that enemies of the Company have become active around the Company's dominion. Seeks permission to send his Gorkha troops to accompany the British forces in this adventure.

OR 217 f 1; CR 22, pp. 397-98, no. 10.

April 13 267. Seton to Amar Singh Thapa of Nepal. Acknowledges his letter offering the writer a military aid. Says that since Amir Khan has crossed over to Ganga no military aid is required from the addressee.

OR 218,[4] *f 1; CR 22, pp. 398-400, no. 10(2).*

April 13[5] 268. From Chautria Hastdial Shah. Refers to the dispatch of Harikishan on his part to the addressee five-six months back.

[1]Enclosed with a letter from the Agent to the Governor-General at Headquarter, dated 1 April 1805.

[2]The document does not bear the date of receipt, however, this date is written over the folder (?).

[3]Copy of the letter enclosed with a letter from the Agent to Governor-General.

[4]Copy enclosed with a letter from the Agent at Bareilly to the Governor-General, dated 2 April 1805.

[5]The date of receipt given on the document by A. Seton is 2 April 1805, however, the date on the folder of the document is 13 April 1805.

Says that as the enemies have been busy in sporadic activities in the Company's domination, if desired the Gorkha troops may be sent to join the Company's forces.

OR 219,[1] f 1; CR 22, p. 400, no. 1.

April 13 269. Seton to Hastdial Shah, Chautria. Acknowledges receipt of the addressee's letter. Refers to his previous letter along with a box of American tea sent to the addressee. Further says that since Amir Khan, under apprehension has already crossed over to Ganga there is no need of military aide from the addressee.

OR 220,[2] f 1; CR 22, pp. 201-03, no. 11 (1).

April 13[3] 270. Intelligence report from the newswriter at the camp of Lord Lake to the Agent to the Governor-General at Farrukhabad. Conveys news regarding a meeting of Rai Ratan Lal, *wakil* of Raja Ranjit Singh of Bharatpur and other officials with Lord Lake and Mercer to measure sword with Jaswant Rao Holkar and Daulat Rao Sindhia on account of skirmishes between the two enemies, etc., etc.

OR 221,[4] f 1.

April 17 271. Intelligence report from the newswriter at Kabul. Informs about:

(a) the halt of Shah Shuja al-Mulk at Dera Ghazi Khan.
(b) appointment of Ata Muhammad Khan as the *subedar* of Peshawar following the dismissal of Rahmat-Allah Khan.
(c) dispatch of troops by Bagh Singh Ahluwalia to help Saheb Singh, the Raja of Patiala.
(d) *nazr* of Rs. 5 lakh from Bahawal Khan *subedar* of Bahawalpur, begging pardon for his previous misdeeds.
(e) a *nazr* from Raja of Leh to the king of Kabul.

OR 222,[5] f 1; CR 22, pp. 403-4, no. 12.

April 17 272. Intelligence report from Dulha Rai at Multan. Conveys the intention and plan of Shah Shuja al-Mulk to direct his attention towards Hindustan after setting down the affairs at Multan. Also informs about the precious presents offered by Shahnawaz Khan of Multan and Lala Chandan Lal, the *wakil*

[1]Copy enclosed with a letter from Seton.

[2]Copy enclosed with a letter from Seton at Bareilly, dated 2 April 1805.

[3]The date of receipt does not come forth from the document, however, the date of its translation is 13 April.

[4]Enclosed with a letter from Lloyd, Acting Agent at Farrukhabad.

[5]Enclosed with a letter from the Resident at Delhi, dated 2 April 1805.

of Jaswant Rao Holkar to the king of Kabul and vice versa. Also expresses his loyalty to the family of the addressee.

OR 223, f 1; TR 51, pp. 276-77, no. 83; CR 22, pp. 390-92, no. 8; AR 20, p. 9.

April 18 273. Amar Singh to Seton. Acknowledging the friendly relation between Nepal and the Company to fight against the enemy (*pindaris*) who have created commotion and disturbance as far as Najibabad and Muradabad. Dated 24 March 1805.

OR[1] 224, f 1; WS, WC, CR 22, pp. 412-14, no. 15; TR 51, pp. 277-79, no. 84; AR 20, p. 13.

April 18 274. From Seton. Statement of the amount of duties levied by the *zamindars* of Nawwab Wazir on the *qand* (loaf sugar) and *misri* (sugar) of the Company.

OR 225,[2] f 1; CR 22, p. 414; no. 16; TR 51, p 279, no. 85; AR 20, p. 13.

April 18[3] 275. Seton to Thapa Amar Singh of Nepal. Acknowledges receipt of the addressee's letter where in he has offered military aid to the Company to fight against the *pindaris*. States that he will shortly send this letter to the Governor-General for his consideration. Dated 5 April 1805.

OR 226,[4] f 1; CR 22, pp. 406-8, no. 13 (1); TR 51, pp. 289-90, no. 88; AR 20, p. 13.

April 18 276. Seton to Hastdial Shah of Nepal. To the same effet as the foregoing.

OR 226, OR 227, f 1; CR 22, pp. 409-11, no. 13 (2); TR 51, p. 290, no. 88; AR 20, p. 13.

April 18 277. Hastdial Shah to Seton. Offers a contingent of troops

[1]Enclosed with a letter from the Agent in the Ceded Provinces to the Secretary, dated 5 April 1805.

[2]Copy enclosed with a letter from the Agent in Ceded Provinces, dated 9 April 1805.

[3]The date in TR is 28 April but OR 227 which is the copy of original letter bears 18 April as the date of its receipt, while OR 226 does not bear any date or endorsement. The difference may have been caused as both the letters OR 226 and OR 227 have been addressed to Thapa Amar Singh and Chautria Hastdial Shah respectively.

[4]Enclosed with a letter from the Agent to the Governor-General in Ceded Provinces.

to fight against the enemy of the Company. Dated 2 *Zilhijja* 1219 AH.

24 March 1805, OR 228,[1] *WS, WC, f 1; CR 22, pp. 411-12, no. 14; TR 51, p. 279, no. 84; AR 20, p. 13.*

April 19 278. From Daulat Rao Sindhia. States that persons who are guilty of disrespect and improper proceedings towards the gentlemen (British) of the Residency shall he punished by the writer.

OR 229,[2] *WS, WC, f 1; CR 22, pp. 414-18, no. 17; TR 51, pp. 280-84, no. 86; AR 20, p. 8.*

April 19[3] 279. Mirza Sikandar Shukoh to Col. Collins. Denies of having ever written any intelligence injurious to the reputation of Nawwab Wazir.

OR 230,[4] *f 1; CR 22, pp. 420-23, no. 19.*

April 19[5] 280. Mirza Sikandar Shukoh to Col. Collins. To the same effect as the foregoing.

OR 231, f 1; CR 22, pp. 420-23, no. 19.

April 19 281. From A. Seton to Nasr Allah Khan (of Rampur). Asks the addressee to release Munir Khan as he has not been found guilty of helping Rahmat Khan knowingly but unknowingly. Dated 19 April 1805.

OR 251[6] *(h) f 1).*

April 21 282. Ranjit Singh of Bharatpur to Mercer. Promisary note executed by the writer for the repayment of Rs. 20 lakh taken from the Company. Also gives the break-up of the annual instalment.

OR 232, f 1; CR 23, pp. 418-19, no. 18(i).

April 21 283. Rai Ratan Lal and Jani Daya Shankar, *wakils* of Raja Ranjit Singh to Mercer. Request to issue a memorandum for

[1]Enclosed with a letter from the Agent in the Ceded Provinces to the Secretary of Political Department, dated 5 April 1805.

[2]Enclosed with a letter from the Resident at Sindhia's court, dated 3 April 1805.

[3]The date of receipt does not come forth from the document, however, the date of despatch is 11 April 1805.

[4]Copy enclosed with a letter from the Resident at Lucknow, dated 11 April 1805.

[5]The date of receipt does not come forth from the document.

[6]Enclosed with a letter of A. Seton, dated 29 April 1805.

the exemption of outstanding amount of Rs. 5 lakh as dues on the said Raja.

OR 233,[1] *f 1; CR 22, pp. 419-20, no. 18(2).*

April 21 284. To Nawwab Wazir. Referring to the letter of Col. Collins expresses his (writer's) sincere thanks to the addressee for supplying 12 elephants to the Company on the request of Col. Collins.

CI 41, pp. 89-91, no. 9A; TI 51, pp. 108-10, no. 39; AI 20, p. 69.

April 22 285. To Daulat Rao Sindhia. Acknowledges and recapitulates addressee's letter dated 23 February. Commends addressee's declaration for maintaining peace and friendly relation with the Company. Objects addressee's advances towards north, while Close has been ordered to move towards south from north. Asks him to return immediately from north in order to occupy the remaining possession of Holkar in Malwa and to adopt measures for the stability of his government.

CI 41, pp. 92-101, no. 10; TI 51, pp. 111-19, no. 40; AI 20, p. 48.

April 22 286. From Raja Chhatarsal (of Kotah). Requests for the restoration of the writer's property.

OR 234, WS, WC, f 1.

April 23 287. Surji Rao Ghatke to Lord Lake. Informs that he (the writer) will reach Bharatpur soon to settle certain issues between Raja Ranjit Singh, Jaswant Rao Holkar and the Company. Dated 11 April 1805.

OR 235[2] *(a), f 1; CR 22, pp. 423-25, no. 20(1).*

April 22 288. General Lake (Commander-in-Chief) to Surji Rao Ghatke. Asks the addressee not to come to Bharatpur as the issues pending between the Company and Ranjit Singh of Bharatpur (which the addressee is desirous to resolve) have been settled. Also informs about the departure of Holkar from Bharatpur.

OR 235[3] *(b), f 1; CR 22, pp. 425-27, no. 20(2).*

April 22 289. To Daulat Rao Sindhia. Commends the addressee's declaration for maintaining peace and friendly relation with

[1]Copy enclosed with a letter from Mercer, dated 18 April 1805.
[2]Ibid., dated 11 April 1805.
[3]Ibid., dated 11 April 1805.

the Company; objects his advances towards north contrary to the terms and conditions of the defensive alliance; asks his immediate return in order to occupy the remaining possession of Holkar in Malwa; also asks to adopt measures for the stability of his government.

CI 41, pp. 92-101, no. 10; TI 51, pp. 111-19, no. 40; AI 20, p. 48.

April 25 290. Surji Rao Ghatke to Mir Alam. Acknowledges receipt of addressee's letter. Requests for payment of about Rs. 10,000 as loan to Sakha Ram Pandit (writer's *wakil* at the addressee's court) immediately. Also requests to prosecute Eknath Marwari who has misappropriated wheat and other grain of about Rs. 40,000 from the area of Din Dayal *mutasaddi* and pay the said amount to the writer.

OR 236,[1] *f 1; CR 22, pp. 427-29, no. 21.*

April 28 291. Copy of newsletter from Abbas Quli Khan at Multan to the Resident at Delhi. Furnishes reports about the departure of Shuja al-Mulk from Shikarpur towards Multan and Dera Ghazi Khan-crossing over river Kotmatan at Ghat Badani; fight between Ahmad Khan Durrani Noorzai and the Afghan miscreants and the subsequent defeat of the latters. Presentation of *nazr* by Shahnawaz Khan and *wakil* of Jaswant Rao Holkar, etc., preparation of the journey of the king from Multan. Rumors regarding arrival of Gul Muhammad Khan along with Nawwab Ahmad Khan and his troops; also report about the payment of Rs. 12,000 per annum to Murshidzada through the *subedar* of Multan to meet the expenses.

OR 237,[2] *f 1.*

April 28 292. Newsletter from Abbas Quli Khan at the camp of Shuja al-Mulk to the Resident at Delhi. Informs that Ahmad Khan Durrani has crossed the river Attock to suppress Bahawal Khan and other miscreants; informs about his (writer's) arrival in the Royal court of Kabul along with Muhammad Yaqub Khan. Also says about the warm welcome given to them at Kabul where they were also bestowed with *khilat,* jewels and other fabulous items, etc. Dated 15 March 1805.

OR 238,[3] *f 1; TR 51, pp. 284-88, no. 87; AR 20, p. 11.*

[1]Enclosed with a letter from the Resident at Hyderabad, dated 25 April 1805.
[2]Enclosed with a letter from the Resident at Delhi, dated 20 April 1805.
[3]Ibid., dated 13 April 1805.

April 28 293. Intelligence from the *deorhi* of Daulat Rao Sindhia. Gives details of court proceedings and refers to the preparation made by Jaswant Rao Holkar and Amir Khan against the Company, etc. Dated 23 *Muharram* 1220 AH (24 April 1805).

OR 249 (a), f 1.

April 28 294. Intelligence from the *deorhi* of Daulat Rao Sindhia. Gives details of the court proceedings and refers to the two letters from Raja of Kotah addressed to Jaswant Rao Holkar and Daulat Rao Sindhia in respect of the possible tussel between them and the Company's government, etc. Dated 24 *Muharram* 1220 AH (25 April 1805).

OR 249 (b), f 1.

April 28 295. Intelligence from the *deorhi* of Daulat Rao Sindhia. Gives details of the court proceedings and refers to the meeting of the *wakils* of the Raja of Jaipur and Surji Rao Ghatke with Daulat Rao Sindhia and Jaswant Rao Holkar in respect of the planning of the expected tussel with the Company's forces, etc.

OR 249(c), f 1.

April 28 296. Intelligence from the *deorhi* of Daulat Rao Sindhia. Gives details of the court proceedings and refers to the meetings of Jaswant Rao Holkar and Amir Khan and also that of the *wakils* of Raja of Kotah and Jaipur, etc., with Daulat Rao Sindhia for the proposed movement against the Company's government, etc.

OR 249 (d), f 1.

April 30. 297. From Nawwab Muin al-Mulk (Dilawar Jang of Murshidabad). Complementary with a present of five *pitara* (baskets) of *murabba* and *achaar* (preserves and pickle). Dated 29 April 1805.

OR 240, WS, WC f 1; TR 51, p. 290, no. 89; AR 20, p. 9.

April 30[1] 298. From Bishambhar Pandit (*wakil* of Raghuji Bhonsla). Notifies the marriage of his brother Hari Bhadra Pandit.

OR 241, WS, WC, f 1; TR 51, p. 291, no. 90; AR 20, p. 6.

April 30 299. Hafiz Sher Muhammad Khan of Baghdad to Jones, the Resident at Baghdad. Complementary.

OR 242,[2] f 1; CR 22, pp. 429-30, no. 22.

[1]Date of receipt in TR 51, p. 291 is 31 April 1805 (?).

[2]Enclosed with a letter from the Resident at Baghdad, dated 15 February 1805.

April 30 300. Copy of a letter from the King of Persia (Fath Ali Shah) to Prince Husain Ali Mirza. Conveys a detailed information regartding attack of Russian forces on Iran (Tibtis region); the battles fought by the Iranian forces against the Russian invaders and the defeat and sloughter of the Russian army . . ., etc. Dated *Jumada II*, 1219 AH (September-October 1804).

OR 234[1] (a) f 1 ; CR 22, pp. 439-45, no. 26(1).

April 30 301. Copy of a letter from the king of Persia to his minister. Informs about the departure of Muhammad Hasan Khan (probably second minister of Persia) along with dead bodies of some martyrs. Asks the addressee to make proper arrangements for them. Also refers to the Russian attack and the victory of Persian army over them . . ., etc.

OR 243[2](b) f 1; CR 22, pp. 452-54, no. 26(5).

April 30 302. Aqa Muhammad Nabi Khan, the envoy of Persia in India to Harford Jones, the Resident at Baghdad. Expresses his emotions on their separation and assures of all assistance to the addressee while he (addressee) visits Bushire, Iran or any other place.

OR 243[3] (c), f 1; CR 22, p. 455, no. 26(6).

April 30 303. Aqa Muhammad Nabi Khan, the envoy of Persia in India, to Jones, the Resident at Baghdad. Requests for a loan of six thousand (6,000) *tuman* from the addressee and assures of its repayment when he (the writer) arrives in Bombay. Dated 17 *Shaban* 1219 AH. (21 November 1804).

OR 243[4] (d), f 1; CR 22, pp. 445-46, no. 26(2).

April -- 304. Nawwab Nasr Allah Khan (of Rampur) to A. Seton. Expresses gratitude to the Governor-General for the *khilat* bestowed upon him (the writer) and Nawwab Ahmad Ali Khan. Dated 18 *Zilhijja* 1219 AH (24 February 1805).

OR 244,[5] f 1; CR 22, pp. 367-71, no. 1.

[1]Copy enclosed with a letter from Harford Jones, the Resident at Baghdad, dated 24 November 1804.

[2]Ibid.

[3]Ibid., dated 31 December 1805.

[4]Ibid., dated 24 November 1804.

[5]Enclosed with a letter form Seton to Edmonstone, dated 28 March 1805.

April -- 305. Intelligence from the newswriter at the camp of General Lake, the Commander-in-Chief. Informs that the forces of the Company and that of Holkar are at their previous positions; gives details of the defensive measures taken by Raja Ranjit Singh around the fort of Bharatpur; also gives information about the plunder of Kanod by Narayan Rao Dakhni. Also reports about the movements of other British Generals in different directions around Bharatpur to reinforce the Company's forces.

OR 245, f 1.

April -- 306. A. Seton to Nawwab Nasr Allah Khan. Clarifies that the *khilat* bestowed upon Nawwab Ahmad Ali Khan was not due to the addressee's recommendation but due to his own good relation and loyalty to the Company and hence the addressee should not take it as a scorn to his status. Dated 28 March 1805.

OR 245[1] (A), f 1; CR 22, pp. 371-73, no. 2.

April -- 307. From Saiyid Shukr Allah to the Resident at Lucknow. To the same effect as OR 213(a).

OR 246[2] (a), f 1; CR 22, pp. 383-85, no. 6(4).

April -- 308. Jaswant Rao Holkar to Nawwab Saadat Ali Khan (of Awadh). To the same effect as OR 213 (b).

OR 246,[3] f 1; CR 22, pp. 383-85, no. 6(4).

April -- 309. Nawwab Wazir to Edmonstone. Informs about the departure of Ramazan Ali Khan to Calcutta to see the Governor-General and execute some mission on behalf of the writer. Requests the addressee to help the said Khan to have an audience with the Governor-General. Dated 17 *Muharram* 1220 AH (18 April 1805).

OR 247,[4] f 1; CR 22, p. 431, no. 23.

April -- 310. Babu Rao Sindhia to General Manson. Acknowledges receipt of Rs. 75,000 (seventy-five thousand rupees only) for the payment of troops. Dated 28 *Rabi I*, 44 *Julus* (of Shah Alam II) = 29 July 1802.

29 July 1802, OR 248, f 1; CR 22, p. 433, no. 24.

April -- 311. Abbas Quli Khan to the Resident at Delhi. Informs

[1]Copy enclosed with a letter from Seton, dated 28 March 1805.
[2]Enclosed with a letter from the Resident at Lucknow, dated 2 April 1805.
[3]Ibid.
[4]Ibid. Also see OR 239.

about the arrival of Fath Khan, a *sardar* (chief) from Herat to Qandhar to collect some Durrani troops to fight against Fath Ali Qujar in Khurasan; the Wazir has asked Ahmed Khan for an audience to prevent him from proceeding towards Multan with the intention of its destruction, etc., etc.

OR 250, f 1.

April -- 312. From Wazir Ali Khan (of Lucknow) to Husaini Begam. Expresses great pleasure for her letter but records his complaint for such painful delay in writing of letters by the addressee. Enquires about the health and welfare of her son Mirza Muhammad Ali Khan and others.

OR 252, f 1.

April -- 313. Muhammad Nabi Khan to . . . ?. Enquires into the reason that delayed the funeral of late Haji Khalil Khan.

CR 22, pp. 457-58, no. 26 (8).

April -- 314. From . . . to Muhammad Nabi Khan. Explains in detail the reasons that delayed the funeral of late Haji Khalil Khan.

CR 22, pp. 458-62, no. 26 (9).

May 1 315. Newsletter from Karoli dated 14 *Muharram* 1220 AH (15 April 1805). Reports the march of Jaswant Rao Holkar and Surji Rao Ghatke from Bharatpur and camped at Karoli. Reports that Jawahar Mal and Thakur Das met Raja of Karoli. The Raja asked about the old friendly relationship between him (Jaswant Rao) and Raja Ranjit Singh. They said that the paramountcy of the English was a fact and was increasing day by day. Further said that Raja of Jaipur by provoking Ranjit Singh made him an enemy of the English. Reports that Jaswant Rao expressed his enmity against English and said if Daulat Rao Sindhia joined hands with him it would be good. Notwithstanding he would never bow before the Company and said he would destroy Jaipur. Reports that in the night Surji Rao Ghatke and Jaswant Rao Holkar went to meet Daulat Rao Sindhia.

OR 254[1] f 1; TR 51, pp. 291-93, no. 91; AR 20, p. 14.

May 2 316. To Raja Ram Raj Bahadur of Travancore and Diwan Rai Keshav Das. Expresses concern on the rebellion of Nair battalion and satisfaction on its prompt and in time suppression. Mentions and appreciates Lt. Col. Macaulay for

[1]Enclosed with a letter from Mercer, dated 18 April 1805.

his promt action taken to releive the addressee from the above-mentioned danger. Suggests that the treaty concluded between the Company and addressee's predecessors needed modificaton as the danger posed by Tipu Sultan has subsided with the latter's death. Assures to maintain friendly relation and make endeavour for the common causes of the two governments.

Further appreciates Diwan Rai Keshav Das for his wisdom, integrity and talent displayed in conclusion of the treaty.

CI 41, pp. 81-85, no. 12; TI 51, pp. 119-24, no. 41; AI 20, p. 62.

May 3 317. To Mir Muhammad Sadiq Gulistana. States that paper regarding the addressee's claim of inheritance and *mukhtrkari* along with other enclosures and translation of letters received from Iran on this subject have been forwarded to the Judge of the court of appeal at Murshidabad.

SI 1, pp. 7-8, no. 8.

May 4 318. Secretary to Mirza Kamil Khan. Condoles with the addressee on the death of his father.

SI 1, p. 8, no. 10.

May 6 319. From Shamsh al-Nisa Begam of Awadh. Complimentary letter requesting for a letter regarding the addressee's health and welfare.

OR 255,[1] WS, WC, f. 1; TR 51, p. 293, no. 92; AR 20, p. 38.

May 6 320. Daulat Rao Sindhia to Lord Lake. Suggests the Company to sign a treaty with Holkar and assures that their territories will remain safe till the question of peace is not decided.

OR 256, f 1; CR 22, pp. 481-84, no. 3.

May 8[2] 321. From Saadat Ali Khan (of Awadh). Inform the addressee about the departure of Ramazan Ali Khan to Calcutta to execute some mission on behalf of the writer. Requests the addressee to grant him some favour in the execution of his

[1]Copy enclosed with a letter from the Resident at Lucknow to the Persian Secretary to the Government, dated 27 April 1805.

[2]Date of receipt on the cover of the letter. The date given in TR 51, AR 20, and on folder of document is 8 April. This may be copier's error.

mission. Dated 27 *Muharram* 1220 AH (28 April 1805).[1]

OR 239,[2] WS, WC, f 1; TR 51, pp. 272-73, no. 80; AR 20, p. 41; CR 22, pp. 373-74, no. 4.

May 8 322. From Nawwab Wazir. Requests for an audience to Ramazan Ali Khan who is going to Calcutta and issue a *parwanagi* to him fulfilling his requests. Dated 17 *Muharram* 1220 AH (18 April 1805).

OR 257,[3] f 1; CR 22, pp. 288-89, no. 6; TR 51, pp 272-73, no. 80; AR 20, p. 41.

May 8 323. Chiragh Ali Khan to Capt. Parsley. States that necessary measures have been taken for the recovery of the plundered property of the British merchants; urges immediate attention towards the affairs of Combroom (?) which has been taken over by the Sultan of Muscat.

OR 258[4]/a, f 1; CR 22, pp. 489-91, no. 7(1).

May 8 324. Chiragh Ali Khan to Capt. Pasley. Intimates of the writer's departure from Bushehr (Bushire).

OR 258/b, f 1; CR 22, pp. 492-94, no. 7(2).

May 8 325. Chiragh Ali Khan to Capt. Pasley. Explains how and why the salary of Shaikh Rahmah Abdullah Khan may be released in his absence.

OR 258[5]/c, f 1; CR 22, pp. 494-96, no. 7(3).

May 8 326. Extract from the journal of Munshi Muhammmad. Demands that predecessors of Amir al-Daulah have made wealth during their life. Further states that some troops have been collected according to the order of the king. Adds that Shaikh Rahmah and Shaikh Nasir Khan should be arrested and their business seized and they be finally terminated.

OR 258[6]/d, f 1; CR 22, pp. 496-97, no. 7(4).

May 8 327. Daulat Rao Sindhia to the Nizam. Acknowledges receipt of his letter informing about submission of the post of *wakalat* to Surji Rao Ghatke and the arrival of Sakha Ram Pandit.

[1]See OR 240 wherein 28 *Muharram* 1220 AH is falls on 29 April 1805.

[2]Enclosed with a personal letter from Col. Collins to Edmonston, dated 29 April 1805.

[3]Copy enclosed with a letter from Col. Collins to Edmonstone.

[4]Enclosed with a letter from Capt. Parsley, dated 10 April 1805.

[5]Ibid., dated 13 April 1805.

[6]Ibid.

Reiterates that the friendship of the two governments is an established fact and beyond doubt which has been testified from time to time.

OR 259,[1] *f 1; CR 22, pp. 516-17, no. 15.*

May 8 328. Surji Rao Ghatke to the Nizam. Acknowledges receipt of his letter informing about the submission of the post of *wakalat* and his conversation with Maharaja and also the arrival of Sakha Ram Pandit along with the letter of Maharaja. Reiterates that the friendship between the two governments is an established fact hopes that the friendship will remain intact.

OR 260,[2] *f 1; CR 22, pp. 517, no. 16.*

May 9 329. To Raja Raghuji Bhonsla. Complementary in reply to addressee's letter with a present of clothes and jewels as a token of congratulation on the victory of British forces against Maratha.

TI 51, pp. 125-26, no. 42; AI 20, p. 61.

May 9 330. To Nawwab Wazir. In reply to addressee's complementary letter. Acknowledges receipt of presents of fruits.

TI 51, p. 126, no. 43; AI 20, p. 69.

May 10 331. From Muhammad Abbas. Informs that he left Shahjahanabad and met the Nizam where he was bestowed with the *khilat*. Also says that he has sent a letter of *Wazir al-Mamalik* confirming his friendly relation with the Company. Expressing his loyalty to the Company offers his services.

OR 261, f 1; CR 22, p. 536; TR 51, p. 287, no. 93; AR 20, p. 10.

May 10 332. From Hafiz Muhammad. Informs that his son Abbas Ali Khan has come back from Shahjahanabad to see him (the addressee). Hopes that his friendly relation with the Company would further be strengthened by this meeting. Offers his services for the Company.

OR 262, f 1, WS; CR 22, p. 534; TR 51, p. 289, no. 94; AR 20, p. 10.

May 11 333. To Raja Raghuji Bhonsla. Acknowledges the addressee's letter complementing the writer on the victory of Lord Lake and General Frazer in India. Expresses thanks for the gift sent

[1]Copy received with a letter from the Resident at Hyderabad.
[2]Ibid., dated 23 April 1805.

along the said letter on this occasion.

CI 41, pp. 426-30, no. 168.

May 12 334. Lord Lake, Commander-in-Chief to Daulat Rao Sindhia. Acknowledges receipt of addressee's letter dated 29 April 1805. Refers to the treaties of friendly relation between the Company and the addressee and accuses him of committing treachery and disloyalty by helping Jaswant Rao Holkar and other enemy of the Company, etc.

OR 263,[1] *f 1; CR 22, pp. 498-504, no. 9.*

May 14 335. News report from the *deorhi* of Daulat Rao Sindhia dated 27 April 1805. Refers to a report on the Maharaja for 28 April which would have come to his notice. Further reports that on 29 April 1805 Maharaja Surji Rao and other chieftains including Bakhshi Tatia and Gopal Rao Bhao had camped at Sabalgarh and were involved in the discussion, thereafter they marched and camped on river Kolon. Reports that due to scarcity of water many men and animals died.

OR 264,[2] *f 1.*

May 14 336. From Nawwab Saadat Ali Khan. Referring to a request of Colonel John Collins for the supply of some elephants for the formation of a new Regiment. Informs that 12 elephants have been supplied from Kanpur to the said colonel and were accepted. Refers his help to the Company during the war with Jaswant Rao Holkar. Also expresses his loyalty to the Company's government. Dated 4 *safar* 1220 AH (4 May 1805).

OR 265,[3] *WS, f 1; CR 22, pp. 513-16, no. 14;*
TR 51, pp. 297-98, no. 95; AR 20, p. 41.

May 14 337. From Nawwab Wazir. To the same effect as OR 265.

OR 266,[4] *f 1; CR 22, pp. 508-11, no. 12;*
TR 51, pp. 297-98, no. 95; AR 20, p. 41.

May 14 338. Hari Ram, Mukund Ram and others to A. Seton stating that they had borrowed a loan of Rs. 20,000 (twenty thousand rupees) from Gopal Das and Babu Dwarka Das and had

[1]Enclosed with a letter from Mercer.

[2]Copy received from Mercer.

[3]Copy enclosed with a letter from the Resident at Lucknow to the Governor-General.

[4]Enclosed with a letter from Col. Collins, dated 5 May 1805.

returned Rs. 7,200 to them and only Rs. 12,800 have to return. Adds that they have already suffered a lot by the hands of Amir Khan. Request that being loyals of the government they may be helped to collect the money so that they may be able to return the money.

OR 267, f 1; CR 22, pp. 511-13, no. 13.

May 14 339. To Nawwab Wazir. Thanks the addressee for the fruits sent by him to the writer.

CI 41, pp. 425-26, no. 167.

May 17 340. From Muin al-Mulk. Sends a gift of fifty baskets of mangoes. Dated 17 *Safar* 1220 AH (17 May 1805).

OR 268 WS, WC, f 1; TR 51, pp. 298-99, no. 96; AR 20, p. 9.

May 18 341. From Ashraf al-Nisa Begam. Stating that her grand-father Mir Ruh al-Din Husain Khan Bahadur Sipahdar Jang was getting a pension of Rs. 5,000 (five thousand) from the Company government after whose death Rs. 1,200 were issued to her mother and father. Informs of the death of her father on 27 *Muharram* 1220 AH (28 April 1805) and requests that her share of Rs. 900 (nine hundred) may be issued to her along with Rs. 300 to look after the other dependens of her father.

OR 269[1] f I, WS; CR 22, pp. 484-86, no. 4; TR 51, pp. 299-302, no. 97; AR 20, p. 2.

May 18 342. Secretary to Babu Jagannath. Acknowledges the addressee's application regarding the grant of a *dastak-e-rahdari* (passport) in favour of his dependents for a journey from Lucknow to Farrukhabad but requests his inability to issue any *dastak* from Lucknow to Kanpur as that region falls in the territory of Nawwab Wazir. Asks the addressee to submit his application to the Resident at Lucknow seeking the said passport.

SI 1, pp. 8-9, no. 11.

May 18 343. Secretary to Babu Bishambhar Das. Acknowledges addressee's letter delievered by Lala Ram Bakhsh. States that the addressee's case has been forwarded to Edmonston. Assures all possible help at the best of his (writer) capabilities.

SI 1, p. 9, no. 12.

[1]Enclosed with a letter from the Superintendent of Nizamat affairs, dated 10 May 1805.

May 18 344. Secretary to Babu Rao Kishan. Congratulates the addressee on the *mu-tarashi* (head shaving) ceremony of his son Babu Baijnath.

SI 1, pp. 9-10, no. 13.

May 18 345. Secretary to Raja Udit Narayan Singh of Benares. Complementary reply in return of addressee's good wishes on Christmas.

SI 1, p. 10, no. 14.

May 18 346. Secretary to Nawwab Khan Jahan Khan of Hoogly. In reply to addresssee's letter sent on the occasion of the writer's complete recovery from illness and on the success of the English troops on the fortress of Dieg.

SI 1, pp. 10-11, no. 15.

May 18 347. Secretary to Salam Allah Khan. Intimates him of the safe arrival of Maclo in England.

SI 1, pp. 11-12, no. 16.

May 18 348. Secretary to Rai Ram Singh. Informs the addressee that as soon as the *dastak* is signed by the Governor-General it will be sent to the addressee through Lala Ram Parsad.

SI 1, pp. 12-13, no. 17.

May 20 349. Maharaja Daulat Rao Sindhia to Colonel Close. Refers his (addressee) earlier letters in connection with the invitation by the Governor-General to see him on the matter of ambassadorship in his court. Requests that his arrival at Kuru is imperative to hold some talks with him. Dated 30 *Muharram* 1220 AH (31 April 1805).

OR 270[1] (a) f 1 and OR 271(a) f 1; CR22, pp. 520-21, no. 16(2); TR, pp. 302-03, no. 98; AR 20, p. 14.

May 20 350. Colonel Close to Maharaja Sahib (Daulat Rao Sindhia) Acknowledges receipt of his earlier letters. Refers to his letters which would have been received by him. Says that since Jenkins has been entrusted with the affairs of the state he should not hesitate in holding talks with him.

OR 270[2](b) f 1 OR 271 (b) f 1; CR 22, pp. 518-20, no. 16 (2); TR 51, pp. 303-05, no. 98; AR 20, p. 14.

[1]Copy enclosed with a leter from Col. Close to the Persian Secretary to the Government.

[2]Ibid.

May 20 351. From Sri Kishan Arjunji Nathji Tiwari of Surat. Expresses his gratitude on the bestowal of *khilat,* the Jewellary, the clothes, etc., on him (writer) by Jonathan Duncon. Persents 25 *asharfi* as a good gesture.

OR 272, WS, WC, f 1.

May 20 352. From . . . . Informs about his illness during his journey to Murshidabad after meeting him (the addressee). Adds that he would perform the journey of Benares after his recovery from illness. Dated 10 May 1805.

OR 273, WC, f 1.

May 20 353. Secretary to Rai Ram Singh. Acknowledges addressee's three letters on the subject of granting *dastak* and seeking extension for his stay at Benares due to some eye ailments.

SI.1, p. 7, no. 9.

May 23 354. Newswriter at the palace of Daulat Rao Sindhia to Col. Close. Furnishes details of the help that the addressee received from Maulavi Fath al-Din and Saiyid Noor al-Din Khan; also describes their displeasure due to the misbehaveour of Jenkins to them. Explains and emphasizes their importance for the success of the Company and their assistance in various litigated issues in regard to Company's affairs and further describes how they have pursuaded and tamed Chhatar Muhammad Khan Pindari and Wazir Muhammad Khan to join the Company's government. Suggests that the British forces should be mobilized towards Malwa as this region is lying unoccupied and unattended by the local Chieftains, etc., etc.

OR 274, ff. 4; CR 22, pp. 521-44, no. 17(a);
TR 51, pp. 307-20, no. 100(a).

May 23 355. Maulavi Fath al-Din and Nur al-Din Khan to Muhammad Hanif, *munshi* of Col. Close. Express all the troubles and hardship which the writers expreinced only to see Col. Close, but as they failed to see him in person, request him (Muhammad Hanif Munshi) to forward their application to Col. Close. Request to write to Shaikh Yusuf regarding their (writers) arrival at Nagpur and also asks to communicate to Col. Close in a proper manner, etc. Dated 29 April 1805.

OR 275 ff 2; CR 22, pp. 459-51, no. 17 (2); TR 51,
pp. 323-27, no. 100(c); AR 20, p. 14.

May 26 356. Colonel Close to Maharaja Daulat Rao Sindhia. Referring his earlier letter expresses displeasure that Jenkins and other have yet not joined the army. Informs that Rao Gopal Janardhan has returned after meeting him. Desires that they must be sent to meet him with all safety and security. Dated 12 May 1805.

OR 276, f 1; CR22, pp. 551-52, no. 18.

May 26 357. To Daulat Rao Sindhia. Assures that the British government has no desire to commit any act of hostility against the addressee and the troops in question are proceeding to their station at Bombay.

CI 41, pp. 107-09, no. 12; TI 51, pp. 127-28, no. 44; AI 20, p. 48.

May 27 358. Colonel Close to Colonel John (Collins). Acknowledge receipt of his letter and says that Saiyid Noor al-Din and Maulavi Fath al-Din Khan have also conveyed him details of the affairs. Hence *bandobast* has to be made by General Lake and Jenkins and it is their duty to conduct the *bandobast,* keeping in mind all the pros and cons.

OR 277[1] (a), f 1; CR 22, pp. 552-53, no. 19(1); TR 51, pp. 340-41, no. 102; AR 20, p. 14.

May 27 359. Colonel John (Collins) to Colonel Close. Expressing his loyalty to the Company informs that on behalf of the Maharaja, Saiyid Noor al-Din Khan and Maulavi Fath al-Din Khan, his two confidents had held discussion with Jenkins on the issue of army stationing at Sagar and had agreed to ractify the matter, but even after a month or so in the absence of a written document he (writer) had to leave the place. Informs that Khan lost all the *jagirs* and *wajuhat* that he possessed under the Maharaja's government. Adds that as Khan was deputed to ractify the matter he was looted by the *pindaris* on his way to meet the addressee. However, he fulfilled all his necessities to continue his journey and further details will be furnished.

OR 277[2] (b), ff 2; CR 22, pp. 553-56, no. 19 (2); TR 51, pp. 342-45; no. 104; AR 20, p. 14.

May 27 360. Colonel Close to Mirza Amber Beg. Acknoweleges receipt of his letter and says that Saiyid Nur al-Din Khan and Maulavi Fath al-Din Khan have been explained the matter and hopes

[1]Copy of the letter enclosed with a desdpatch from Col. Close.

[2]Copy of the letter enclosed with a despatch from Col. Close to the Persian Secretary, dated 6 May 1805.

that the two will further explain the matter regarding *bandobast* to him.

OR 278[1] *(a), f 1; OR 280 (b), f 1; CR 22, p. 556, no. 19(3); TR 51, pp. 341-42, no. 103; AR 20, p. 14.*

May 27 361. Mirza Amber Beg to Colonel Close. Informs that as per the orders he is encamping at Bhilsa with a contingent of 3 platoon and 1,000 troops. Hopes that Saiyid Nur al-Din Khan and Maulavi (Fath al-Din) Sahib would fully explain all the matter before him which would be self-explanatory of their friendly relation. Referring to a promise by Jenkins to send a writtern document clarifying all the issues but did not, and thus in the absence of such orders the Colonel is staying there while the forces of the Maharaja (Daulat Rao Sindhia) have been despatched. Further says that Saiyid Sahib and Maulavi Sahib were looted by the *Pindaris* on the way and there after the Colonel has again to provide them necessary goods for their journey.

OR 278[2] *(b), ff 2; OR 280 (a) f 1; CR 22, pp. 557-58, no. 19(4); TR 51, pp. 345-47, no. 105; AR 20, p. 14.*

May 27 362. Col. Baptiste to Col. Close. Expressing his loyalty to the Company government says that at whatever place at Sagar were the forces of the Maharaja (Daulat Rao Sindhia), Saiyid Nur al-Din Khan and Maulavi Fath al-Din Khan, the two confidents of the Maharaja had held discussion on the issues with Jenkins and the two assured to rectify all the issues and a charter of demands along with the details of the property was given to Jenkins. Adds that he stayed at Sagar and Bhilsa waiting for the reply. Informs that Khan due to non-receipt of a letter from the addressee has lost all his *jagirs* and other priviledges that he has been availing under the Maharaja. To ractify the matter he marched to meet him and was looted by the *Pindaris* on his way to whome he provided all the necessities to reach him and explain the matter and waits for the reply.

OR 279[3] *(a), ff 2; CR 22, p. 553, no. 19(5), TR 51, p. 336, no. 102; AR 20, p. 14.*

[1]Copy enclosed with a despatch from Col. Close to the Persian Secretary, Dated 6 May 1805.

[2]Ibid.

[3]Copy of the letter.

May 27 363. Colonel Close to Colonel Baptiste. Acknowledges receipt of his letter and informs that the matter has been explained fully by Noor al-Din Khan and Maulavi Fath al-Din Khan. Informs that such *bandobast* has to be done by General Lake and Jenkins whom he has already directed on these lines. Says that being loyal to the Company he should not worry.

OR 279[1] (b) f 1; CR 22, p. 552, no. 19; TR-51, p. 334, no. 102; AR 20, p. 14.

May 27 364. From Azim al-Daulah Amir al-Hind. Informs that the revenue of Carnatic (Karnataka) as well as arrears has been sent.

OR 281, WS, WC, f 1; CR 22, pp. 558-59, no. 20; TR 51, pp. 347-48, no. 106; AR 20, p. 2.

May 28 365. From Khan Jahan son of Fath Ali Khan. Requests for his maintenance.

OR 282, WS, WC, f 1; CR 22, pp. 563-66, no. 22; TR 51, pp. 351-54, no. 107; AR 20, p. 19.

May 28 366. George Guthrie to Kaji Amar Singh, Chautria Hastdil Shah and Randhir Singh referring to their request to oust Prakaram Kunwar, brother of Raja of Srinagar who has been hiding in the house of Raja Ram Dayal Gujar with a nefarious design to create disturbance in the upper hilly region defends him and lauds of his goods conduct.

OR 284[2] (a), f 1; CR 22, pp. 566-69, no. 23(1); TR 51, pp. 335-39, no. 101; AR 20, p. 11.

May 28 367. Kaji Amar Singh to George Guthrie. Acknowledges receipt of his letter along with the letter of George Seton. Stating that he has no difference with him (the addressee) and as such he has communicated the same to the Governor-General at Calcutta and has sent the reply of A. Seton's letter. Informs that Prakaram Kunwar, brother of Raja of Srinagar is hiding in the house of a relative of one Ram Dayal Gujar who is intending to create disturbance in the upper hilly region, should be arrested. Raja Gujar should also not provide shelter in his territory.

OR 284[3](b), f 1; CR 22, pp. 570-71, no. 23(2); TR 51, pp. 332-35, no. 101 (b); AR 20, p. 11.

[1]Copy of the letter.
[2]Copy enclosed with a letter from the Collector at Saharanpur.
[3]Ibid.

May 30 368. Jangi Khan to Muhammad Nasr Allah Khan. Informs that he along with Jaswant Rao Holkar was encamping at Bharatpur. Meanwhile an accord occurred between the Company and the Raja of Bharatpur. Jaswant Rao Holkar left Bharatpur and crossed over to river Chambal. Adds that he too, crossed over Chambal and camped at Fatehpur Sikri where he got a message from General Lake inviting him to attend him with an assurance to be pardoned of all his misconduct and would be awarded as the Chieftain of Hindustan, hence he met General Lake in his camp. Hopes that he would meet the addressee today.

OR 285[1] *(a), f 1; CR 22, pp. 571-73, no. 24(1).*

May 30 369. Arab Khan to Nawwab Nasr Allah Khan. Informs that he was encamping at Bharatpur along with Maharaja Jaswant Rao Holkar. Meanwhile an accord concluded between the Company and the Raja of Bharatpur. As a result Maharaja left Bharatpur and crossed over to river Chambal. Adds that he left the camp of Maharaja and encamped at Fatehpur Sikri where he got a message form General Lake to meet him. Rest to the same effect as the foregoing.

OR 285 (b), f 1; CR 22, pp. 573-75, no. 24(2).

May 31 370. *Dastak* issued in favour of Bapu Mahip Rao and other servants of Raghunath Bhonsla who are going from Calcutta to Nagpur having essential commodities with them. Directs the *rahdars* and *guzarbans* not to harass them on their way for any type of tax.

OR 287 f 1.

May -- 371. Conversation held between Maharaja Ranjit Singh and Munshi Saiyid Ghulam. Communicates that on 6 *Muharram* 1220 AH (7 April 1805) he met Maharaja Ranjit Singh at Phulbari. The Maharaja expressed deep concern over the happenings. However, he requested for the restoration of new territories to make the instalments easy. In reply he put forward the conditions described by Lord Lake to pay an amount of Rs. 20 lakh in three instalments and restoration of the fort of Bharatpur and Deig. The Maharaja desired to make the instalment easier. Agreeing with his request he demanded some security from the Maharaja and therefore the latter agreed to surrender one of his sons for the purpose. Thereafter Maharaja

[1]Copy enclosed with a private letter from Letin to Edmonston.

Janswat Rao Holkar was also forced to leave Maharaja Ranjit Singh's territory as was the condition in the agreement.

OR 288, f 1 and OR 289, f 1; CR 22, pp. 467-74, no. 1.

May -- 372. *Iqrarnama* under the seal of David Ochterlony declaring that the offences of Sardar Gurudatt Singh have been pardoned. However, *mahal* Karnal and Jhanjana which had been brought under the administration of the Company government will remain under the Company itself. Adds that Sardar Gurudatt Singh should ensure his loyalty to the government and should come with his forces as and when it would be required. He should also not interfare in the affairs of Azimabad Baladri which are under the possession of Gulsher Khan.

OR 290,[1] *f 1; CR 22, pp. 486-89, no. 5.*

May -- 373. From Muhabbat Khan at Lucknow. Expressing his gratitude for the attention paid to the safety of his brothers and their families during the disturbances.

OR 291,[2] *f 1; CR 22, pp. 497-98, no. 8.*

May -- 374. Maulavi Fath al-Din Khan and Noor al-Din Khan to Colonel Close. Informs that as per the orders of Jenkins they left the camp of Daulat Rao Sindhia but on their way they were looted by the *Pindaris*. However, Colonel John Baptiste who was present at the Sagar agreement and had reached Bhilsa provided them with all the necessities and gave a letter in his (addressee) name affirming his commitment to honour the agreement. Add that they marched to Nagpur after facing a lot of troubles in their way but failed to see him (addressee). State that they met Elphinstone who insisted them to see the Colonel and they followed it. Thus they met him (addressee) at Amroli and narrated the entire story. Also refer to the news report of Muhammad Yusuf. Dated 28 *Muharram*.

OR 292, f 1 and OR 293, f 1; CR 22, pp. 547-49, no. 17(1); TR 51, pp. 320-23, no. 100 (b); AR 20, p. 14.[3]

June 3 375. From Nawwab Nusrat Jang[4] (of Dacca). Congratulates on the success of British forces in capturing the fort of

[1]Copy enclosed with a letter from the Resident at Delhi.
[2]Enclosed with a letter from Seton.
[3]Enclosed with a letter from Col. Close.
[4]The date and seal are on the cover.

Darara under the command of Lord Lake. Also greets on the agreement concluded with Maharaja Ranjit Singh wherein he has agreed to pay Rs. 20 lakh and keep his son as captive in Company's custody till he clears out the payment of the said amount. Further requests for favours and prays for the welfare and glory of the Company's rule. Dated 26 May 1805

OR-295,[1] WS, WC f 1; TR-51, pp. 363-64; no. 110; AR 20, p. 26.

June 3 376. From Mahdi Ali Khan and others, the sons of late Nawwab Ali Ibrahim Khan. Say that the Company's government had fixed a sum of Rs. 500 (five hundred) only as pension for the maintenance of the family following the demise of their father. Now their elder brother does not give them (the petitioners) their proper shares. Hence Request for the equal distribution of the pension among the successors of their father as per norms of the *sharia.*

OR 296,[2] f 1; CR 22, pp. 581-82, no. 1.

June 4 377. From Nawwab Munni Begam. Complains that she has not received any letter from the addressee for a long time and hence requests for the same for the consolation. Dated 26 *Safar* 47 *Julus* of (Shah Alam II) (26 May 1805).

OR 297, WS, WC, f 1; CR 22, pp. 589-90, no. 3; TR 51, pp. 364, no. 111; AR 20, p. 22.

June 5 378. From Ramazan Ali Khan to the Persian Secretary to Governor-General. Says that he has arrived from Murshidabad to see him but as his luggage and other material had not arrived so far, he would visit him on its arrival and also talk about the appointment of Munshi Muhammad Ahsan. Further says that Huzoor-e-Purnoor (Nawwab Wazir) has demanded 1,000 *bandooq-e-chaqmaqi* (matchlock guns). But this is not possible without prior permission of the Governor-General. So requests to help him getting the permission and also procuring the said guns.

OR 298, f 1; TR 51, pp. 365-66, no. 112; AR 20, p. 35.

June 5 379. Col. Collins to Nawwab Wazir. Refers to the letter of Governor-General regarding decision of the Council in

[1]Letter delivered by the *wakil.*

[2]Copy enclosed with a letter from A. Brook, Agent at Banda.

connection with the measures adopted to suppress the rebels. Seeks permission for mobilizing the Company's forces in the territory of the addressee. Also requests to issue a public notice asking all the officials and the public to extend all essential assistance to the British forces. Dated 17 May 1805.

OR 299,[1] f 1; CR 22, pp. 590-94, no. 4(1).

June 5 380. Col. Collins to Nawwab Wazir. To the same effect as OR no. 299.

OR 300,[2] f 1; CR 22, pp. 590-94, no. 4(1).

June 5 381. Nawwab Wazir of Awadh to Col. John Collins. Refers to the addressee's letter seeking permission for the mobilization of the Company's forces in the territory of the writer (Nawwab Wazir). Welcomes the idea and assures that the Company's forces will be provided all essential assistance in suppressing and apprehending the rebels. Further says that he will accept the terms and conditions regarding release of Bisheshar Das who is under arrest due to lapses in the accounts. Dated 26 *Safar* 1220 AH (26 May 1805).

OR 301,[3] f 1; CR 22, pp. 594-98, no. 4(2).

June 5 382. Nawwab Wazir to Col. Collins. To the same effect as OR 301.

OR 302,[4] f 1; CR 22, pp. 594-98, no. 4(2).

June 5 383. Col. Collins to Nawwab Wazir. Refers to a letter from A. Seton stating that the rebels Maan Singh and Bheja Singh are still at large and busy in creating disturbance, thus a plan to curb their activities and apprehend them has been decided. In this connection it is essential to mobilize the forces and capture them before the rainy season starts. Therefore the writer (Col. Collins) requests the addressee to allow the Company's forces to enter into his territory in order to chase and arrest the aforesaid rebels.

OR 303,[5] f 1; CR 22, pp. 599-602, no. 4 (3).

[1]Copy enclosed with a letter from the Resident at Lucknow, dated 27 May 1805.

[2]Ibid., dated 27 May 1805.

[3]Ibid., dated 27 May 1805.

[4]Ibid., dated 26 May 1805.

[5]Ibid., dated 27 May 1805.

June 5 384. Col. Collins to Nawwab Wazir. To the same effect as OR 303.

OR 304,[1] f 1; CR 22, pp. 599-602, no. 4(3).

June 5 385. Muhammad Ali Khan, *tahsildar* of *pargana* Katehar to A. Seton, the Resident at Lucknow. Describes the details of the progress in regard to the arrest of Jaswant Singh and Keri Singh who have taken away the cattle from the Company's territory and now absconding in the territory of Mirza Hakim Mahdi who is not ready to cooperate and concludes that the area of Katehar and Baranpur have become desolate due to the terror of the aforesaid rebels, hence it is very difficult to manage the food provisions and move against the rebels. Therefore requests to arrange food provisions and issue proper orders to Mirza Hakim Mahdi so that speedy action could be taken against the said rebels.

OR 305,[2] f 1; CR 22, pp. 602-07, no. 4.

June 5 386. Col. Collins to Nawwab Wazir of Awadh. Refers to the petition of Muhammad Ali Khan, *tahsildar* of Katchar (*pargana*) describing the non-cooperation of addressee's official Mirza Hakim Mahdi in regard to the arrest of the rebels who have taken shelter in addressee's territory and are in a practice of taking away the cattle from Company's territory in connivance of the local people. Requests the addressee to issue proper orders to the said Mirza and other officials to cooperate with the Company's staff who are deputed to execute this duty.

OR 390,[3] f 1; CR 22, pp. 607-10, no. 4(5).

June 5 387. Col. Collins to Nawwab Wazir of Awadh. To the same effect as OR 306.

OR 307,[4] f 1; CR 22, pp. 607-10, no. 4(5).

June 6 388. From Qutlugh Sultan Begam. Complementary letter with presents of golden and silver rings on the eve of *chahar shamba* of the month of Safar.

OR 308,[5] WS, WC, f 1; CR 22, pp. 627-28, no. 6: TR 51, p. 366, no. 113; AR 20, p. 22.

[1]Copy enclosed with a letter from the Resident at Lucknow, dated 27 May 1805.

[2]Ibid.

[3]Ibid.

[4]Ibid.

[5]Enclosed with a letter from the Acting Agent at Benares to the Persian Secretary to the Government, dated 30 May 1805.

June 6 389. Muhammad Ali Khan, *tahsildar* of *pargana* Katehar to Seton. To the Same effect as OR 305.

OR 309,[1] *f 1; CR 22, pp. 602-607, no. 4.*

June 6 390. Nawwab Wazir to Col. Collins. Acknowledges receipt of the addressee's letter along with a copy of the petition of Muhammad Ali Khan, *tahsildar* of Katehar in connection with the non-cooperation of Mirza Hakim Mahdi to the Company's officials for suppressing and apprehending the rebels who have taken away cattle from the Company's territory. Assures that Mirza Hakim Mahdi would be punished if found guilty and also says that he would issue orders to the concerned officials to give all assistance to Company's officials. Dated 27 May 1805.

OR 310,[2] *f 1; CR 22, pp. 616-18, no. 5.*

June 6 391. Nawwab wazir to Col. Collins. To the same effect as the OR 310.

OR 311,[3] *f 1; CR 22, pp. 616-18, no. 512.*

June 6 392. Col. Collins to Nawwab Wazir. Requests the addressee to allow the Company's forces to enter his (addressee) territory in order to chase, apprehend and vanquish the rebels and miscreants who take shelter in his territory after committing crime in the Company's territory. Narrates the case of Bisheshar Das in the light of the favourable letter from Scott to prove his innocence and advocates for his release from the confinement. Also seeks permission for his (Bisheshar Das) family to come over to Bareilly. Dated 28 May 1805.

OR 312,[4] *f 1; CR 22, pp. 618-25, no. 5(3).*

June 6 393. Col Collins to Nawwab Wazir. To the same effect as the OR 312.

OR 313,[5] *f 1; CR 22, pp. 618-25, no. 5(3).*

[1]Copy enclosed with a letter from the Agent to the Governor-General, dated 24 May 1805.

[2]Enclosed with a letter from the Resident at Lucknow, dated 29 may 1805.

[3]Duplicate copy enclosed with a letter from the Resident at Lucknow, dated 29 May 1805.

[4]Copy enclosed with a letter from the Resident at Lucknow, dated 24 May 1805.

[5]Duplicate copy enclosed with a letter from the Resident at Lucknow, dated 27 May 1805.

June 6 394. Col. Collins to Nawwab Wazir. Requests the address that the decision in the case against Hakim Ali Khan should not be given only on the basis of the statement of the accused because there are several things to be taken into consideration which has not been considered. Hence insists that the statements of the witnesses are essential to decide the case in a just manner. Dated 29 May 1805.

OR 314,[1] *f 1; CR 22, pp. 625-27, no. 5(4).*

June 6 395. Col. Collins to Nawwab Wazir. To the same effect as the OR 314.

OR 315[2]*, f 1.*

June 8 396. General Lake to Amar Singh. Acknowledges receipt of addressee's letter along with a piece of China silk. Says that Maharaja Shamsher Singh has agreed to cooperate with the Company's forces as per agreement with the Company. Asks the addressee to be ready to perform the works assigned to him in cooperation of the Company's forces. Dated 28 May 1805.

OR 316[3] *(a), f 1; CR 22, pp. 633-34; no 8(2);*
TR 51; pp. 367-68; no. 114; AR 20; p. 14.

June 6 397. General Lake to Hastdial Shah. To the same effect as the OR 316. Dated 28 May 1805.

OR 316[4] *(b), f 1; CR 22, pp. 630-31, no. 7(2);*
TR 51, pp. 367-68, no. 114; AR 20, p. 14.

June 8 398. Amar Singh to General Lake. Acknowledges receipt of addressee's letter and says that the rebels who were active in Najibabad have been suppressed. Further expresses willingness to invade Rajas of hilly region and assures to be abiding by the terms and conditions of the agreement concluded with the Company. Dated 10 *Safar* 1220 AH (10 May 1805 AD).

OR 317[5] *(a), f 1; CR 22, pp. 628-30, no. 7(1);*
TR 51, pp. 369-71, no. 115; AR 20, p. 14.

[1]Copy enclosed with a letter from the Resident at Lucknow, dated 29 May 1805.

[2]Ibid.

[3]Copy enclosed with a letter from Mercer to the Secretary to the Governor-General, dated 28 May 1805.

[4]Copy enclosed with a letter from Mercer, Secretary to the Government, dated 28 May 1805.

[5]Copy enclosed with a letter from Mercer, dated 20 May 1805.

June 8 399. Hastdial Shah to General Lake. To the same effect as OR 317 (a).

OR 317[1] (b), f 1; CR 22, pp. 631-33, no. 8(1); TR 51, pp. 369-71, no. 115; AR 20, p. 14.

June 8 400. Nawwab Wazir to Col. Collins. Reiterates his alliance with the Company and expresses his confidence. Encloses a copy of the petition of Bisheshar Das in defence of the charges levelled against him by the son of Kashmiri Mal. Dated 28 *Safar* 1220 AH (28 May 1805 AD).

OR 318,[2] f 1; CR 22, pp. 649-50, no. 14(1).

June 8 401. From Bisheshar Das. States that he has no relation to the loan raised from Nawwab Haider Beg Khan and what ever evidence has been presented by son of Kashmiri Mal, in this regard is forged and fabricated. However the facts may be checked from the Registers and ***khatas***.

OR 319,[3] f 1; WC; CR 22, pp. 650-52, no. 14(2).

June 11 402. From Raja Narendergir. States that the last rites of his deceased father have been completed and now he is the successor of him (the deceased) who had declared this in presence of John Bellie during his lifetime and further repeated the same at the time of his death.

OR 320,[4] f 1; CR 22, pp. 644-45, no. 12.

June 11 403. From Maharaja Kanchangir Himmat Bahadur. To the same effect as the OR 320.

OR 321,[5] f 1; CR 22, pp. 642-44, no. 11.

June 13 404. From Nawwab Nasir al-Mulk. Expresses his financial difficulties due to burden of expenditure and says that Thomas is well aware of his position. Requests for increment in his pension to meet the expenditure. Also seeks an audience with the Governor-General.

OR 322, f 1.

[1]Copy enclosed with a letter from Mercer, dated 20 May 1805.

[2]Copy enclosed with a letter from the Resident at Lucknow, dated 30 May 1805.

[3]Ibid.

[4]Enclosed with a letter from the Commander in Cuttack to Secretary to Government, dated 31 May 1805.

[5]Ibid.

June 15 405. From Nawwab Munni Begam. Expresses grief on the departure of Pattle to England. Dated 13 *Rabi I*, 47 *Julus* of (Shah Alam II) (12 June 1805).

OR 323, f 1, WS, WC; CR 22, pp. 656-58, no. 16.

June 17 406. Daulat Rao Sindhia to Col. Close. Informs that Atma Ram, Shiv Ram and Balaji Yashwant at Nagpur have been informed by the writer to act according to the wishes of the addressee. Further insures of his solidarity with the Company. Expresses that he will discuss other issues when the addressee will arrive there. Dated 25 *Muharram*, 1205 *Deccani* Calender (24 April 1805).

OR 324,[1] *f 1; CR 22, pp. 658-61, nos. 17 and 18; TR 51, pp. 371-72, no. 116; AR 20, p. 14.*

June 17 407. From Daulat Rao Sindhia. Expresses anxiety for non-receipt of any reply from the addressee (Governor-General) as a number of issues have to be arranged in order only after receiving his (Governor-General) reply. Emphasizes continuance of the friendly relation between them and says his agent Bhagwant Rao may describe various points to the addressee. Requests to communicate the provisions of the treaty. Dated 23 April 1805.

OR 325, f 1; WS, WC; TR 51, pp. 373-75, no. 117; AR 20, p. 8.

June 17 408. Rafi al-Daulah, *nazim* of Bharoch. States that he is the son and successor of Sultan Changez and has arrived at Calcutta to present his case before the Governor-General as recommended by General Wellesley, Col. Close, Col. Malcolm and Kirkpatrick, etc. Says that the estate of Bharoch was granted to his predecessors by Emperor Akbar as *Al-tamagha*. But due to mischief of Diwan Lallu, he (the writer) has become bankrupt for the last 32 years. Now Bharoch has been brought under the Company's territory, it should be restored to the writer. Further assures of his loyalty to the Company.

OR 326, ff 2, WC; TR 51, pp. 376-83, no. 118; AR 20, p. 35.

[1]Persian Translation of Marathi letter with original enclosed with a letter from Col. Close, dated 30 May 1805.

June 19 409. From Nawwab Wazir. States that the friendship between the two states has been further strengthened by Col. John Collins. However, a number of following issues could not be decided. Says that the permit rules in respect of trade between two states should be adopted in such a way that it may be beneficial for both the states. Further put forth certain provisions to resolve the issue relating to the arrears from *talluqa* Sheoram (?), accounts of Dula Ram, transportation of essential commodities to writer's territory as previous, payment of revenue duties from *pargana* Najwal (?), repatriation of criminals from each others territory, etc., etc. Dated 8 *Rabi II* 1220 AH (7 June 1805).

OR 327,[1] *ff 2, WS, WC; CR 22, pp. 662-68, no. 19; TR 51, pp. 383-93, no. 119; AR 20, p. 41.*

June 20 410. Mir Muhammad Quli to Nawwab Wazir. Calls upon the witnesses who witnessed the conversation between the writer and Rahman Khan in respect of the where abouts of one Bheja Singh who has taken shelter on the border at Muhammadi or Katehar after committing crime in the territory of Nawwab Wazir.

OR 328,[2] *f 1; CR 22, pp. 669-76, no. 20; TR 51, pp. 393-406, no. 120; AR 20, p. 15.*

June 20 411. Mir Muhammad Qali to Nawwab Wazir. To the same effect as the OR 328.

OR 329,[3] *f 1; CR 22, pp. 669-76, no. 20; TR 51, pp. 393-406, no. 120; AR 20, p. 15.*

June 20 412. Hakim Mahdi Ali Khan to Nawwab Wazir. Refutes the charges levelled against the writer by Muhammad Ali Khan, the *amil* of Katehar in respect of the search of one Bheja Singh. Requests to enquire into the matter and proclaim justice.

OR 330,[4] *f 1; CR 22, pp. 676-79, no. 21(1).*

June 20 413. Hakim Mahdi Ali Khan to Nawwab Wazir. To the same effect as OR 330.

OR 331,[5] *f 1; CR 22, pp. 676-79, no. 21(1).*

[1]Enclosed with a letter from the Resident at Lucknow.

[2]True copy enclosed with a letter from the Resident at Lucknow, dated 12 June 1805.

[3]Ibid.

[4]Ibid.

[5]Ibid.

June 20 414. Nawwab Wazir to Col. Collins. Encloses an application along with the statement of Mohammad Ali Khan, the *tahsildar* of Katehar in respect of the deeds of Hakim Mahdi Ali Khan in connection with the arresting of a miscreant who has created disturbances in the territory of the Company and thereafter took shelter in the writer's territory

OR 332,[1] f 1; CR 22, pp. 680-81, no. 21(2).

June 20 415. Nawwab Wazir to Col. Collins. To the same effect as OR 332.

OR 333,[2] f 1; CR 22, pp. 680-81, no. 21(2).

June 22 416. From Nawwab Murtaza Khan. States that the Company's government had fixed a pension of Rs. 5,000 per month to his family. But after the demise of his mother Fazilat al-Nisa Begam and step-mother Saliha Begam the collectorate did not pay Rs. 2,000 per month which had been spent by the deceased. Requests to issue orders to the concerned officials for the renewal and continuence of the pension at the rate of Rs. 5,000 per month and also pay the arrears at the rate of Rs. 2,000 per month since the death of writer's mother. Dated 20 *Rabi I*, 47 *Julus* of (Shah Alam II) (19 June 1805).

OR 334[3] (a) f 1, WS, WC;
CR 22, pp. 718-20, no. 24(1).

June 22 417. Middleton to Nawwab Murtaza Khan. States that the addressee is responsible for the welfare and looking after of the successors and dependents of Late Nawwab Sadiq Ali Khan and hence any payment for their maintenance would be given to them non other than the addressee. Dated 19 June 1805.

OR 334 (b), f 1; CR 22, pp. 718-20, no. 24(2).

June 23 418. To Rana Kirat Singh of Gohad. Referring to the treaty of Bayana concluded with the addressee. Offers thanks for extending the military aid at Etawah.

CI 41, pp. 109-10, no. 13; TI 51, pp. 128-29, no. 45; AI 20, p. 63.

[1]Copy enclosed with a letter from the Resident at Lucknow, dated 12 June 1805.

[2]Ibid.

[3]Copy enclosed with a letter from the Resident at Lucknow.

June 24 419. From Khan Jahan Khan to Governor-General. Requests the address to issue orders for the repair work of the building in which he stays.

OR 335, f 1, WC; TR 51, pp. 406-09, no. 121, AR 20, p. 19.

June 24 420. Col. Close to Daulat Rao Sindia. Acknowledges receipt of addressee's letter. Expresses his inability to visit the addressee due to some reason at present.

OR 336,[1] *f 1; CR 22, pp. 723-26, no. 26; TR 51, pp. 409-10, no. 122; AR 20, p. 14.*

June 25. 421. From Amat al-Zahra (the Begum of Faizabad). States that tranquillity and peace prevail in her territory under the patronage and guidance of the Company's government. Assures of her loyalty to the Company. Refers to the addressee's visit of Kanpur and says that her representative Darab Khan had met him to convey her message. Further says that she is still waiting for the response from addressee's side. Dated 13 June 1805.

OR 337[2]*, WS, WC, ff 2; CR 22, pp. 726-29, no. 27; TR 51, pp. 411-14, no. 123; AR 20, p. 5.*

June 25 422. From Amat al-Zahra (the Begam of Faizabad). To the same effect as OR 337.

OR 338,[3] *f 1; CR 22, pp. 740-43, no. 29; TR 51, pp. 411-14, no. 123; AR 20, p. 5.*

June 27 423. Copy of the treaty concluded between the Company and Nizam of Hyderabad regarding transfer of Berar to the Nizam in liue of the maintenance of ten *Risalas* of forces, each consisting of one *risaladar*, two *jamadar*, ten *dafadar* and 1,000 (one thousand) *sawars* and paying them monthly salary. The treaty contains nine clauses bearing detailed agreements on various aspects of the status of the *risalas* and its officers, etc.

OR 339, ff 2; CR 22, pp. 634-38, no. 9.

June 28 424. Surji Rao Ghatke to Sakha Ram Pandit, *wakil* (of Daulat Rao Sindhia). Acknowledges receipt of addressee's letter bearing details of the situation. Informs the address that village

[1]Enclosure to a letter from Col. Close, dated 5 June 1805.
[2]Enclosed with a letter from the Resident at Lucknow, dated 16 June 1805.
[3]Ibid.

Virur has been assigned to Mir Alam and he has been directed to collect the arrears of the revenue due from 1413 *Fasli*. Asks the addressee to serve the enclosed letter addressed to Mir Alam at the earliest and tell him to send detailed information of the developments in this regard. Dated 7 *Safar*.

OR 340,[1] *f 1; CR 22, pp. 744-46, no. 31.*

June 29 425. Middleton, the magistrate. To the *zamindars*, *taluqadars*, *mustajirs*, etc., of *pargana* Mahmud Shahi, Kesho Nagar, Brahmapur, Begamabad, etc., of *taluqa thana* Kotah, etc. Informs them that the boat of Captain (?) has drawned in the river near Kotah and travellers are now in great trouble. Directs them to give all assistance to the victims. Dated 31 May 1805.

OR 341, f 1; CR 22, pp. 750-51, no. 33;
TR 51, pp. 414-16, no. 124; AR 20, p. 23.

June -- 426. Col. James Kirkpatrick to Mir Alam. Refers to a letter received from Capt. Sidhnam Bahadur intimating about the misunderstanding of the officials of the Maharaja Rao Pandit Pardhan in respect of the collection of *chauth*. Requests to send a letter to Raja Mahipat Ram in respect of the deposition of Rs. 2 lakh of *chauth*. Also desires a direct settlement for the collection of *chauth* in future.

OR 342,[2] *f 1; CR 22, pp. 638-42, no. 10.*

June -- 427. Narayan Rao to Sakha Ram Pandit. States that he will arrive in the vicinity of Bharatpur till 19 *Muharram*. Informs about his meeting with Yashwant but expresses discontentment. Says that the Maharaj has written for the expenditure many times but the *hundi* of Rs. 10,000 that was given by the government was bounced which would be sent latter on. Suggests the addressee to raise amount from the Company's government to meet out the expenditure, etc.

OR 343,[3] *f 1; CR 22, pp. 646-49, no. 13.*

June -- 428. Lord Lake to Daulat Rao Sindhia. Asks the addressee to releive Jenkins (the Company's officer) along with some others immidiately from the addressee's court. Threatens that if

[1]Enclosed with a letter from Krikpatrick, dated 14 May 1805.

[2]Copy enclosed with a letter from the Resident at Lucknow, dated 10 June 1805.

[3]Enclosed with a letter from Col. Kirkpatrick, dated 26 May 1805.

Jenkins does not arrive at the British camp the friendly relations between the Company and the addressee will be terminated.

OR 344,[1] *f 1; CR 22, pp. 652-56, no. 150.*

June -- 429. Lord Lake to Daulat Rao Sindhia. To the same effect as OR 344.

OR 345,[2] *f 1; CR 22, pp. 652-56, no. 15.*

June -- 430. Col. Collins to Nawwab Wazir. Refers to the letter of Strachy, the District Judge of Kanpur complaining against the addressee's officials who have started demanding octroi duty on the food grains form the Company's men and has caused a sharp price hike in the market of Kanpur. Requests the addressee to issue orders to the ***kotwal, ummals***, etc., of Kanpur to abstain from demanding taxes/duty from the officers of Company in transporting the food grains. Dated 9 November 1805.

OR 346[3] *(a), f 1; CR 22, pp. 681-82, no. 22(1).*

June -- 431. Strachy, Judge at Kanpur to Col. Collins. Complains of the rising prices of grain in the market of Kanpur that is only due to the dishonesty and cheating of the *Ummals*. Dated 17 October 1804.

OR 346[4] *(b), f 1; CR 22, pp. 682-84, no. 22(7).*

June -- 432. Nawwab Wazir to Col. Collins. Refers to a letter from the Judge of Kanpur explaining reasons for the scarcity and dearness of the grain due to undue demand of taxes by the local officials. Assures that the orders may be issued in this effect that such undue taxes are not demanded any more. Further assures that the writer would never deviate from the agreement agreed upon by the two governments. Dated 7 *Shaban* 1219 AH (11 November 1804) .

OR 347[5] *f 1; CR 22, pp. 685-86, no. 22(2).*

June -- 433. Col. Collins to Nawwab Wazir. Refers to the addressee's letter and says that Col. William Scott has written many letters to the addressee and has also sent the Code of Rules regarding tax demands from the grain merchants according to the agreement concluded between the two governments in regard

[1]Enclosure to a letter from Mercer, dated 4 June 1805.

[2]Copy Enclosed with a letter from Mercer, dated 4 June 1805.

[3]Enclosed with a letter from the Resident at Lucknow, dated 10 June 1805.

[4]Ibid.

[5]Ibid.

to the trade relations. Dated 19 November, 1804.

OR 348, f 1; CR 22, pp. 686-89, no. 22(3).

June -- 434. Nawwab Wazir to Col. Collins. Requests to establish a system of revenue collection on transportation of food grain through mutual understanding that may be favourable to both the governments and beneficial to the merchants.

OR 349[1] *f 1; CR 22, pp. 689-91, no. 22(4).*

June -- 435. Col. Collins to Nawwab Wazir. Refers to the petitions of two merchants Udai Ram and Beni Prasad received through the Collector (revenue) at Kanpur complaining against the illegal collection of taxes from them by Bakhshi and Balak Ram, *daroghas* while they were carrying their goods. Asks the addressee to arrange repayment of their amounts and direct the officials to abstain from such collection from the merchants. Dated 11 *Shawwal* 1219 AH (13 January 1805).

OR 350,[2] *f 1; CR 22, pp. 691-92, no. 22(5).*

June -- 436. Col. Collins to Nawwab Wazir. Acknowledges receipt of addressee's letter regarding appropriate orders issued to Beni Parsad and Hakim Mahdi Ali Khan in response to the petitions of grain merchants. Complains against Bakhshi Ram and Balak Ram who are regularly in practice of violating clause VIII of the agreement concluded between the two governments on 10 November 1801. Asks the addressee to check such officials so that the merchants could not be harassed for undue demand of taxes. Also explains the terms of treaty in respect of trade, etc. Dated 15 January 1805.

OR 351,[3] *f 1.*

June -- 437. Nawwab Wazir to Col. Collins. Acknowledges receipt of addressee's letter reminding adherence to the agreement concluded between the two governments. Emphasizes the need of quick finalization of the clauses of trade agreement and its immediate implementation in order to avoide delay in transportation of grain and other food items. Dated 20 January 1805.

OR 352,[4] *f 1; CR 22, pp. 696-99, no. 22(7).*

[1]Enclosed with a letter from the Resident at Lucknow, dated 10 June 1805.
[2]Ibid.
[3]Ibid.
[4]Ibid.

June -- 438. Col. Collins to Nawwab Wazir. Acknowledges receipt of addressee's letter. Informs that addressee's proposals regarding settlement of trade agreement has been sent to Governor-General for his perusal. Assures the addressee that the orders of the Governor-General will be dispatched at the earliest. Dated 21 January 1805.

OR 353, f 1; CR 22, p. 700, no. 22(8).

June -- 439. Nawwab Wazir to Col. Collins. Says that the merchants Shiv Bakhsh, Ram Bakhsh and Mir Kazim who have taken shelter in Kanpur, Allahabad and Korh (Fatehpur) without clearing their accounts with the writer's government. Accuses that they owe huge amount of dues and are not paying heed to the notices sent to them in this regard. Asks the addressee to arrange their extradition from the Company-held territories. Dated 28 *Shawwal* 1219 AH (30 January 1805).

OR 354,[1] f 1; CR 22, pp. 701-03, no. 22(9).

June -- 440. The Resident (*Sahib-e-kalan*) at Lucknow to Nawwab Wazir. Acknowledges receipt of addressee's letter in respect of the merchants who have not cleared their accounts with the addressee's government and now they have taken shelter in the Company's territory. Says that the writer has directed the judges of Allahabad and Kanpur to send the said merchants to Lucknow to clear their dues and settle their accounts with the addressee's government. Dated 2 February 1805.

OR 355,[2] f 1; CR 22, pp. 703-04, no. 22(10).

June -- 441. Nawwab Wazir to Col. Collins. Acknowledges receipt of addressee's letter and says that the villages of Suram, etc., were taken into possession by Faiz Allah Khazanchi through Almas Ali Khan at the time of division of the territory and the revenue was deposited to Company's government. Ascertains his right over these villages and asks the addressee to issue orders to the collector of Allahabad to hand over these villages to the writer's government. Dated 29 *Zulqada* 1219 AH (2 March 1805).

OR 356[3] f 1; CR 22, pp. 704-05, no. 22(11).

[1]Copy enclosed with a letter from the Resident at Lucknow, dated 10 June 1805.

[2]Ibid.

[3]Ibid.

June -- 442. Col. Collins to Nawwab Wazir. Acknowledges receipt of addressee's letter in respect of transfer of Suram village, etc., to the writer and says that he has ordered the Collector of Allahabad to look into the matter and report. Assures that as soon as the report of Collector is received it will be conveyed to addressee. Dated 3 March 1805.

OR 357,[1] *f 1; CR 22, pp. 705-06, no. 22(12).*

June -- 443. Col. Collins to Nawwab Wazir. Refers to his earlier dispatch regarding the issue of Suram *pargana*, etc. Informs about the reply received from the Collector of Allahabad stating that according to the agreement concluded between the two governments on 10 November 1801, the district of Allahabad came under the possession of the Company's government in its entirety and no *pargana* was excluded from it. Dated 21 March 1805.

OR 358,[2] *f 1; CR 22, pp. 706-07, no. 22(13).*

June -- 444. Nawwab Wazir to Col. Collins. Acknowledges letter from the addressee regarding the issue of the transfer of *pargana* Suram, etc., to the writer. States that the agreement of November 1801 contains the clause that the said *parganas* out of Allahabad district will be in writer's possession. Asks the addressee to reconfirm it with the copy of agreement and issue orders to the Collector of Allalhabad to restore these *parganas* to the writer. Dated 25 February 1805.

OR 359,[3] *f 1; CR 22, pp. 708-09, no. 22(14).*

June -- 445. Col. Collins to Nawwab Wazir. Acknowledges receipt of addressee's letter regarding rsetoration of the *parganas* of Suram, etc., to him as per treaty of November 1801. Further says that the *parganas* of Suram, etc., were brought under the possession of the Company long before the conclusion of the said treaty that brought the district of Allahabad in the possession of the Company. That is why the *parganas* of Suram, etc., have not been mentioned in the aforesaid treaty. Informs that the orders have been sent to the Collector of Allahabad to enquire into

[1]Copy enclosed with a letter from the Resident at Lucknow, dated 10 June 1805.

[2]Ibid.

[3]Ibid.

the matter and send the report along with necessary papers and records. Dated 13 April 1805.

OR 360,[1] f 1; CR 22, pp. 709-10, no. 22(15).

June -- 446. Nawwab Wazir to Col. Collins. Says that Shiv Bakhsh *mustajir* who owes Rs. 11,000 to the writer's government has taken refuge in Kanpur, the territory of the Company. Asks the addressee to issue order to the Judge of Kanpur to extradite the said *mustajir* to Lucknow so that the said amount due on him can be recovered.

OR 361,[2] f 1; CR 22, pp. 710-11, no. 22(16).

June -- 447. Col. Collins to Nawwab Wazir. Acknowledges receipt of addressee's letter in respect of extradition of Shiv Bakhsh merchant from Kanpur to Lucknow in order to settle the account with the addressee's government. Says that the Judge of Kanpur has already been directed to do the needful but no reply has so far been received. Assures that the addressee will be informed with the response of the judge. Dated 21 April 1805.

OR 362,[3] f 1; CR 22, pp. 711-13, no. 22(17).

June -- 448. Col. Collins to Nawwab Wazir. States that orders were issued to the judge of Kanpur in respect of the search of Kesar Singh, the merchant who have taken refuge in Kanpur. Informs that the said judge has replied that the said merchant is not traceable in Kanpur, however, he has assured that as soon as he (the merchant) arrives in this area will be arrested and extradited to the addressee. Dated 4 May 1805.

OR 363,[4] f 1; CR 22, pp. 713-14, no. 22(18).

June -- 449. Nawwab Mualla Jah of Kalpi to Col. Collins. Gives a detailed account of the hereditary Jagir at Kalpi and ascertain the writer's right over it.

OR 364,[5] f 1; CR 22, pp. 729-40, no. 28.

June -- 450. Mir Alam to Raja Mahipat Ram refers to the letters of

[1]Copy enclosed with a letter from the Resident at Lucknow, dated 10 June 1805.

[2]Ibid.

[3]Ibid.

[4]Ibid.

[5]Ibid.

Sidhnam Bahadur and Col. Close and says that it has been learnt from them that the addressee is not allowing the *taluqadars* of the Peshwa enter the *mahals* and collect the amount of *chauth*, etc., urges him to help them collect the *chauth* etc.

OR 365,[1] *f 1; CR 22, pp. 743-44, no. 30.*

June -- 451. Mir Alam to the Resident at Hyderabad. Proposes a schedule for the composition and arrangement of a body of troops regarding the Company's government.

OR 366,[2] *f 1; CR 22, pp. 746-50, no. 32.*

June -- 452. Raja Churaman Rai of Badaun and others to Captain Roughridge. Acknowledges receipt of Rs. 200 (two hundred) *kaldar* only against his salary as per order of Col. Edward from the *kachehri* of the said *pargana* through Fath Ali, *Sazawal*. Dated 26 *Magh* 1212 *Fasli* (21 January 1805).

OR 367 (a), f 1; CR 22, p. 752, no. 34(1).

June -- 453. Bikramajit Singh of Badaun to Captain Raughridge. Acknowledges receipt of Rs. 100 (one hundred) *kaldar* only against his salary as per order of Col. Edward from the *kachehri* of the said *pargana* through Fath Ali Khan, *Sazawal.* Dated 10 *Magh* 1212 *Fasli* (25 January 1805).

OR 367(b), f 1; CR 22, p. 753, no. 34(2).

June -- 454. Receipt of Rs. 50 *kaldar* only executed by Raj Kumar Babu Baikunth Singh, *jagirdar* of *pargana* Badaun received against the salary as per order of Col. Edward from the *kachehri* of the said *pargana* through Fath Ali Khan, *Sazawal*. Dated 31 January 1805.

OR 367 (c) f 1; CR 22, pp. 753-54, no. 34(3).

June -- 455. Receipt of Rs. 150 (one hundred and fifty) *kaldar* only executed by Shiv Prasad Singh, *diwan* of Badaun received against his salary from the *kachehri* of the said *pargana* through Fath Ali, *Sazawal.* Dated 21 January 1805.

OR 367 (d), f 1; CR 22, pp. 754-55, no. 34(4).

June -- 456. Receipt of Rs. 425 (four hundred twenty-five) only executed by Maharaja Munshi Nath Singh, *zamindar* of Ramgarh

[1]Copy enclosed with a letter from the Resident at Hyderabad, dated 10 June 1805.

[2]Ibid.

received against the salary of the *barqandaz* (musketeer) posted at Hazaribagh to guard the *chhawni* (cantonement). Dated 14 *Baisakh* 1212 *fasli* (27 April 1805).

OR 368, f 1; CR 22, pp. 755-56, no. 35.

June -- 457. Intelligence from the newswriter at Lucknow. Narrates the fight that took place on 2 June between Hasan Beg and Shaikh Ajmeri which resulted into the death of the both. Also explains the disturbance created at the *deorhi* of Shaikh Masud Ali by the *sawars* for the non-payment of their salaries.

OR 369,[1] *f 1.*

June -- 458. Duplicate of OR 369.

OR 370, f 1.

July 3 459. To Nawwab Murtaza Khan. Acknowledges receipt of addressee's applications regarding continuance of the pension of his late mother in his name. Informs the addressee that the final settlement of the pension will be done after the receipt of the report of the committee for the revision of *nizamat* establishment. However, orders have been issued to the Collector for the continuance of Rs. 1,000 to the addressee as pension and discharge of the accumulated arrear from the date of the death of addressee's mother.

CI 41, pp. 112-15, no. 15;
TI 51, pp. 130-33, no. 46.

July 3 460. To Nawwab Nasir al-Mulk. Acknowledges addressee's petition for the continuance of the pension of late Saliha Begam in the name of her successors. Says that the final settlement of the pension may be done after receipt of the report of the committee appointed for the revision of *nizamat* establishment. However, the Collector of Mushidabad has been ordered to release the payment of the pension of Rs. 1,000 per mensum to Saliha Begam's two granddaughters and discharge of arrear from the date of the Begam's death.

CI 41, pp. 111-12, no. 14;
TI 51, pp. 133-35, no. 47.

July 4 461. Strachy, the Judge of Kanpur to Col. Collins. Explains the reasons for the scarcity and dearness of grains in the Company's territory due to the delay in the transportation caused due to

[1]Copy enclosed with a letter from the Resident at Lucknow, dated 6 June 1805.

intervention of Nawwab Wazir's officials for appropriating taxes from the merchants carrying grain and passing through the territory of the Nawwab. Dated 27 October 1804.

OR 371/18 (b),[1] *f 1; CR 22, pp. 773-75, no. 1(2/b).*

July 4 462. Col. Collins to Nawwab Wazir. Refers to a dispatch from the Judge of Kanpur explaining the reasons for the scarcity and dearness of the grain and says that the addressee would issue orders to the *ummals* (officials) of the roads to abide by the terms of the treaty concluded between the two governments in respect of trade and supply of food grain and other provisions. Dated 5 *Shaban* 1219 AH. (11 November 1804).

OR 371/18 (a),[2] *f 1; CR 22, pp. 772-73, no. 1(2/a).*

July 4 463. Col. Collins to Nawwab Wazir. Acknowledges receipt of addressee's letter. Says that the Governor-General had assured of the compensation of the loss to the addressee's government further says that he (the writer) has no authority to go against the terms of the treaty, etc. Dated 15 *Shaban* 1219 AH. (19 November 1805).

OR 371/16,[3] *f 1; CR 22, pp. 777-80, no. 1(4).*

July 4 464. Nawwab Wazir to Col. Collins. Acknowledges receipt of the letter of the addressee dated 5 *Shaban* referring to the causes of the scarcity and dearness of grain as expressed by Strachy, the Judge of Kanpur. Says that he (the addressee) may order the *kotwal* and *mahajans* of Kanpur to abstain from appropriating the taxes from the merchant as this would be against the terms of the treaty. Dated 17 *Shaban* 1219 AH (2 November 1804).

OR 371/17,[4] *f 1; CR 22, pp. 776-77, no. 1(3).*

July 4 465. Resident at Lucknow (*Sahib-e-Kalan*) to Nawwab Wazir. Refers to the letter received from Robert Grant, the Collector (Revenue) at Kanpur complaining that the addressee's official (*bakhshi*) posted at *chawki* of Roop Pur has misappropriated

[1]Copy enclosed with a letter from the Resident at Lucknow, dated 10 June 1805.

[2]Ibid.

[3]Ibid.

[4]Ibid.

Rs. 16 from Udai Ram, merchant who has been carrying 17 packs of grain to Kanpur. Asks the addressee to check these officials and direct them to abstain from such misappropriation of taxes. Also asks the addressee to refund the misappropriated amount to Udai Ram. Dated 13 January 1805.

OR 371/1,[1] *f 1; CR 22, pp. 780-81, no. 1(5).*

July 4 466. Nawwab Wazir to Col. Collins. Acknowledges receipt of addressee's letter asking the writer to issue orders to Bakshi Ram and Balak Ram to return the amount to concerned merchants that they have appropriated revenue for carrying their merchandise. Says that Beni Parsad and Hakim Mahdi Ali Khan have been directed to do the needful in this regard. Further says that it had been decided that the terms of the trade affairs between the Company and writer's governments would be decided by mutual understanding. But no action has so far been taken in this respect by the Company's government. In this situation the transportation of merchandise between the two states are great source of monetary loss to the writer's government. Asks the addressee to expedite the process. Dated 11 *Shawwal* 1219 AH (13 January 1805.)

OR 371/15,[2] *f 1 CR 22, pp. 781-83, no. 1(6).*

July 4 467. Col. Collins to Nawwab Wazir. Acknowledges receipt of the addressee's letter (dated 13 *Shawwal* 1219 AH =15 January 1805) regarding redressal of the grievances of the merchants, etc. Further complains that the deeds of Bakshi Ram and Balak Ram have been against article, '8' of the treaty of November 1801. Also gives the 8 article of the said treaty. Dated 13 *Shawwal* 1219 AH (15 January 1805).

OR 371/14,[3] *f 1.*

July 4 468. Nawwab Wazir to Col. Collins. Acknowledges receipt of addressee's letter dated 13 *Shawwal* (1219 AH)=15 January 1805) wherein he has assured of the quick communication of Governor-General's reply regarding trade treaty between the two governments. Emphasizes the need of quick settlement of the terms of the said treaty so that the deadlock may be removed for the easy supply of food items and collection

[1]Copy enclosed with a letter from the Resident at Lucknow, dated 10 June 1805.

[2]Ibid.

[3]Ibid.

of revenue, etc. Dated 18 *Shawwal* 1219 AH (20 January 1805.)

OR 371/13,[1] f 1; CR 22, pp. 786-789, no. 1(8).

July 4 469. Col. Collins to Nawwab Wazir. Acknowledges receipt of addressee's letter dated 18 *Shawwal* 1219 AH (20 January 1805) and says that what ever the latter has claimed, have been communicated to the Governor-General for his perusal. Further assures that the addressee will soon be informed of the reply of the Governor-General in repect of his claims and demands. Dated 19 *Shawwal* 1219 AH (21 January 1805).

OR 371/12,[2] f 1; CR 22, pp. 789-90, no. 1(9).

July 4 470. Nawwab Wazir to Col. Collins. States that Shiv Bakhsh, Ram Bakhsh and Mir Kazim Ali, merchants owe a huge amount of debt due to the writer's government and now they have taken refuge at Kanpur, Allahabad and Fatehpur respectively. Refers to his (addressee's) orders to the Collectors of the said districts regarding extradition of these merchants to the writer's government in order to recover the amount of debt from them. Expresses displeasure over the cold and confused response of these officers and ask the addressee to manage the extradition of the said merchants to writer's government. Dated 28 *Shawwal* 1219 AH (30 January 1805).

OR 371/6,[3] f 1; CR 22, pp. 797-99, no. 1(15).

July 4 471. Resident at Lucknow to Nawwab Wazir. Acknowledges receipt of the addressee's letter regarding extradition of Shiv Bakhsh, Ram Bakhsh and Mir Kazim Ali who owe huge amount of dues to the addressee's government and have taken refuge in the Company's territory. Informs the addressee that orders have been issued to the Collectors of Allahabad and Kanpur to capture and extradite them to Lucknow in order to settle their accounts with the addressee's government. Dated 2 February 1805.

OR 371[4]/5, f 1; CR 22, pp. 79-801, no. 1(16).

[1]Copy enclosed with a letter from the Resident at Lucknow, dated 10 June 1805.

[2]Ibid.

[3]Ibid.

[4]Copy enclosed with a duplicate letter from the Resident at Lucknow, dated 10 June 1805.

July 4 472. Nawwab Wazir to Col. Collins. States that the village of Suram, etc.; from the district of Allahabad has been under the possession of Faiz Allah Khazanchi since long back. Even when district of Allahabad was handed over to the Company the said villages were retained under the same state according to the treaty (of November 1801). Asks the addressee to write to the Collector of Allahabad to leave the said villages under the possession of Faiz Allah Khazanchi and whatever amount have been appropriated by the Company's officials from these villages may be returned to the said *khazanchi*. It is dated 29 *Zulqada* 1219 AH (1 March 1805).

OR 371/11,[1] *f 1; CR 22, pp. 791, no. 1(10).*

July 4 473. Col. Collins to Nawwab Wazir. Acknowledges receipt of the addressee's letter regarding case of *pargana* Suram, etc., in district Allahabad. Communicates the acceptance of the proposal by the Governor-General that the district of Allababad has been taken over by the Company in its entirety. Dated 21 March 1805.

OR 371/9,[2] *f 1; CR 22, pp. 793-94, no. 1(12).*

July 4 474. Col. Collins to Nawwab Wazir. Acknowledges receipt of addressee's letter in respect of the transfer of *pargana* Suram, etc., to the territory of Faiz Allah Khazanchi against the treaty. Informs the addressee that orders have been issued to the Collector of Allahabad to redress the problem. Assures that the addressee will soon be informed of the reply of the said Collector. Dated 1 *Zilhijja* 1219 AH (23 March 1805).

OR 371/10,[3] *f 1; CR 22, pp. 791-92, no. 1(11).*

July 4 475. Nawwab Wazir to Col Collins. Acknowledges receipt of addressee's letter stating that the *pargana* of Suram, etc., were not excluded from district of Allahabad under the agreement of November 1801 and this district was taken over by the Company in its entirety. Says that the proposal of the inclusion of Suram was not accepted and it is mentioned in the treaty that Suram is excluded from the region of Allahabad w.e.f. 1296 *Fasli*. Asks the addressee to issue orders to the Collector of

[1]Copy enclosed with a letter from the Resident at Lucknow, dated 10 June 1805.

[2]Ibid.

[3]Ibid.

Allahabad to leave the said *taluqa* (Suram) and whatever have been collected from here during previous years be deposited to the writer's government. Dated 23 *Zilhijja* 1219 AH (24 March 1805).

OR 371/8;[1] *f 1; CR 22, pp. 794-95; no. 1(13).*

July 4 476. Col. Collins to Nawwab Wazir. Acknowledges receipt of addressee's letter dated 23 *Zilhijja* 1219 AH (25 March 1805) regarding *pargana* Suram's ownership. Refers to addressee's letter of 1216 AH (1801-02) to Henery Wellesley in this regard and says that all the representation and other facts have been sent to the Governor-General for his perusal. Assures that whatever order may come from him it will be soon communicated to the addressee. Dated 13 April 1805.

OR 371/7,[2] *f 1, CR 22, pp. 795-97, no. 1(14).*

July 4 477. Nawwab Wazir to Col. Collins. States that Shiv Bakhsh merchant who owes an amount of Rs. 11,000 (eleven thousand) only to the government has taken refuge in Kanpur and now planning to move to Bundelkhand. Asks the addressee to direct the Collector of Kanpur to send the said merchant to the writer in order to settle the accounts. Dated 21 *Muharram* 1220 AH (22 April 1805).

OR 371/4, f 1, CR 22, pp. 801-02, no. 1(17).

July 4 478. Col. Collins to Nawwab Wazir. Acknowledges receipt of addressee's letter regarding extradition of Shiv Bakhsh, merchant who owes an amount of Rs. 11,000 (eleven thousand) only to the addressee's government and now staying in Kanpur with a plan to move towards Bundelkhand. Says that the writer has directed the Collector of Kanpur to summon the said merchant and send him to the addressee where he can settle the account and pay the said dues. Dated 22 *Muharram* 1220 AH (23 April 1805).

OR 371/3,[3] *f 1; CR 22, pp. 802-03, no. 1(18).*

July 4 479. Col. Collins to Nawwab Wazir. States that he had directed the Judge of Kanpur to search the absconding taluqadar Kesar Singh earlier. Informs about the reply of the Judge that the said taluqadar is not traceable in Kanpur but as soon as he arrives

[1]Copy enclosed with a letter from the Resident at Lucknow, dated 10 June 1805.

[2]Ibid.

[3]Ibid.

in the area he will be arrested and extradited to the addressee. Dated 4 Safar 1220 AH (4 May 1805).

OR 371/2,[1] f 1; CR 22, pp. 803-05, no. 1(19).

July 4 480. Nawwab Wazir to Governor-General. States that a few issues which have not been settled at the time of the conclusion of the treaty (in November 1801) relating to the trade between the two states, status of Suram *pargana*, some building belonging to the pious persons, etc., now require proper and urgent attention for their logical settlement. Asks the addressee to issue orders to concerned authorities to settle these issues after discussing with the writer. Dated 8 *Rabi* I, 1220 AH (4 July 1805).

OR 371/19,[2] f 1; CR 22, pp. 765-72, no. 1(1).

July 7 481. From Ahmad Yab Khan. Refers to the visit of his brother to the addressee's court with a recommendation of Baji Rao regarding the *sardari* and ownership of the *pargana* of Bawani that have been left to him (writer) by his late father. Says that he has already decided to leave the worldly affairs and spend the rest of his life in prayers and meditation, hence he has no problem to bequeath the *sardari* and *zamindari* of *pargana* Bawani to his brother and *wakil* (of Mualla Jah) Muhammad Yab Khan as the pleasure of the Company is more important to him than the *sardari* and *zamindari* of *pargana* Bawani.

OR 372/1,[3] f 1; CR 22, pp. 817-25, no. 3(1).

July 7 482. Imad al-Mulk to Nasir al-Daulah. Appoints the addressee as his successor and grants him a salary of Rs. 700 per month along with Rs. 2,000 *hundawan* (?) till his stay in Poona, also grants an amount of Rs. 100 per month to Muhammad Panah Khan for life-long under the condition that he remains loyal to the writer. In the same way grants *jagirs* and allowances to other broters with some terms and condition.

OR 372/ii,[4] f 1; CR 22, pp. 825-27, no. 3(2).

[1]Copy enclosed with a duplicate letter from the Resident at Lucknow, dated 10 June 1805.

[2]Ibid.

[3]Ibid.

[4]Enclosed with a letter from the Commissioner of Rohilkhand, dated 19 June 1805.

July 7 483. (I.) Shah Alam II to Nasir al-Daulah Chin Qulich Khan. Expresses deep concern over the sad demise of Asaf Jah and hopes that the addressee will act according to the wishes and desires of his (addressee) late father.

(II.) Shah Alam II to Peshwa Baji Rao. Inform the addressee about the accession of Nasir al-Daulah to the seat of his late father Asaf Jah. Asks the addressee to treat him (Nasir al-Daulah) in the same respect as he (the addressee) treated late Asaf Jah.

(III.) Akbar Shah (*Wali-ahad*) to Nasir al-Daulah. Informs about the dispatch of two letters to Peshwa and Daulat Rao Sindhia through Ata Allah Khan.

OR 372/iii,[1] *f 1, CR 22, pp. 827-31, no. 3(3).*

July 7 484. To Amrit Rao. Refers to his correspondence with the addressee. Says that the engagements concluded as the result of addressee's discussion with General Arthur Wellesley in respect of the former's monetary assistance have been conveyed to the writer. In this regard T. Brook, the Acting Agent at Benares has been directed to pay the amount of Rs. 1 lakh to the addressee. Further the addressee, as per terms of the engagement may get a territorial assignment commensurate to fetch an annual amount of Rs. 7 lakh or by cash with the consultation of the *Peshwa*. Furthermore appreciates the addressee and his followers and adherents for their cooperation and amity towards the Company.

CI 41, pp. 116-19, no. 16; TI 51, pp. 135-39, no. 49.

July 8 485. Bishambar Pandit to Governor-General. Requests for the restoration of his (writer's) *jagir* in Shah Bandar, the details of which has already been submitted to Edmonston.

OR 373,[2] *WS, WC, f 1; TR 51, pp. 416-17, no. 125; AR 20, p. 6, no. 125.*

July 8 486. Bishambhar Pandit to Edmonston, the Persian Secretary to Governmentt. Encloses a memorandum for the addressee's perusal on the subject of the restoration of his *jagir* in Shah Bandar.

OR 374, f 1, WS, WC; TR 51, pp. 418-19, no. 126; AR 20, p. 6, no. 126.

[1]Enclosed with a letter from the Commissioner of Rohilkhand, dated 19 June 1805.

[2]Enclosed with a letter from the Resident.

July 8 487. Memorandum from Bishambhar Pandit to Edmonston, the Persian Secretary to the Governmentt. Explains the status of the *jagir* in Shah Bandar that had been granted to the writer as *inam al-tamgha* by the Company but was not given by the misrepresentation of Kaji Pandit. Requests the addressee to look into the matter and issue orders to the Commissioner at Cuttack to restore the said *jagir* to the writer.

OR 375, f 1; TR 51, pp. 319-21, no. 126, AR 20, p. 6, no. 126.

July 8 488. Nasir al-Mulk (of Murshidabad). Sends a gift of mangoes through Mir Kamal al Din Husain Khan.

OR 376, f 1, WS, WC.

July 10 489. From Umarao Begam (of Murshidabad). Requests for the grant of monetary assistance for the marriage of her two daughters.

OR 377,[1] *f 1, WS, WC; CR 22, pp. 331-33, no. 4; TR 51, pp. 421-23, no. 127; AR 20, p. 30, no. 127.*

July 10 490. From Muin al-Mulk (Nawwab Dilawar Jang). Explains his partial recovery from various types of ailments as a result of the regular and sincere treatment by Dr. Russel. Seeks permission to go for a river journey as prescribed by the said doctor for a climatic change on river Ganges up to Kishan Nagar or Munger. Dated 10 July 1805.

OR 378, f 1, WS, WC; TR 51, pp. 423-26, no. 128.

July 10 491. Prince Mirza Sulaiman Shukoh to the Governor-General. Informs that one Haji Muhsin, a pious man of the Emperor's court has proceeded for the audience of the addressee towards Calcutta. Asks the addressee to give him a favourable and suitable treatment.

OR 379, f 1, WS, WC; CR 22, pp. 838-39, no. 6; TR 51, pp. 427-28, no. 129; AR 20, p. 23, no. 129.

July 10 492. From Purnaiya. Informs him about the growing population of Srirangapattam as a result of the renovation work of the demolished fort and the sufferings due to lack of water in this locality. Further informs about the survey of the area for digging of canals to connect river Lachhman Tirath with Kaveri near Tappur and Chunchun Katta and further

[1]Enclosed with a letter from the agent to the Governor-General at Murshidabad.

to Srirangapattam for a regular supply of water for drinking and irrigation purposes. This survey was conducted by Col. Melcom Olex and the writer. Requests for the approval of the project and its timely execution in order to save the population form starvation. Dated 14 June 1805.

OR 380,[1] *ff 2, WS, WC; CR 22, pp. 833-37, no. 5; TR 51, pp. 428-35, no. 130; AR 20, p 31, no. 130.*

July 10 493. Emperor Shah Alam II. Says that one Haji Muhsin Marandazani Karbalai has been robbed off near Shahjahanabad in Jahangirabad while returning from Mecca and Madina. Recommends pecuniary help to the said Haji and asks the addressee to arrange for the recovery of his properties worth Rs. 4,000.

OR 381, ff 2, WS, WC; CR 22, pp. 839-41, no. 7; TR 51, pp. 435-37, no. 131; AR 20, p. 19, no. 131.

July 12 494. From Nasir al-Mulk (of Murshidabad). Requests to dispose off the papers submitted by the writer regarding *nizamat* affair before the addressee's departure to England. Dated 11 *Rabi* II, 47 *Julus* (of Shah Alam II) = 9 July 1805.

OR 382, WS, WC, f l; CR 22, pp. 841-43, no. 8.

July 13 495. From Raja Bakht Bali. Recounts his services to Col. Pool during the campaign against Nawwab Shamsher Bahadur and requests for the restoration of his ancestral *jagir* along the fortresses of Ajaygarh and Bhuragarh occupied by the said Nawwab some time back along with an amount of Rs. 5 lakh.

OR 383,[2] *f 1; CR 22, pp. 844-47, no. 9(1).*

July 13 496 Raja Tej Singh (of Sarila) to John Baillie. Explains the circumstance that resulted in the confiscation of his hereditary *jagir* by Nawwab Shamsher Bahadur of Bundelkhand. Requests the addressee to restore the aforesaid *jagirs* to him (the writer). Also expresses his full confidence in British government and assures of his loyalty.

OR 384,[3] *f 1; CR 22, pp. 847-53, no. 9(2).*

July 13 497. From Raja Narendargir (of Sikandra). Informs about

[1]Enclosed with a letter from the acting Resident in Mysore, dated 14 June 1805.

[2]Enclosed with a letter from Major Baillie.

[3]Copy enclosed with a letter from Capt. Baillie.

the sad demise of his father and the (*kiriya karam*) last rites of the deceased. Also informs that he has been appointed as the successor of his late father as per his will. Refers to John Baillie and Kunwar Kanchangir for further details.

OR 385,[1] f 1; CR 22, pp. 854-55, no. 10(1).

July 13 498. From Kunwar Kanchangir. To the same effect as the foregoing letter OR 385.

OR 386,[2] f 1; CR 22, pp. 855-57, no 10(2).

July 14 499. From Nasir al-Daulah (of Kalpi). Expresses the harsh treatment of the southern officers meted out to the writer and requests for some help from the Governor-General.

OR 387,[3] f 1; CR 22, pp. 865-67, no. 13; TR 51A, pp. 445-47, no. 134; AR 20, p. 29.

July 14 500. From Muhammad Baqar Ali Khan (of Fatehpur). Requests to direct Col. Collins to investigate into the case of his mother's involvement in the affairs related to Hakim Mahdi Ali Khan. Further requests that if she is found innocent she may be allowed to return to Fatehpur.

OR 388,[4] WS, WC, f 1; CR 22, pp. 858-61, no. 11.

July 16 501. Mir Qusim Ali Khan and other, dependents of Nawwab Saiyid Saleh Khan (of Murshidabad). Requests to continue the pension of their late father in their names as they are the real successors.

OR 389,[5] WS, f 1; CR 22, pp. 870-71, no. 15; TR 51A, pp. 447-50, no. 135; AR 20, p. 7.

July 17 502. From Emperor Shah Alam II. Asks the addressee to enhance the monthly allowance of the princes and early payment of Rs. 6 lakh as *peshkash*.

OR 390,[6] WS, f 1; TR 51A, pp. 450-53, no. 136; AR 20, p. 19.

[1]Copy enclosed with a letter from the Commissioner at Bundelkhand.

[2]Ibid.

[3]Enclosed with a letter from Brooke, dated 1 July 1805.

[4]Enclosure to a letter from the Magistrate at Allahabad, dated 4 July 1805.

[5]Enclosed with a letter from the superintendent of Nizamat Affaris, dated 10 July 1805.

[6]Enclosure to a letter from the resident at Delhi to the Secretary to the Government, dated 1 July 1805.

July 17 503. From Shah Alam II.To the same effect as the foregoing letter OR 390.

OR 391,[1] *f 1; TR 51A, pp. 450-53, no. 136; AR 20, p. 19.*

July 17 504. From Harinder Narayan (of Cooch Behar). Complains against the actions of the Provincial court of Rangpur against the writer and requests to issue prohibitory orders to the judges of both the courts.

OR 392, f 1; WS, WC; TR 51A, pp. 452-56, no. 137; AR 20, p. 35.

July 17 505. From the Raja of Cooch Behar. States that the Governor-General had established and appointed the Resident and a judicial court functioning under the control of the British government as the writer was a minor and could not run the government. Requests to restore his authority over the day-to-day administration and the court as he has now come of age.

OR 393, f 1; WS, WC; TR 51A, pp. 456-64, no. 138; AR 20, p. 35.

July 17 506. Nawwab Wazir to Col. Collins. Says that the sons of Ghulam Muhammad Khan were allowed to stay in Lucknow during the time of Col. Scott. Since then the writer has brought their obnoxious activities to the notice of the addressee repeatedly and has also requested to check them. And now they have been found moving in the city with firearm and a few gunmen. Hence requests the addressee to take them from Lucknow to the territory of the British government as a safety measure to the peace and harmony of the city of Lucknow.

OR 395,[2] *f 1, CR 22, pp. 883-86, no. 18(1).*

July 17 507. Nawwab Wazir to Col. Collins. To the same effect as the foregoing letter OR 395.

OR 396,[3] *f 1; CR 22, pp. 883-86, no. 18(1).*

July 17 508. Col. Collins to Nawwab Wazir. Encloses a petition of the sons of Ghulam Muhammad Khan explaining the reason of their movement in the city of Lucknow with firearms.

[1]Copy enclosed with a letter from the Resident at Delhi to the Secretary to the Government, dated 1 July 1805.

[2]Copy enclosed with a letter from the Resident at Lucknow, dated 8 July 1805.

[3]Ibid.

Enquires from addressee whether to inform the Governor-General regarding this matter or not.

OR 397,[1] f 1, CR 22, pp. 886-87, no. 18(2).

July 17 509. Col. Collins to Nawwab Wazir. To the same effect as the foregoing letter OR 397).

OR 398,[2] f 1, CR 22, pp. 886-88, no. 18(2).

July 17 510. Nawwab Wazir to Col. Collins. Says that the sons of Ghulam Muhammad Khan have submitted an application begging pardon for their actions and adds that it is necessary to send them out of Lucknow lest they create some disturbances. Dated 2, *Rabi II*, 1220 AH (30 June 1805).

OR 399,[3] f 1, CR 22, pp. 889-90, no. 18(3).

July 17 511. Nawwab Wazir to Col. Collins. To the same effect as the foregoing letter OR 399.

OR 400,[4] f 1; CR 22, pp. 889-90, no. 18(3).

July 17 512. Abd Allah Khan, Saif Allah Khan and Sayeed Khan (sons of Ghulam Muhammad Khan) to Nawwab Wazir. Refutes the charges levelled against them and explain the necessity of keeping a few gunmen along with them for their personal security. Dated 3 *Rabi I* 1220 AH (29 June 1805).

OR 401,[5] f 1; CR 22, pp. 891-94, no. 18(4).

July 17 513. Abd Allah Khan, Saif Allah Khan and Sayeed Khan (sons of Ghulam Muhammad Khan) to Nawwab Wazir. To the same effect as the foregoing letter OR 401.

OR 402,[6] f 1; CR 22, pp. 891-94, no. 18(4).

July 17 514. Nawwab Wazir to Col. Collins. States that he (the writer) has come to know that John Ahmuty, the *nazim* of Gorakhpur has been proposed to move towards the area of Bahraich with British troop. If this is true he may be allowed to call back all the *amils* posted in that area.

OR 403,[7] f 1; CR 22, pp. 894-97, no. 19(1).

[1]Copy enclosed with a letter from the Resident at Lucknow, dated 8 July 1805.
[2]Ibid.
[3]Ibid.
[4]Ibid.
[5]Ibid.
[6]Ibid.
[7]Ibid.

July 17 515. Nawwab Wazir to Coll. Collins. To the same effect as the foregoing letter OR 403.

OR 404,[1] *f 1; CR 22, pp. 894-97, no. 19(1).*

July 18 516. Col. Collins to Nawwab Wazir. Explains the need of mobilizing troops in the area of the addressee that one rebellious *zamindar* Bhagwant Singh has taken refuge in this area and Ahmad Ali Khan, deputed to arrest the said rebel has committed delay. There is all probability that the said rebel may take refuge in the adjacent territory of the Company and create disturbance. Hence it is essential to depute a Company of troops to arrest the said rebel before the latter could manage to fly from this area.

OR 405,[2] *f 1; CR 22, pp. 897-99, no. 19(3).*

July 17 517. John Ahmuty to Ahamd Ali Khan. States that urgent orders have been issued to Hakim Mahdi Ali Khan to arrest one rebel Bhagwant Singh as desired by the writer and also asks the addressee to direct the *zamindars* of the said area not to interfere in the movement of the Company's troops for this purpose.

OR 406,[3] *f 1; CR 22, pp. 896-97, no. 19(2).*

July 17 518. John Ahmuty to Ahmad Ali Khan. To the same effect as the foregoing.

OR 407,[4] *f 1; CR 22, pp. 896-97, no. 19(2).*

July 17 519. To Nawwab Wazir. Acknowledges addressee's dispositions for the prosperity of the Company. Requests for a loan of Rs. 10 lakh to meet out the expenses of public services. Assures the addressee that the amount will be refunded regularly as per terms of loan.

CI 41, pp. 119-125, no. 17; TR 51, pp. 139-45, no. 50.

July 18 520. To the King. Condoling on the death of addressee's daughter Zubdat al-Nisa Begam.

CI 41, pp. 430-32, no. 169; TI 51, p. 146, no. 51.

[1]Copy enclosed with a letter from the Resident at Lucknow, dated 8 July 1805.
[2]Ibid, dated 9 July 1805.
[3]Ibid, dated 8 July 1805.
[4]Ibid, dated 9 July 1805.

July 18 521. To Nawwab Dilawar Jang. Acknowledges receipt of addressee's application seeking permission to leave to Munger on health grounds. Permits the addressee to go for a visit of Munger.

CI 41, pp. 432-34, no. 170; TI 51, p. 146, no. 52.

July 20 522. Mir Nazar Ali to Monkton. Requests for a *rahdari* (Passport) for himself to travel from Calcutta to Lucknow along with his belongings consequent upon delivery of presents to the Governor-General from Nawwab Wazir.

OR 408, f 1.

July 20 523. From Ramazan Ali Khan. Requests for a *dastak-i-rahdari* for himself to travel from Calcutta to Lucknow along with horses, wooden furniture and Chinese glass utensils, etc.

OR 409, f 1.

July 20 524. From Ramazan Ali. Requests that the materials required by Nawwab Wazir consisting horse, wooden furniture, China glass utensils, etc., may be sent from Calcutta to Lucknow with Mir Nazar Ali.

OR 410, f 1.

July 21 525. From Nawwab Nusrat Jang (of Dacca). Promises to stand surety to his brother's conduct at Dacca in future and accept all the terms and conditions laid down by the addressee for the release of writer's brother Shams al-Daulah.

OR 411,[1] f 1, WS, WC; CR 22, pp. 901-05, no. 21; TR 51A, pp. 464-66, no. 139; AR 20, p. 26.

July 21 526. From Aqa Nabi Khan (the Persian Ambassador). Explains the hardship of sea journey from Baghdad to Bombay. Says that now he will soon take up the journey to Calcutta through the land route to see the Governor-General to discuss various matters including the issue of French activities.

OR 412, WS, f 1; CR 22, pp. 905-06; TR 51A, pp. 466-70, no. 140; AR 20, p. 1.

July 22 527. From Imdad Husain Khan of Farrukhabad. Acknowledges receipt of Governor-General's letter and request him to give his

[1]Enclosure to a letter from the senior Judge at Decca, dated 15 July 1805.

attention towards the writer's interests and a few points of the government may be solved.

OR 413,[1] f 1, WS, WC; CR 22, pp. 909-10, no. 23; TR 51A, pp. 471-72, no. 141; AR 20, p. 11.

July 22 528. From Mirza Muhammad Wali of Patna. Recounts his services to the Company's government and requests for the means of subsistence from the Governor-General.

OR 414, f 1, WC; TR 51A, pp. 473-76, no. 142; AR 20, p. 23.

July 22 529. Nawwab Wazir to Col. Collins. Acknowledges receipt of addressee's letter regarding mobilization of troops in order to capture one rebel Bhagwant Singh. Says that the writer has issued urgent orders to Mahdi Ali Khan for immediate action in this regard. Dated 11 *Rabi II*, 1220 AH (9 July 1805).

OR 415,[2] f 1, WC; CR 22, pp. 899-900, no. 20(1).

July 22 530. Nawwab Wazir to Mahdi Ali Khan. Directs the addressee to take immediate action in regard to the arrest of the rebel Bhagwant Singh. Dated 11 *Rabi II*, 1220 AH (9 July 1805).

OR 416,[3] f 1; CR 22, pp. 900-01, no. 20(2).

July 22 531. Nawwab Wazir to Col. Collins. To the same effect as the OR 415.

OR 417,[4] f 1; CR 22, pp. 910-11, no. 24(1).

July 22 532. Nawwab Wazir to Mahdi Ali Khan. To the same effect as OR 416.

OR 418, f 1; CR 22, pp. 911-12, no. 24(2).

July 24 533. From Raja Udit Narayan Singh (of Benares). Requests for the restoration of his ancestral *jagir* of Kol-Asla mortgaged to Babu Shiv Parsan Singh against Rs. 1 lakh.

OR 419, f 1, WS, WC; TR 51A, pp. 476-78 no. 143; AR 20, p. 33.

July 24 534. From Raja Udit Narayan Singh (of Benares). Gives a brief history of *jagirs* of Kol-Asla and Majhua and establishes

[1]Enclosure to a letter from the Agent at Farrukhabad to the Persian Secretary, dated 15 July 1805.

[2]Enclosure to a letter from the Resident at Lucknow, dated 13 July 1805.

[3]Ibid.

[4]Ibid.

his demands of revenue from the said *jagirs*.

OR 420, ff 11; TR 51A, pp. 476-78, no. 143; AR 20, p. 33.

July 24 535. To Nawwab Wazir. Comprehensively explains the losses and damages sustained by Prendergast at the hands of Almas Ali Khan who seized the indigo work establishment and indigo farms situated in *pargana* Saket previously given to the former as per an agreement concluded between the two persons in 1798. Further says that the charge levelled against Almas Ali Khan by Prendergast have been found valid by the committee appointed to look into the matter judiciously. Recommends that the said Khan may be brought to book and the loss sustained by Prendergast would properly be compensated by restoring the indigo works and indigo farms to the latter. Other details may be sought from Col. Collins.

CI, pp. 125-30, no. 18; TI 51, pp. 146-52, no. 53.

July 25 536. Petition of Aqa Muhammad Shustari for a *dastak-i-rahdari* for the journey of Mirza Muhammad Raza along with horses and other belongings from Calcutta to Hyderabad via Ganjam. Dated 1 April 1805

OR 421, f 1.

July 25 537. To Maharaja Daulat Rao Sindhia. Asks the addressee to release Jenkins immediately from his court along with attached escorts of Residency to the nearest station of British government. Further informs that Lord Lake has been appointed as the Commander-in-Chief and has been vested with all power to accord any military and political engagement with the states out of British jurisdiction. Expresses hope that the addressee will comply with the directions immediately keeping in mind the treaty of peace concluded earlier between the two governments.

CI 41, pp. 130-37, no. 19; TI 51, pp. 159-68, no. 66.

July 25 538. To Qutlugh Sultan Begam. Complementary in reply to her letter along with present of a ring.

CI 41, pp. 434-35, no. 172; TI 51, p. 153, no. 54.

July 25 539. To Babbu Begam. Complementary in reply of her letter informing of the marriage of the daughters of late Nawwab Mubarak al-Daulah.

CI 41, pp. 437-38, no. 175; TI 51, p. 153, no. 55.

July 25 540. To Shams al-Nisa Begam (widow of late Nawwab Asaf al-Daulah). Complementary in reply to her letter.
CI 41, pp. 435-36, no. 173; TI 51, p. 154, no. 56.

July 25 541. To Munni Begam. Complementary in reply to her letter expressing anxiety on account of the writer's health.
CI 41, p. 441, no. 179; TI 51, p. 154, no. 57.

July 25 542. To Nawwab Dilawar Jang. Complementary in reply to addressee's letters along a number of presents.
CI 41, pp. 439-40, no. 177; TI 51, p. 155, no. 58.

July 25 543. To Nawwab Nusrat Jang. Complementary in reply to the addressee's two letters, the first on the occasion of season and the second on the capture of fortress of Darara by British forces.
CI 41, pp. 441-42, no. 180; TI 51, p. 154, no. 59.

July 25 544. Karim Quli Khan. Complementary in reply to his letter of congratulation on the season.
CI 41, pp. 440-41, no. 178; TI 51, p. 156, no. 60).

July 25 545. To Jagat Seth. In reply to addressee's letter expressing gratitude for allowing him to visit Jagannathji and the attention which he received from the British authorities in Cuttack.
CI 41, pp. 444-45, no. 182; TR 51, p 156, no. 61.

July 25 546. To Bishambhar Pandit. Complementary in reply to addressee's letter announcing the marriage of his brother Hari Bhadra Pandit.
CI 41, pp. 445-46, no. 183; TI 51, p. 157, no. 62.

July 25 547. To Manohar Das. Complementary reply to his letter informing of his arrival at Murshidabad and his intention to stay there for some time for health benefits before resuming his journey to Benares.
CI 41, pp. 436-37, no. 174; TI 51, p. 157, no. 63.

July 25 548. To Imdad Hussain Khan. Complementary in reply to his two letters affording testimony to the propriety of the conduct of Russel and Cuthbert during the period of their respective residence at Farrukhabad and expressing the favourable opinion which the addressee entertains of Lloyd's disposition.
CI 41, pp. 443-44, no. 181; TI 51, pp. 157-58, no. 64.

July 25 549. To Arjunji Nathji, the Sanker of Surat. Acknowledgement to his *arzi* (application). Declines to accept his *nazr* of 25 gold *muhrs* on the occasion of his investiture.

CI 41, pp. 438-39, no. 176; TI 51, p. 158, no. 65.

July 26 550. From mother of Nawwab Ahmad Ali Khan. Informs about the breaking of the proposed engagement of her son to the daughter of Nawwab Khiradmand Khan of Farrukhabad. Dated 12 *Rabi II*, 1220 AH (10 July 1805).

OR 422, f 1, WS, WC; TR 51A, pp. 479, no. 144; AR 20, p. 3.

July 26 551. To Nawwab Nasir al-Mulk. Acknowledges receipt of addressee's letter expressing regret on the news of writer's proposed departure to England. Expresses gratification for the addressee's concern on this subject. Says that (the writer) would make all possible effort to complete the work on the revision of the *nizamat* establishment so far leaving for England. Regrets the addressee's desire to have a meeting with the writer at Calcutta due to latter's utmost engagement in the essential disposition which he has to conclude before his departure to England.

CI 411, pp. 137-41, no. 20; TI 51, pp. 168-72, no. 67.

July 26 552. To Nawwab Munni Begam. To the same effect as the foregoing CI 20 and TI 67.

CI 41, pp. 142-45, no. 21; TI 51, pp. 173-74, no. 68.

July 27 553. From Nawwab Nasir Jang Khiradmand Khan of Farrukhabad. Requests for the payment of the amount of revenue collected by the Company from Farrukhabad for the month of September 1802.

OR 423,[1] f 1; CR 22, pp. 912-14, no. 25.

July 27 554. The Magistrate at Gorakhpur to Gulab Singh, *subedar*. Directs the addressee to accompany Capt. Malcot along with a Company of troops in order to arrest the rebel Bhagwant Singh and send him immediately to the *faujdari* court at Gorakhpur. Dated 13 June 1805.

OR 424,[2] f 1; CR 22, pp. 914-16, no. 26(1).

[1]Copy enclosed with a letter from the Acting Agent at Farrukhabad, dated 15 July 1805.

[2]Copy enclosed with a letter from the Resident at Lucknow to the Secretary to Government, dated 18 July 1805.

July 27 555. The Magistrate at Gorakhpur to Gulab Singh, *subedar* of Bhojpur. To the same effect as the foregoing OR 424.

OR 425,[1] f 1.

July 27 556. The Magistrate at Gorakhpur to Col. Collins. Refers to the letters received from Nawwab Wazir, John Ahmuty and the addressee. Says that a *parwana* should be issued to Gulab Singh, *subedar* of Bhojpur directing him not to let his troops trespass the territory of Nawwab Wazir. Dated 13 July 1805.

OR 426,[2] f 1, CR 22, pp. 917-19, no. 26(2).

July 27 557. The Magistrate at Gorakhpur. To the same effect as the foregoing OR 426.

OR 427,[3] f 1; CR 22, pp. 917-19, no. 26(2).

July 27 558. The Magistrate at Gorakhpur to Gulab Singh, *subedar* of Bhojpur. Directs the said *subedar* to warn the troops stationed for the arrest of Bhagwant Singh not to step into the territory of Nawwab Wazir. Dated 13 July 1805.

OR 428,[4] f 1; CR 22, pp. 919-20, no. 26(3).

July 27 559. The Magistrate at Gorakhpur to Gulab Singh, *subedar* of Bhojpur. To the same effect as the foregoing OR 428.

OR 429,[5] f 1; CR 22, pp. 919-20, no. 26(3).

July 27 560. Prince Akbar to Col. Octerlony. Says that Rs. 36,000 has been fixed as annual stipend in lieu of the five villages Kotah, Dhana, Korli, Bachhra and Sapnawat of *pargana* Dasna. Further says that a few matters will be communicated by his representative Saiyid Razi Khan.

OR 430,[6] f 1, WS, WC; CR 22, pp. 920-21, no. 27.

July 27 561. To the King Shah Alam II. Informs the king that the writer's resignation from the post of Supreme Command of

[1]Copy enclosed with a letter from the Resident at Lucknow to the Secretary to Government, dated 18 July 1805.

[2]Copy enclosed with a letter from the Resident at Lucknow, dated 18 July 1805.

[3]Ibid.

[4]Copy enclosed with a letter from the Resident at Lucknow to the Secretary to Government, dated 18 July 1805.

[5]Copy enclosed with a letter from the Resident at Lucknow, dated 18 July 1805.

[6]Enclosed with a letter from the Resident at Delhi, dated 13 July 1805.

the Company's government has been accepted and soon he will leave the charges of government to his successor Marquess Cornwallis. Expresses hope that the prosperity of addressee's person and state will grow further and the friendly relations of the two states further strengthened under the able governance of Marquess Cornwallis.

CI 41, pp. 146-48, no. 22; TI 51, pp. 175-77, no. 69.

July 27 562. To Qutluq Sultan Begam. To the same effect as the foregoing CI 22 and TI 69.

CI 41, pp. 148-49, no. 23; TI 51, pp. 177, no. 70.

July 27 563. To Mirza Sulaiman Shukoh. To the same tenor and date as the foregoing CI 22 and TI 69.

CI 41, pp. 150-51, no. 24; TI 51, p. 177, no. 71.

July 27 564. To Mirza Shigufta Bakht. To the same tenor and date as the foregoing CI 22 and TI 69.

CI 41, pp. 148-49, no. 23; TI 51, p. 177, no. 72.

July 27 565. To Nawwab Wazir. Informs the addressee that the writer's request for relieving from the duties of Supreme Government of British possession of India has been accepted and now he is waiting for the arrival of his successor Lord Cornwallis at Fort William to devolve the charges to him at the earliest and set out for England. Expresses gratitude for the kind and humble dispositions of the addressee during the writer's administration. Hopes that the subsisting friendly relation between the two states will get a further boost under the governance of his successor Lord Cornwallis.

CI 41, pp. 151-54, no. 25; TI 51, pp. 178-80, no. 73.

July 27 566. To Bahu Begum. To the same effect as the foregoing CI 25 and TI 73).

CI 41, pp. 154-56, no. 26; TI 51, p. 181, no. 74.

July 27 567. To Shams al-Nisa Begam. To the same effect as the foregoing CI 25 and TI 73.

CI 41, pp. 154-56, no. 26; TI 51, p. 181, no. 75.

July 27 568. To Nawwab Nasir al-Mulk. To the same effect as the foregoing CI 25 and TI 73.

CI 41, pp. 163-65, no. 31; TI 51, p. 181, no. 76.

July 27 569. To Nawwab Munni Begam. To the same effect as the foregoing CI and TI 73.

CI 41, pp. 163-65, no. 31; TI 51, p. 181, no. 77.

July 27 570. To Babbu Begam. To the same effect as the foregoing CI 25, and TI 73.

CI 41, pp. 163-65, no. 31; TI 51, p. 181, no. 78.

July 27 571. To the Nizam. To the same effect as the foregoing CI 25 and TI 73).

CI 41, pp. 156-58, no. 27; TI 51, p. 181, no. 79.

July 27 572. To Mir Alam. To the same effect as the foregoing CI 25 and TI 73.

CI 41, pp. 156-58, no. 27; TI 51, p. 181, no. 80.

July 27 573. Raja Raghuji Bhonsla. To the same effect as the foregoing CI 25 and TI 73.

CI 41, pp. 174-75, no. 38; TI 51, p. 181, no. 81.

July 27 574. To the Peshwa. To the same effect as the foregoing CI 25 and TI 73.

CI 41, pp. 160-62, no. 29; TI 51, p. 181, no. 82.

July 27 575. To Daulat Rao Sindhia. To the same effect as the foregoing CI 25 and TI 73.

CI 41, pp. 162-63, no. 30; TI 51, p. 181, no. 83.

July 27 576. To Nawwab Azim al-Daulah, the Nawwab of Carnatik. To the same effect as the foregoing CI 25 and TI 73.

CI 41, pp. 158-60, no. 28; TI 51, p. 181, no. 84.

July 27 577. To the Raja Ram Raj of Travancore. To the same effect as the foregoing CI 25 and TI 73.

CI 41, pp. 172-74, no. 37; TI 51, p. 181, no. 85.

July 27 578. To Raja Sawai Jagat Singh of Jainagar. To the same effect as the foregoing CI 25 and TI 73.

CI 41, pp. 167-69, no. 34; TI 51, p. 181, no. 86.

July 27 579. To Imdad Hussain Khan. To the same effect as the foregoing CI 25 and TI 73.

CI 41, pp. 176-78, no. 39; TI 51, p. 181, no. 87.

July 27 580. To Umrao Begam. To the same effect as the foregoing CI 25 and TI 73.

CI 41, pp. 176-78, no. 39; TI 51, p. 182, no. 88.

July 27 581. To Khiradmand Khan. To the same effect as the foregoing CI 25 and TI 73.

CI 41, pp. 176-78, no. 39; TI 51, p. 182, no. 89.

July 27 582. To Nawwab Ahmad Ali Khan. To the same effect as the foregoing CI 25 and TI 73.

CI 41, pp. 180-82, no. 41; TI 51, p. 182, no. 90.

July 27 583. To Nawwab Nasr Allah Khan. To the same effect as the foregoing CI 25 and TI. 73.

CI 41, pp. 180-82, no. 41; TI 51, p. 182, no. 91.

July 27 584. To Nawwab Nusrat Jang. To the same effect as the foregoing CI 25 and TI 73.

CI 41, pp. 182-84, no. 42; TI 51, p. 182, no. 92.

July 27 585. To Amrit Rao. To the same effect as the foregoing CI 25 and TI 73.

CI 41, pp. 160-62, no. 29; TI 51, p. 182, no. 93.

July 27 586. To Nawwab Dilawar Jang. To the same effect as the foregoing CI 25 and TI 73.

CI 41, pp. 182-84, no. 42; TI 51, p. 182, no. 94.

July 27 587. To the Raja of Nepal. To the same effect as the foregoing CI 25 and TI 73.

CI 41, pp. 178-79, no. 40; TI 51, p. 182, no. 95.

July 28 588. To Raja Udit Narayan Singh. To the same effect as the foregoing CI 25 and TI 73.

CI 41, pp. 165-66, no. 32; TI 51, p. 182, no. 96.

July 29 589. To Raja Kishan Raj of Mysore. To the same effect as the foregoing CI 25 and TI 73.

CI 41, pp. 169-70, no. 35; TI 51, p. 182, no. 97.

July 27 590. To Purnaiya. To the same effect as the foregoing CI 25 and TI 73.

CI 41, pp. 170-72, no. 36; TI 51, p. 182, no 98.

July 27 591. To Maharaja Man Singh of Jodhpur. To the same effect as the foregoing CI 25 and TI 73.

CI 41, pp. 166-67, no. 33; TI 51, p. 182, no. 99.

July 28 592. Mirza Murad Bakhsh (son of Shah Alam II) to Col.

Ochterlony. Accepts the offer of Governor-General to pay Rs. 1,000 per month to the Company in lieu of village Suhani as *tayul*.

OR 431,[1] *f 1, WS, WC; CR 22, pp. 922-23, no. 28.*

July 29 593. From Mahabat Ali Khan. Requests for the grant of a proper means of subsistence as he has served the Company for a long period of 35 years.

OR 432, f 1, WS, WC; TR 51A, pp. 479-81, no. 145; AR 20, p. 29.

July 29 594. To King Shah Alam II. Acknowledges receipt of addressee's letter dated 17 July 1805 regarding arrangement of fund for the support of the addressee's relief. Informs the addressee that the arrangement for the required support could not be done due to regular engagement of Company's government in ongoing war in Hindustan. Further says that an amount of Rs. 6 lakh will be deposited to the addressee's treasury as soon as the causes of its delay are subsided.

CI 41, pp. 184-87, no. 43; TI 51, pp. 183-85, no. 100.

July 30 595. From Nawwab Muhammad Ali Khan of Farrukhabad. Requests to continue a debit of Rs. 500 monthly from the writer's allowance as a recovery of the loan raised by the writer for the marriages of himself and his brother.

OR 433,[2] *f 1, WS, WC; CR 22, pp. 923-24, no. 29; TR 51A, pp. 485-86, no. 147; AR 20, p. 24.*

July 31 596. To King Shah Alam II. Informs the addressee of his (writer's) appointment and taking charge of Governor-General at Fort William on 30 July 1805. Assures the address that the relation between the two states will remain intact and he (the writer) will make utmost effort to see the comfort and dignity of the addressee growing day by day.

CI 41, pp. 188-89, no. 44; TI 51, pp. 185-86, no. 101.

July 31 597. To Qutluq Sultan Begam. To the same effect as the foregoing CI 44 and TI 101.

CI 41, pp. 189-90, no. 45; TI 51, p. 187, no. 102.

[1]Enclosed with a letter from the Resident at Delhi, dated 13 July 1805.

[2]Enclosed with a letter from the Acting Agent at Farrukhabad, dated 18 July 1805.

July 31 598. To Mirza Sulaiman Shukah. To the same effect as the foregoing CI 44 and TI 101.

CI 41, pp. 189-90, no. 45; TI 51, p. 187, no. 103.

July 31 599. To Mirza Shigufta Bakht. To the same effect as the foregoing CI 44 and TI 101.

CI 41, pp. 189-90, no. 45; TI 51, p. 187, no. 104.

July 31 600. To the Nizam. Informs the addressee that he (the writer) has been appointed and taken charge of Governor-General on 30 July 1805. Further assures that the prevailing friendship between the two states may further be cemented during the writer's governance.

CI 41, pp. 194-96, no. 48; TI 51, pp. 187-90, no. 105.

July 31 601. To Mir Alam. To the same effect (with a slight variation of second paragraph). As the foregoing CI 48 and TI 105.

CI 41, pp. 196-98, no. 49; TI 51, p. 190, no. 106.

July 31 602. To Nawwab Wazir Informs that the writer has been appointed and has taken charge of the Governor-General on 30 July 1805. Assures that the prevailing friendly relation will be further strengthened and the writer will strive his best for the prosperity of the two states.

CI 41, pp. 191-92, no. 46; TI 51, pp. 190-92, no. 107.

July 31 603. To Bahu Begam. To the same effect as the foregoing CI 46 and TI 107.

CI 41, pp. 192-93, no. 47; TI 51, p. 192, no. 108.

July 31 604. To Shams al-Nisa Begam. To the same effect as the foregoing CI 46 and TI 107.

CI 41, pp. 192-93, no. 47; TI 51, p. 192, no. 109.

July 31 605. To Nawwab Nasir al-Mulk. To the same effect as the foregoing CI 46 and TI 107.

CI 41, pp. 201-202, no. 52; TI 51, p. 192, no. 110.

July 31 606. To Munni Begam. To the same effect as the foregoing CI 46 and TI 107.

CI 41, pp. 201-02, no. 52; TI 51, p. 192, no. 111.

July 31 607. To Babbu Begam. To the same effect as the foregoing CI. 46 and TI 107.

CI 41, pp. 201-02, no. 52; TI 51, p. 192, no. 112.

July 31 608. To Maharaja Raghuji Bhonsla. To the same effect as the foregoing CI 468 TI 107.

CI 41, pp. 204-06, no. 54; TI 51, p. 192, no. 113.

July 31 609. To Nawwab Azim al-Daulah. To the same effect as the foregoing CI 46 and TI 107.

CI 41, pp. 202-04, no. 53; TI 51, p. 193, no. 114.

July 31 610. To Raja of Travancore. To the same effect as the foregoing CI 46 and TI 107.

TI 51, p. 193, no. 115.

July 31 611. To Maharaja Sawai Jagat Singh of Jainagar (Jaipur). To the same effect as the foregoing CI 46 and TI 107

CI 41, pp. 218-19, no. 63; TI 51, p. 193, no. 116.

July 31 612. To Imdad Hussain Khan. To the same effect as the foregoing CI 46 and TI 107.

CI 41, pp. 208-09, no. 56; TI 51, p. 193, no. 117.

July 31 613. To Umrao Begam. To the same effect as the foregoing CI 46 and TI 107.

CI 41, pp. 208-09, no. 56; TI 51, p. 193, no. 118.

July 31 614. To Khiradmand Khan. To the same effect as the foregoing CI 46 and TI 107.

CI 41, pp. 208-09, no. 56; TI 51, p. 193, no. 119.

July 31 615. To Ahmad Ali Khan. To the same effect as the foregoing CI 46 and TI 107.

CI 41, pp. 214-16, no. 60; TI 51, p. 193, no. 120.

July 31 616. To Nasr Allah Khan. To the same effect as the foregoing CI 46 and TI 107.

CI 41, pp. 214-16, no. 60; TI 51, p. 193, no. 121.

July 31 617. To Nawwab Nusrat Jang of Dacca. To the same effect as the foregoing CI 46 and TI 107.

CI 41, pp. 212-14 no. 59; TI 51, p. 193, no. 122.

July 31 618. To Amrit Rao. To the Same effect as the foregoing CI 46 and TI 107.

CI 41, pp. 200-01, no. 51; TI 51, p. 193, no. 123.

July 31 619. To Nawwab Dilawar Jang. To the same effect as the foregoing CI 46 and TI 107.

CI 41, pp. 216-17, TI 51, p. 193, no. 124.

July 31 620. To the Raja of Nepal. To the same effect as the foregoing CI 46 and TI 107.

CI 41, pp. 211-12, no. 58; TI 51, p. 193, no. 125.

July 31 621. To Raja Udit Narayan Singh. To the same effect as the foregoing CI 46 and TI 107.

CI 41, pp. 217-18, no. 62; TI 51, p. 193, no. 126.

July 31 622. To Maharaja Kishan Raj, the Raja of Mysore. To the same effect as the foregoing CI 46 and TI 107.

CI 41, pp. 206-207, no. 55; TI 51, p. 194, no. 127.

July 31 623. To Purnaiya. To the same effect as the foregoing CI 46 and TI 107.

CI 41, p. 207, no. 55; TI 51, p. 194, no. 128.

July 31 624. To Daulat Rao Sindhia. To the same effect as the foregoing CI 46 and TI 107.

TI 51, p. 194, no. 129.

July 31 625. To Maharaja Man Singh of Jodhpur. To the same effect as the foregoing CI 46 and TI 107.

CI 41, p. 220, no. 64; TI 51, p. 194, no. 130.

July 31 626. To the Peshwa. To the same effect as the foregoing CI 46 and TI 107.

CI 41, pp. 198-99, no. 50; TI 51, pp. 194-96, no. 131.

July 31 627. To the Peshwa Pandit Pardhan. To the same effect as the foregoing CI 46 and TI 107.

CI 41, pp. 198-99, no. 50; TI 51, pp 194-96, no. 131.

July 31 628. From Raja Kesri Singh (of Jaitpur). *Iqrarnama* submitted by the writer to Brooke for the grant of 52 villages (tax free) to the former at the time when the Company's troops made entry in Bundelkhand to chastize the rebels.

OR 434,[1] f 1; CR 22, pp. 805-12, no. 2 (1).

July 31 629. To Raja Kesri Singh of Jaitpur. Conveys the addressee about

[1]The document is bilingual in Hindi and Persian.

a tax-free grant of 52 villages to him by the Company with a condition of his obedience and loyalty to the Company and its government. Dated 4 July 1805.

OR 435,[1] f 1; CR 22, pp. 812-17, no. 2(2).

July -- 630. Bahu Begam to Edmonstone. Acknowledges the letter from the addressee through Col. Collins and assures of her sincerity and integrity to the Company's government. Dated 4 *Rabi II* 1220 AH (2 July 1805).

OR 436,[2] f 1; CR 22, pp. 867-69, no. 14.

July -- 631. Col. Collins to Nawwab Wazir. To the same effect as OR 405.

OR 437,[3] f 1; CR 22, pp. 897-99, no. 19(3).

July -- 632. Wazir Ali Khan to Hussaini Begam. Informs about his ill health and complains of his restlessness on not receiving of her letters. Dated 5 July 1805.

OR 438, f 1.

Aug. 4. 633. From Nasir al-Mulk. Expresses concern on departure of the addressee to Europe (England) and also feels sorry on being deprived of a personal audience with him. Expresses hope that his successor Marquess Cornwallis will continue the friendly relations.

OR 441, WS, WC, f 1; CR 23, pp. 1-4, no. 1; TR 51A, pp. 493-96, no. 150; AR 20, p. 28.

Aug. 5 634. From Nawwab Munni Begam. Expresses deep concern on the departure of the address without having made any proper arrangement in regard to the *nizamat* affairs. Also informs that Mirza Muhammad Kamil Khan has been appointed as *wakil* in the place of his late father Nasir Muhammad Khan. Dated 4 *Jumada* 1, 1220 AH (31 July 1805).

OR 440, WS, WC, f 1; CR 23, pp. 5-8, no. 3; TR 51A, pp. 497-500, no. 151; AR 20, p. 28.

Aug. 5 635. From Nawwab Shamsher Bahadur.Expresses desire to have an audience with the addressee and says that Capt. John

[1]The document is bilingual in Hindi and Persian.
[2]Copy enclosed with a letter from the Resident at Lucknow, dated 5 July 1805.
[3]Ibid.

Baillie is proceeding to pay respect to the addressee who may inform the particulars of the writer.

OR 442, WS, WC, f 1; TR 51A, pp. 501-02, no. 152; AR 20, p. 38.

Aug. 5 636. To Daulat Rao Sindhia. Informs the addressee that the writer has been appointed and taken charge of the supreme government of the British possessions in India on 30 July 1805 after arriving at Fort William. Expresses his satisfaction that the addressee has lately intended to release Jenkins along other gentlemen and conduct them safely to the British station. Further says that General Lake has been authorized to discuss all the points with addressee's Agent pending so far in order to preserve the relation of friendship and amity between the two states.

CI 41, pp. 220-23, no. 65; TI 51, pp. 196-99, no. 132.

Aug. 5 637. Raj Narayan son of late Neelmani, *kirani* (clerk) to the Persian Secretary. Says that his late father served the addressee as *kirani* for long years following his death the writer has no means of subsistence and his one brother, four sisters and mother are now passing through severe starvation. Requests the addressee to do some favour as he is an educated man and has studied Persian and Bangla, etc.

OR 443, f 1; CR 23, pp. 4-5, no. 2; TR 51A, p. 503, no. 153; AR 20, p. 29.

Aug. 6 638. To Nasir al-Mulk from the Persian Secretary. Acknowledges receipt of addressee's letter along a copy of the letter of Courtney Smith addressed to former wherein he has used some disrespectful language. Says that the writer has presented the same before the Governor-General for his perusal. Further says that the Governor-General has taken a strong disapproval of the language used by Smith and has directed him to tender an apology to the addressee. Assures that the dignity and prosperity of the two states will never be compromised.

CI 41, pp. 223-26, no. 66; TI 51, pp. 199-200, no. 133.

Aug. 7 639. From Burra Phukan Partap Ballabh of Assam. Informs about the payment of Rs. 10,032 5 *annas* and 9 *gandas* spent by Chait Singh, *risaladar* through Kanwal Lochan. Also informs about the presents being sent to Governor-General. Dated 25 December 1804.

OR 445, f 1; TR 51A, pp. 507-09, no. 155; AR 20, p. 4.

Aug. 7 640. From Seth Abhay Chand of Murshidabad. Informs the addressee about the ill intentions of Maya Ram Burra in regard to payment of money. Further requests to direct Kanwal Lochan to collect the amount for which orders were issued in his name.

OR 446, WS, WC, f 1; TR 51A, pp. 514-19, no. 157; AR 20, p. 39.

Aug. 7 641. From Nawwab Nasir al-Mulk (of Murshidabad). Expresses deep concern on the departure of address to England. Further assures that he expect the same friendly relations with the Company's government during the Governorship of addressee's successor Lord Cornwallis. Dated 7 *Jumada I*, 1220 AH (3 August 1805).

OR 447, WS, WC, f 1; CR 23, pp. 11-13, no. 5; TR 51A, pp. 519-20, 158; AR 20, p. 28.

Aug. 7 642. From Nawwab Munni Begam. To the same effect as the foregoing OR 447. Dated 8 *Jumada I*, 1220 AH (4 August 1805).

OR 448, WS, WC, f 1; CR 23, pp. 18-21, no. 7; TR 51A, p. 520, no. 159; AR 20, p. 23.

Aug. 7 643. Nawwab Muin al-Mulk (of Bengal). To the same effect as the foregoing OR 448 and 447.

OR 449, WS, WC, f 1; TR 51A, pp. 520-21, no. 160; AR 20, p. 9.

Aug. 7 644. From Sikandar Shukoh. Explains his financial situation and requests for a respectable pecuniary assistance.

OR 450,[1] *WS, WC, f 1; CR 23, pp. 14-18, no. 6; TR 50A, pp. 509-14, no. 156; AR 20, p. 24.*

Aug. 7 645. From Burra Phukan Partap Ballabh (of Assam). Complains that Mirza Ghulam Ali and Kalyan Singh have plundered and devastated the area of Chauki Kandar. Requests the addressee to arrest these *sardars* and save the region from their atrocities.

OR 451, WS, WC, f 1; CR 23, pp. 8-10, no. 4; TR 51A, pp. 504-07, no. 154; AR 20, p. 4.

Aug. 7 646. To the King, Shah Alam II. Expresses intention to proceed on a journey to the upper provinces and if situation remain conducive he may avail the opportunity to visit the addressee in person.

CI 41; pp. 226-27, no. 67; TI 51, p. 201, no. 134.

[1]Enclosed with a letter from the Resident at Lucknow, dated 27 July 1805.

Aug. 7 647. To Nawwab Wazir. Expresses his (writer's) inability to see the addressee while proceeding on a journey to the upper provinces due to urgency of his duties. Assures that he (writer) may find some leisure to gratify the addressee by spending some time with him.
CI 41, pp. 229-30, no. 70; TI 51, pp. 201-02, no. 135.

Aug. 7 648. To Mirza Sulaiman Shukoh. To the same effect as the foregoing CI 70 and TI 135.
CI 41, pp. 227-28, no. 69; TI 51, p. 203, no. 137.

Aug. 7 649. To Bahu Begam. To the same effect as the foregoing
CI 41, pp. 227-28, no. 70; TI 51, p. 203, no. 137.

Aug. 7 650. To Shams al-Nisa Begam. To the same effect as the foregoing CI 70 and TI 135.
CI 41, pp. 230-31, no. 71; TI 51, p. 203, no. 138.

Aug. 7 651. To Nasir al-Mulk. To the same effect as the foregoing CI 70 and TI 135.
CI 41, pp. 232-33, no. 73; TI 51, p. 203, no. 139.

Aug. 7 652. To Munni Begam. To the same effect as the foregoing CI 70 and TI 135.
CI 41, pp. 231, no. 72; TI 51, p. 203, no. 140.

Aug. 7 653. To Babbu Begam. To the same effect as the foregoing CI 70 and TI 135.
CI 41, p. 231, no. 71; TI 51, p. 203, no. 141.

Aug. 7 654. To Qutluq Sultan Begam. To the same effect as the foregoing CI 70 and TI 135.
CI 41, pp. 227-28, no. 68; TI 51, p. 203, no. 142.

Aug. 7 655. To Mirza Shigufta Bakht. To the same effect as the foregoing CI 70 and TI 135.
CI 41, pp. 227-28, no. 68; TI 51, p. 203, no. 143.

Aug. 7 656. To Amrit Rao. To the same effect as the foregoing CI 70 and TI 135.
CI 41, p. 233, no. 74; TI 51, p. 203, no. 144.

Aug. 7 657. To Raja Udit Narayan Singh. To the same effect as the foregoing CI 70 and TI 135.
CI 41, pp. 233-34, no. 75; TI 51, p. 203, no. 145.

Aug. 7 658. To Imdad Husain Khan. To the same effect as the foregoing CI 70 and TI 135.

CI 41, pp. 234-35, no. 76; TI 51, p. 203, no. 146.

Aug. 7 659. To Khiradmand Khan. To the same effect as the foregoing CI 70 and TI 135.

CI 41, pp. 234-35, no. 76; TI 51, p. 204, no. 147.

Aug. 7 660. To Nawwab Dilawar Jang. To the same effect as the foregoing CI 70 and TI 135.

CI 41, pp. 235-36, no. 77; TI 51, p. 204, no. 148.

Aug. 7 661. From Babu Ram Narayan Singh son of late Jagat Singh. Requests for the restoration of village Uncha and Chauka Ghausabad to the writer that had been escheated from his late father Babu Jagat Singh following his conviction in a case.

OR 452, f 1 TR 51A, pp. 521-23, no. 161; AR 20, p. 7.

Aug. 8 662. Nawwab Babbu Begam. Expresses deep concern for the departure of the addressee to England and expresses her loyalty to Company's government under his successor Lord Cornwallis.

OR 453, WS, WC, f 1; CR 23, pp. 25-28, no. 10; TR 51A, pp. 523-24, no. 162; AR 20, p. 6.

Aug. 8 663. From Nawwab Qasim Ali Khan. Complementary.

OR 454, WS, WC, f 1; CR 23, pp. 23-25, no. 9; TR 51A, p. 524, no. 163; AR 20, p. 7.

Aug. 8 664. From Nawwab Sharaf Ali Khan. Complementary.

OR 455, WS, WC, f 1; CR 23, pp. 21-23, no. 8; TR 51A, p. 524, no. 164; AR 20, p. 1.

Aug. 9 665. From Nawwab Nasir al-Mulk. Requests the address to send two double barrel and two single barrel guns and also two bull dogs from England. Dated 9 *Jumada I*, 48 (*Julus of Shah Alam II*)/5 August 1805.

OR 456, WS, WC, f 1; CR 23, pp. 28-29, no. 11; TR 51A, pp. 524-25, no. 165; AR 20, p. 28.

Aug. 9 666. From Mirza Jan Tapish. Repents for his mistakes and requests for his release with the assurance that he (the writer) would never indulge in such misdeeds as he committed earlier.

OR 457, WC, f 1; TR 51A, pp. 487-89, no. 148.

Aug. 10 667. From Nasir al-Mulk Nusrat Jang (of Dacca). Congratulates the addressee (Lord Cornwallis) on his arrival to Calcutta and taking charge of the office of Governor-General. Dated 4 August 1805.

OR 458, WS, WC, f 1; TR 51A, p. 526, no. 167; AR 20, p. 26.

Aug. 12 668. From Inayat Ali Khan (servant of Ahmad Ali Khan of Rampur). Explains the reason for his arrest that one day he was engaged in discussion with the men of Nawwab Nasr Allah Khan the paternal uncle of Nawwab Ahmad Ali Khan on some issue. On the complaint of the men of Nawwab Nasr Allah Khan he was arrested and brought to Bareilly and then to Lucknow and then to Allahabad where he has been kept in captivity for six months. Requests the addressee to enquire the matter and order for his (writer's) release.

OR 459,[1] *f 1; CR 23, pp. 29-31, no. 12; TR 51A, pp. 526-29, no. 168; AR 20, p. 15.*

Aug. 12 669. From Basant Rai (of Azimabad). Expresses his miserable condition due to usurpation of his share in the *zamindari* of Azimabad by his elder brother Kalyan Singh following the death of their father Maharaja Shitab Rai. Requests the addressee to order for the equal division of the said *zamindari* among him and his brother.

OR 460, WS, f 1; TR 51A, pp. 529-31, no. 169; AR 20, p. 36.

Aug. 13 670. From Husaini Begam and Bibi Kallo, wives of Wazir Ali. Request the addressee to arrange a separate *haveli* for them either in Munger or Bhagalpur or Calcutta as they are not getting a respectable treatment from the family members where they are living in Munger.

OR 461, WS, f 1; CR 23, pp. 32-33, no. 13.

Aug. 15 671. From Amrit Rao. Expresses gratitude for the generosity and kind favour shown by General Wallesley at Benares; explains his financial difficulties and requests for some pecuniary help from the Company's government till his claims with Baji Rao is adjusted. Also requests for regular payment of his allowances. Dated 4 August 1805.

OR 463,[2] *f 1; TR 51A, pp. 540-44, no. 175; AR 20, p. 3.*

[1]Enclosed with a letter from the Magistrate at Allahabad, dated 1 August 1805.

[2]Translation of the Hindi letter enclosed to a letter from the agent, dated 6 August 1805.

Aug. 14 672. From Maharaja Jagat Singh (of Jaipur). Acknowledges receipt of two letters from the addressee and expresses his friendly feelings towards the Company's government. Says that he has despatched a very confidential agent to General Lake to make him aware of some important matters.

OR 464, WS, WC, f 1; TR 51A, pp. 531-32, no. 170; AR 20, p. 32.

Aug. 14 673. From Nasir al-Mulk Nusrat Jang (of Dacca). Expresses deep concern for the departure of the addressee from Calcutta to England and wish that his excellency may return to India again.

OR 465,[1] *WS, WC, f 1; CR 23, pp. 33-38, no. 14; TR 51A, 533, no. 171; AR 20, p. 26.*

Aug. 14 674. From Muin al-Mulk Dilawar Jang. Congratulates the addressee (Lord Cornwallis) on coming over to India as Governor-General. Expresses and assures of his loyalty towards the Company's government and expects the same kind and friendly relations with the Company in future under his (addressee's) Governorship. Also sends a welcome letter along with *nazr-o-nisar* as per tradition.

OR 466, WS, WC, f 1; TR 51A, pp. 533-34, no. 172; AR 20, p. 9.

Aug. 14 675. From Babbu Begam. Complementary on the eve of arrival of the addressee (Lord Cornwallis) to India as Governor-General and assures of her loyalty. Dated 11 August 1805.

OR 467, WS, WC, f 1; CR 23, pp. 119-21, no. 37; TR 51A, p. 578, no. 205; AR 20, p. 6.

Aug. 14 676. From Babbu Begam. To the same effect as OR 467.

OR 468, WS, WC, f 1; CR 23, pp. 122-25, no. 38; TR 51A, p. 578, no. 204; AR 20, p. 6.

Aug. 14 677. From Amrit Rao. Intimates his (writer's) arrival at Benares for pilgrimage. Also explains the events occurred during the journey and his efforts for obtaining the friendship of Baji Rao. Further explains his reliance on the generosity of the addressee. Dated 7 *Jumada I* 1220 AH (3 August, 1805)

OR 469,[2] *f 1; TR 51 A, pp. 534-40, no. 174; AR 20, p. 3.*

[1]Enclosed with a letter from the second judge of the court at Dacca to the Persian Secretary to government, dated 10 August 1805.

[2]Enclosed with a letter from the Agent at Benares, dated 6 August 1805.

Aug. 15 678. From Nawwab Nasir al-Mulk. Complementary. Further informs that the writer has dispatched Rai Manik Chand to wait on addressee.

OR 470, WS, f 1; TR 51A, p. 576, no. 202; AR 20, p. 28.

Aug. 15 679. From Nawwab Munni Begam. Congratulatory on the arrival of Lord Cornwallis in India as Governor-General. Assures of her loyalty to Company's government and expects the some friendly relation between the two governments. Dated 15 *Jumada I*, 1220 AH (11 August 1805).

OR 471, WS, WC, f 1; TR 51A, p. 576, no. 201; AR 20, p. 23.

Aug. 15 680. From Nasir al-Mulk (of Murshidabad). To the same effect as the foregoing OR 471.

OR 472, WS, WC, f 1; TR 51A, pp. 573-74, no. 200; AR 20, p. 28).

Aug. 15 681. From Nawwab Munni Begam. Expresses deep concern on the departure of the Governor-General to Europe and informs about the departure of Manik Chand to get an audience of the addressee. Dated 12 August 1805.

OR 473, WS, WC, f 1; CR 23, pp. 18-20, no. 7.

Aug. 16 682. Harak Chand Jagat Seth. Expresses his eagerness for an audience of the addressee. Conveys dispatch of his agent Munshi Gobind Chand to present the *nazr* to the addressee.

OR 474, WS, WC, f 1; TR 51A, p. 579, no. 206; AR 20, p. 17.

Aug 15[1] 683. Basanti Ram to Col. Broughton. Acknowledges receipt of Rs. 50 against the price of a shawl sold to the addressee by the writer. Dated 10 June 1805.

OR 475, f 1; CR 23, p. 38, no. 15(a).

Aug. 15 684. Ganesh Chand *Sarraf* to Col. Broughton. Acknowledges receipt of Rs. 15 8 *annas* against the price of one *than* of muslin and one scarf sold to the addressee. Dated 10 June 1805.

OR 476, f 1; CR 23, pp. 38-39, no. 15(b).

[1]The date does not come forth from the documents, however, the date on folder is 15 August.

Aug. 16 685. Saiyid Jafar Khan to Edmonstone. Submits a report on the mission in Nadaun for which the writer was sent there by Col. Scott; asks the addressee to reimburse the arrears of the monthly allowance of the writer; also encloses a recommendation letter from Raja Sansar chand.

OR 477,[1] *WS, WC, f 1; CR 23, pp. 39-47, no. 16(1); TR 51A, pp. 544-54, no. 176; AR 20, p. 15.*

Aug. 16 686. Saiyid Jafar Khan to Edmonstone. To the same effect as the foregoing OR 477. Dated 4 *Jumada I*, 1220 AH (31 July 1805).

OR 478, f 1; CR 23, pp. 47-51, no. 16(2).

Aug. 16 687. From Company's Agent at the Court of Mughal Emperor Shah Alam II. Informs about the arrival of Nawwab Nasir al-Daula Khan at the court on 31 July and his discussion with the Emperor. The emperor expressed his satisfaction to the policies of the Company but complained that the addressee could not settle the differences between the Emperor and *Wazir al-Mumalik*.

OR 479,[2] *f 1.*

Aug. 16 688. From Raja Sansar Chand of Nadaun. Memornadum presented to the addressee demanding that the writer may be appointed as the channel for the communication of all orders and directives to the chiefs of the hill; promises to give aide to the British cause in all expeditions in the region and requests to grant a few *taluqas* to the writer which had been in the possession of his father in his lifetime.

OR 480, f 1; CR 23, p. 52, no. 16(b).

Aug. 16 689. To Zaib al-Nisa Begam. Refers to the discussion held between Lord Wellesley, Lord Lake and the addressee regarding transfer of her *jagirs* on the other side of river Jamuna (Yamuna). Informs about the confirmation of the *jagirs* possessed by the addressee. Expresses gratitude for providing essential help to Guthrie, the Collector of Saharanpur, at the time of danger. Deputes Guthrie for further communications.

TI 41, pp. 236-40, no. 78; TI 51, pp. 204-8, no. 149.

[1]Enclosed with a letter from the Resident at Lucknow, dated 6 August 1805.
[2]Enclosed with a letter from the Resident at Delhi.

Aug. 17 690. From Muin al-Mulk Bahadur. Regrets his inability to visit the addressee due to latter's journey to the upper provinces.
OR 481, WS, WC, f 1; TR 51A, pp. 558-59, no. 178; AR 20, p. 9.

Aug. 18 691. From Patni Mall (of Murshidabad). Informs about the arrival of Muhammad Hasan Kashmiri with the bundles of *pashmina* ordered by Mercer with an advance of Rs. 5,000; enquires as to whom the said bundles should be delivered as Mercer is out of town.
OR 482, f 1; CR 23, pp. 54-55, no. 17(3).

Aug. 18 692. Muhammad al-Din Ahmad Khan alias Muhammad Mian, *tahsildar* of Najibabad to A. Seton. Enquires about the receipt of *pashmina* worth Rs. 5000 sent with Manik Chand and Roop Chand. Also informs that the said item was insured. Dated 1 August 1805.
OR 483, f 1; CR 23, pp. 52-53, no. 17(1).

Aug. 18 693. Muhammad Hasan Kashmiri to Manik Chand and Roop Chand, the bankers at Najibabad. Enquires whether the bundles of *pashmina* sent to A. Seton have been delivered to him or not.
OR 484,[1] *f 1, CR 23, pp. 56-57, no. 17.*

Aug. 18 694. Resident at Lucknow to Rai Patni Mall (of Murshidabad). To the same effect as the foregoing OR 484.
OR 485, f 1; CR 23, pp. 53-54, no. 17(2).

Aug. 18 695. To Nawwab Nasir al-Mulk. In reply to addressee's letter informing about his mission of Rai Manikchand to wait on the Governor-General.
CI 41, pp. 447-50, no. 185; TI 51, p. 208, no. 150).

Aug. 18 696. To Nawwab Munni Begam. To the same effect as the foregoing CI 185 and TI 150.
CI 41, pp. 450-52, no. 187; TI 51, p. 209, no. 151.

Aug. 18 697. To Nawwab Nasir al-Mulk. In reply to addressee's letter congratulating on the writer's return to the Presidency.
CI 41, pp. 449-50, no. 186; TI 51, p. 209 no. 152.

[1]Copy enclosed with a letter from A. Seton, 1 August 1805.

Aug. 18 698. To Nawwab Munni Begam. To the same effect as the foregoing CI 186 and TI 152.

CI 41, pp. 450-52, no. 187; TI 51, p. 209, no. 153.

Aug. 18 699. To Babbu Begam. To the same effect as the foregoing CI 186 and TI 152.

CI 41, pp. 152-53, no. 188; TI 51, p. 210, no. 154.

Aug. 18 700. To Nawwab Mir Mumtaz Khan. To the same effect as the foregoing CI 186 and TI 150.

CI 41, pp. 453-54, no. 189; TI 51, p. 210, no. 155.

Aug. 18 701. To Jagat Seth. In reply to addressee's letter dated 16 August 1805 informing about his proceeding to see the Governor-General but was prevented from doing so. Hopes to receive his visit on writer's return to the Presidency.

CI 41, pp. 454-55, no. 190; TI 51, p. 211, no. 156.

Aug. 19 702. A. Seton to Nawwab Nasr Allah Khan of Rampur. Acknowledges the receipt of a letter from Munshi Gopalji regarding murder of one of the servants of Company by an Afghan resident of Rampur on the border of Rampur. Asks that the assassin be apprehended and extradited to the writer. Dated 4 August 1805.

OR 486,[1] *f 1.*

Aug. 19 703. Nawwab Nasr Allah Khan of Rampur to A. Seton. Informs about the murder of one of the Company's men by an Afghan at the border of the said state further states that the assassin has been arrested and being sent to the addressee escorted by Shah Alam Khan and his men for the trial. Dated 1 August 1805.

OR 487,[2] *f 1.*

Aug. 19 704. Gopalji Das to A. Seton, Agent to Governor-General. Informs that the assassin of the Company's servant is being sent to the addressee for trial and justice under the escort of Shah Alam Khan and his Company.

OR 488,[3] *f 1.*

Aug. 19 705. Nawwab Wazir to Col. Collins. Acknowledges receipt of

[1]Enclosed with a letter from A. Seton, dated 4 August 1805.
[2]Copy enclosed with a letter from A. Seton, the Agent to Governor-General.
[3]Enclosed with a letter from A. Seton, Agent of Governor-General at Bareilly.

addressee's letter dated 13 *Jumada I* 1220 AH (9 August 1805) and expresses great pleasure on the arrival of Lord Cornwallis as Governor-General at Calcutta. Also informs about the dispatch of Rs. 2,000 (two thousand) only as *nazr* to be distributed among the beggars and orphans.

OR 489,[1] f 1; CR 23, pp. 60-61, no. 19; TR 51A, p. 559, no. 179; AR 20, p. 41.

Aug. 19 706. To Nawwab Nusrat Jang (from the Vice-President). Communicates the addressee that the final orders and arrangement for the release and journey of his brother Nawwab Shams al-Daulah in conformity with the resolution of the late Governor-General Marquess Wellesley. Further reminds the addressee that he will be considered responsible for the future conduct of his brother and that his brother's real enlargement depends on his future course of action. Informs that the collector of Dacca has been directed to pay an amount of Rs. 750 per month to Nawwab Shams al-Daulah from his enlargement and Rs. 500 per month to his wife which she is getting from the time of her husband's confinement be continued to her. Suggests the addressee to contact S. Bird, the Senior Judge of the Court of Appeal at Dacca for any further particulars.

CI 41, pp. 240-44, no. 79; TI 51, pp 211-16, no. 157.

Aug. 20 707. From Qutluq Sultan Begam. Expresses pleasure on the arrival of Lord Cornwallis as Governor-General and requests for confirmation of her son Mirza Khurram Bakht as the rightful successor to the throne of the state after the death of his father. Reassures of her loyalty to the Company's government.

OR 490,[2] f 1: CR 23, pp. 61-63, no. 20; TR 51A, pp. 559-62, no. 180; AR 20, p. 20.

Aug. 20 708. From Raja Sharfuji Bhonsla of Tanjor. Expresses great pleasure on the arrival of Lord Cornwallis as Governor-General in India. Expresses his earnest expectation for favour and guidance from the addressee.

OR 492,[3] f 1; TR 51A, pp. 562-64, no. 181; AR 20, p. 36.

[1]Enclosed with a letter from the Resident at Lucknow, dated 10 August 1805.

[2]Enclosure to a letter from W. A. Brook to Lumsden, dated 10 August 1805.

[3]Persian translation of Marathi letter enclosed with a letter from the Chief Secretary at Fort St. George to the secretary political department, dated 31 July 1805.

Aug. 20 709. From Nawwab Wazir. Writes on the issue of the region of Indiar (Idiar) which is pending from the time of Lord Wellesley. Requests to deal with this issue according to the treaty concluded between the two states. Dated 13 *Jumada I* 1220 AH (9 August 1805).

OR 493,[1] *ff 2, WS, WC; CR 23, pp. 64-66, no. 21; TR 51A, pp. 564-66, no. 182; AR 20, p. 41.*

Aug. 20 710. Khan-i-Jahan Khan to Sir George Barlow Burnet, the Vice-President. Complementary on the appointment of the addressee as the Vice-President of Fort William in the absence of the Governor-General.

OR 494, WS, WC, f 1; TR 51A, p. 566, no. 184; AR 20, p. 19.

Aug. 21 711. From Nawwab Nasir al-Mulk. Requests the addressee to pay attention to the *nizamat* affairs after his return from the Upper provinces. Implores upon the necessity of building of a palace for the writer's residence, therefore requests to direct Major Theming to start the work immediately after the rains. Dated 20 August 1805

OR 495, WS, f 1; TR 51A, pp. 576-77, no. 203; AR 20, p. 26.

Aug. 23 712. To Saiyid Jafar Khan. Refers to addressee's letter describing his endeavour to placate Raja Sansar Chand of Nadaun in favour of Company's government. Refutes addressee's supposition of British incursion into the territory of Raja Ranjit Singh of Lahore and other Sikh territory. Asks the addressee to give a clarification in writing to the said Raja and impress upon him that the British government always desire to kept all the local chiefs and allies of the Company in good friendly relations. Further assures that the British government would not interfare in the affairs of Nadaun. However, wants to establish an everlasting friendly relation with the state of Nadaun. Suggests to contact Col. Collins for further communications.

CI 41, pp. 244-50, no. 80; TI 51, pp. 216-23, no. 158.

Aug. 24 713. From Qutluq Sultan Begam. Complementary on the arrival of Governor-General at Calcutta. Expresses eagerness

[1]Enclosed with a letter from the Resident at Lucknow, dated 10 August 1805.

of her son Khurram Bhakht Mirza to get an audience with the addressee.

OR 496, WS, f 1; CR 23, pp. 80-82, no. 26; TR 51A, pp. 567-68, no. 187; AR 20, p. 20.

Aug. 25 714. From Bahu Begam. Expressses deep concern over the departure of the addressee to England. Anticipates that the addressee would convey favourable note regarding the writer to his successor Lord Cornwallis.

OR 497, WS, f 1; CR 23, pp. 70-73, no. 23; TR 51A, pp. 568-69, no. 188; AR 20, p. 5.

Aug. 25 715. From Shams al-Nisa Begam. Complementary on the arrival of Lord Cornwallis as the Governor-General. Expresses that the writer may get the same favour from the addressee as have been earlier.

OR 498,[1] f 1; CR 23, pp. 73-74, no. 24; TR 51A, p. 569, no. 189; AR 20, p. 38.

Aug. 25 716. From Raja Mahipat Rai (of Benares). Requests for an audience with the addressee to discuss the plans of maintaining 10,000 troops; also encloses the details.

OR 499,[2] ff 2; CR 23, pp. 74-80, no. 25.

Aug. 25 717. Nawwab Sikander Jah. Refers to the negotiations between the addressee and the Company regarding establishment of a body of *silahdar* horse to preclude the depredations of freebooters. States that the British troops stationed at Hyderabad may not serve this purpose.

CI 41, pp. 250-55, no. 81; TI 51, pp. 223-29, no. 159.

Aug. 25 718. To Mir Alam. To the same effect as the foregoing CI. 81 and TI 159.

CI 41, pp. 250-55, no. 81; TI 51, p. 229, no. 160.

Aug. 26 719. Saiyid Jafar Khan to Edmonstone. Submits a report in respect of the mission on which he had been sent to Nadaun by Col. Scott. Requests for the payment of the arrears of his

[1]Enclosure to a letter the Magistrate at Patna, dated 17 August 1805.

[2]Enclosed with a letter from the Resident at Hyderabad, dated 11 August 1805.

monthly allowances. Also encloses a note of request from Raja Sansar Chand. Dated 31 July 1805.

OR 500,[1] *f 1; CR 23, pp. 82-97, no. 27(1).*

Aug. 26 720. Saiyid Jafar Khan to Edmonstone. To the same effect as the OR no. 477 and 478.

OR 501,[2] *f 1; CR 23, pp. 91, no. 27(2).*

Aug. 26 721. From Zaib al-Nisa Begam. Congratulatory on the arrival of Lord Cornwallis as Governor-General of India. Requests for the restoration of her properties, etc. Dated 10 August 1805.

OR 502,[3] *f 1; CR 23, pp. 97-100, no. 28; TR 51A, p. 525, no. 166; AR 20, p. 42.*

Aug. 27 722. To Nawwab Nasir al-Mulk. Regrets for his inability to see the addressee while passing through Murshidabad. Hopes to pay a visit on his return. Offers every possible help and co-operation in the improvement of the *nizamat* affairs. Assures the addressee of his (writer) prime attention to provide him and his family a suitable accommodation. Informs that Sir George Barlow has been directed to take measures to relieve the addressee from the present inconvenience.

CI 41, pp. 258-60, no. 83; TI 51, pp. 230-32, no. 161.

Aug. 27 723. To Khiradmand Khan. Expresses pleasure on assuring the addressee of the removal of all doubts in regard to his (the addressee) conduct at the time of Holkar's incursion into the Doab. Expresses confidence in the addressee's fidelity towards the British government.

CI 41, pp. 255-57, no. 82; TI 51, pp. 232-34, no. 162.

Aug. 28 724. From Nawwab Wazir (of Awadh). Complementary on the arrival of Lord Cornwallis to India as Governor-General. Anticipates the same favourable relation with the addressee as it has been during his predecessors.

OR 503,[4] *WS, f 1; CR 23, pp. 101-03, no. 29.*

[1]Copy enclosed with a letter from the Resident at Lucknow, dated 6 August 1805.

[2]Ibid.

[3]Enclosed with a letter from the Collector at Saharanpur, dated 10 August 1805.

[4]Enclosed with a letter from the Resident at Lucknow, dated 19 August 1805.

Aug. 28 725. *Yaddasht* of *dastak-i-rahdari* under the seal of Ramazan Ali Khan for the transportation of some article from Calcutta to Lucknow.

OR 504, f 1.

Aug. 28 726. From . . . to John Monckton. Sends four bundles of *banat* to Nepal and requests for exemption from duty.

OR 505, WS, f 1.

Aug. 29 727. From Nawwab Khiradmand Khan (of Farrukhabad). Complementary on the arrival of Lord Cornwallis to India as the Governor-General. Dated 22 *Rabi I,* 1220 AH (18 August 1805).

OR 506, WS, f 1; CR 23, pp. 145-47, no. 3; TR 51A, p. 569, no. 191; AR 20, p. 20.

Aug. 29 728. From Shams al-Nisa Begam (of Lucknow). Complementary on the arrival of Lord Cornwallis at Calcutta as Governor-General of India. Anticipates the same friendly relation with the Company's government under the addressee's guidance.

OR 507,[1] WS, f 1; CR 23, pp. 103-05, no. 30; TR 51A, p. 566, no. 183; AR 20, p. 34.

Aug. 29 729. From Nawawb Imdad Husain Khan. Expresses deep concern over the departure of Lord Wellesley to England. Requests to brief his successor Lord Cornwallis of his (Writer's) situation and also to ask him (Cornwallis) to pay proper attention to a few unsettled issues pending for a long time.

OR 508,[2] WS, f 1; CR 23, pp. 111-14, no. 33; TR 51A, p. 571, no. 194; AR 20, p. 11.

Aug. 29 730. From Umrao Begam. Expresses deep concern over the departure of Governor-General (Lord Wellesley) to England.

OR 509,[3] WS, f 1; CR 23, pp. 105-06, no. 31; TR 51A, pp. 571-73, no. 195; AR 20, p. 30.

[1]Enclosure to a letter from the Resident at Lucknow, dated 20 August 1805.

[2]Enclosure to a letter from the Acting Agent at Farrukhabad, dated 16 August 1805.

[3]Enclosure to a letter from the Resident at Farrukhabad.

Aug. 29 731. From Nawwab Khiradmand Khan. Complementary on the arrival of Lord Cornwallis as Governor-General of India. Anticipates a similar favourable relation between the two states. Dated 21 August 1805.

OR 510, WS, f 1; CR 23, pp. 109-10, no. 32; TR 51A, p. 569, no. 196; AR 20, p. 20.

Aug. 29 732. From Nawwab Khiradmand Khan. To the same effect as the foregoing OR 510.

OR 511,[1] WS, f 1; CR 23, pp. 107-08, no. 31.

Aug. 29 733. Intelligence report sent by Abbas Quli Khan from Kabul dated 9 and 10 June 1805. Informs about the arrival of Abd Allah Khan the envoy of Jaswant Rao Holkar at the court of Shah Shuja al-Mulk; says that investigation about him is going on secretly. Further informs that Prince Qaisar has been awarded with a *khilat* and elephant and has been sent to Qandhar to collect Durrani troops. Again informs that Abdullah Khan the envoy of Holkar is developing contact with various *amirs*.

OR 512,[2] ff 2.

Aug. 29 734. To Nawwab Asaf Jah (of Hyderabad) and Mir Alam. Impresses upon the addressees that the deployment of British troops is essential in their territories to maintain a better law and order there.

OR 513,[3] f 1.

Aug. 30 735. From . . . Acknowledges receipt of addressee's letter bearing the news of addressee's departure towards *maghrib* (Europe). Requests the addressee to dispose off the important pending cases.

OR 514, f 1; CR 23, pp. 200-03, no. 20.

Aug. 31. 736. From Nawwab Alif Khan (of Karnul). Acknowledges receipt of addressee's letter and requests that the amount of *peshkash* would not be increased from one lakh per annum as agreed earlier; assures the addressee to extend all military assistance to the Company as and when required. Informs about the departure of two of his *wakils* to see the addressee.

OR 515, WS, f 1; CR 23, pp. 126-31, no. 39; TR 51A, pp. 572-74, no. 197; AR 20, p. 20.

[1]Enclosed with a letter from the Agent at Farrukhabad, dated 10 August 1805.
[2]Enclosure to a letter from the Resident at Lucknow, dated 13 August 1805.
[3]Copy of issue.

Aug. 31 737. Nawwab Saiyid Murtaza Ali Khan. Expresses pleasure on the addressee's arrival as the Governor-General.

OR 516, WS, WC, f 1; CR 23, pp. 118-19, no. 36; TR 51A, p. 579, no. 207; AR 20, p. 39.

Aug. 31 738. From Almas Ali Khan (of Lucknow). Congratulates on the arrival of addressee to Calcutta as Governor-General. Sends 101 *asharfis* as *nazr*.

OR 517, WC, f 1; CR 23, pp. 114-15, no. 34; TR 51A, p. 575, no. 198; AR 20, p. 4.

Aug. 31 739. From Saadat Ali Khan. Expresses his desire to see the addressee at Kanpur while the later will be taking leave for England.

OR 518, WS, WC, f 1.

Aug. 31 740. From Nasir al-Mulk to Pattle. Complains against the order issued to the writer by the Judge of Bhagalpur. Requests the council to issue proper order to the district authorities to abstain from such follies in future.

OR 519, f 1; CR 23, pp. 131-32, no. 40.

Aug. 31 741. From Raja Udit Narayan Singh. Congratulatory on the arrival of the addressee to take over the charge of the government.

OR 520, WS, WC, f 1; CR 23, pp. 236-37, no. 32; TR 51A, p. 575, no. 199; AR 20, p. 33.

Aug. -- 742. From Wazir Ali Khan to Husaini Begam. Informs of his complete recovery from sickness and requests her to write a detailed letter regarding the family affairs. Dated 1 August 1805.

OR 521, f 1.

Sept. 1 743. From Nawwab Imdad Hussain Khan (of Farrukhabad). Complementary on the arrival of the addressee at Calcutta as Governor-General. Assures of his loyalty to the Company's government.

OR 522,[1] WS, WC, f 1; CR 23, pp. 141-45, no. 2; TR 51A, p. 581, no. 218; AR 20, p. 11.

[1]Enclosed with a letter from the acting Agent at Farrukhabad, dated 20 August 1805.

Sept. 1 744. From Umrao Begum (of Farrukhabad). Complementary on the arrival of the addressee to Calcutta as the Governor-General.

OR 523,[1] *WS, WC, f 1; CR 23, pp. 147-49, no. 4; TR 51A, p. 581, no. 219; AR 20, p. 30.*

Sept. 1 745. Sir George Barlow, Vice-President and Deputy Governor of Fort William to the Viceroy of Pegu. Acknowledges addressee's letter complaining that Captain Purser has seized a ship of Dassier in the Rangoon River. Says that a decision will be taken against Capt. Purser after a comprehensive investigation of the case.

TI 51, pp. 234-38, no. 163; AI 20, p. 70.

Sept. 2 746. Nawwab Nasir al-Mulk to the Vice-President Sir George Barlow. Complementary on the addressee appointment as Vice-President of the Company's government during absence of the Governor-General from Calcutta.

OR 524,[2] *WS, WC, f 1; CR 23, pp. 170-72, no. 14; TR 51A, pp. 581-82, no. 220; AR 20, p. 29.*

Sept. 2 747. Nawwab Munni Begam to Sir George Barlow Burnet. To the same effect as the foregoing OR 524.

OR 525,[3] *WS, WC, f 1; CR 23, pp. 172-73, no. 15; TR 51A, p. 582, no. 221; AR 20, p. 23.*

Sept. 2 748. From Prince Mirza Sulaiman Shukoh. Complementary on the arrival of Lord Cornwallis to Calcutta as Governor-General.

OR 526,[4] *WS, WC, f 1; TR 51A, p. 582, no. 222; AR 20, p. 23.*

Sept. 2 749. From Babbar Ali Khan (of Murshidabad). Complementary on the arrival of Lord Cornwallis at Calcutta as Governor-General of India.

OR 527, WS, WC f 1; TR 51A, p. 583, no. 223; AR 20, p. 7.

[1]Enclosed with a letter from the acting Agent at Farrukhabad.

[2]Enclosed with a letter from the superintendent of *nizamat* affairs to the Secretary, Political Department, dated 29 August 1805.

[3]Enclosed with a letter from the superintendent of *nizamat* affairs to the Secretary to Government, dated 29 August 1805.

[4]Enclosed with a letter from the Resident at Lucknow, dated 25 August 1805.

Sept. 2 750. From Maharaja Mitrajit Singh. Informs about the payment of the *malguzari* (rent dues) for the year 1212 *Fasli* (1804-05 AD) in the royal treasury. Also informs that he is now preparing for the payment of next year's rent.

OR 528, f 1; TR 51A, p. 584, no. 224; AR 20, p. 32.

Sept. 2 751. From Madar al-Daulah. Complementary on the arrival of Lord Cornwallis at Calcutta as Governor-General. Dated 23 August 1805.

OR 529,[1] WS, WC, f 1; TR 51A, p. 579, no. 208; AR 20, p. 24.

Sept. 2 752. From Jani Begam. Complementary on the arrival of Lord Cornwallis at Calcutta as Governor-General. Anticipates the same cordial and friendly relation between the two governments as it has been prevailing earlier.

OR 530,[2] WS, WC, f 1; CR 23, pp. 155-57, no. 8; TR 51A, p. 580, no. 215; AR 20, p. 18.

Sept. 2 753. From Nawwab Ali Khan. To the same effect as the foregoing OR 530.

OR 531,[3] f 1; CR 23, pp. 158-60, no. 9; TR 51A, p. 579, no. 210; AR 20, p. 7.

Sept. 2 754. From Akbar Ali Khan. Congratulates and expresses satisfaction on the addressee's arrival at Calcutta as the Governor-General. Seeks permission to have an audience with the addressee. Requests that John Collins be directed in this regard.

OR 532,[4] WS, WC, f 1; CR 23, pp. 160-63, no. 10; TR 51A, p. 579, no. 214; AR 20, p. 4.

Sept. 2 755. From Shams al-Nisa Begam. Complementary. Dated 27 *Jumada I*, 1220 AH (23 August 1805).

OR 533,[5] WS, WC, f 1; CR. 23, pp. 164-65, no. 11.

[1]Enclosed with a letter from the Resident at Lucknow, dated 25 August 1805.
[2]Ibid.
[3]The date does not come forth from the doct.
[4]Enclosed with a letter from the Resident at Lucknow, dated 15 August 1805.
[5]Ibid., dated 25 August 1805.

Sept. 2 756. From Husain Ali Khan. Complementary on the arrival of Lord Cornwallis to India as Governor-General.

OR 534,[1] *WS, WC, ff 2; CR 23, pp. 165-69, no. 12.*

Sept. 2 757. From Maharaja Bhawani Din. Complementary on the arrival of the addressee to India as Governor-General.

OR 535,[2] *WS, WC, f 1; CR 23, pp. 279-81, no. 42; TR 51A, p. 579, no. 213; AR 20, p. 7.*

Sept. 2 758. From Tahsin Ali Khan (eunuch of Nawwab Asaf al-Daula). Complementary along with five *asharfis* as *nazr-i-daakhlai* on the eve of addressee's arrival at *Ashraf al-Bilad* (Calcutta) as Governor-General.

OR 536, WS, WC, ff 2; CR. 23, pp. 169-70, no. 13; TR 51A, p. 579, no. 212; AR. 20, p. 40.

Sept. 2 759. From Imdad Husain Khan (of Farrukhabad). Acknowledges receipt of addressee's letter informing the writer about former's visit of western part of Company's territory (Upper Provinces). Expresses desire to see the addressee on his (the latter's) visit to the west.

OR 537,[3] *WS, WC, f 1; CR 23, pp. 210-12, no. 25.*

Sept. 2 760. From Nawwab Munni Begam to Pattle, superintendent of *nizamat* affairs. Requests for the continuation of the allowance of Rs. 500 to Gauhar al-Nisa Begam, daughter of late Nawwab Mahdi Ali Khan that has been granted to her after her father's death. Further says that the delay in payment has made her condition miserable.

OR 538,[4] *f 1; CR 23, pp. 173-75, no. 16; TR 51A, pp. 58-85, no. 225; AR 20, p. 12.*

Sept. 3 761. From Nawwab Sharaf Ali Khan. Complementary on the arrival of the addressee in India.

OR 539,[5] *WS, WC, f 1; CR 23, pp. 206-07, no. 22; TR 51A, p. 579, no. 211; AR 20, p. 39.*

[1]Enclosed with a letter from the Resident at Lucknow, dated 25 August 1805.

[2]Ibid.

[3]Enclosed with a letter from the acting Agent at Farrukhabad, dated 30 August 1805.

[4]Enclosed with a letter from the superintendent of *nizamat* affairs, dated 31 August 1805.

[5]Enclosed with a letter from the Resident at Lucknow, dated 25 August 1805.

Sept. 3 762. From Nawwab Muhammad Ali Khan (of Farrukhabad). Complementary on the arrival of the addressee at Calcutta. Assures of his loyalty to the Company's government.

OR 540,[1] *WS, f 1; CR 23, pp. 207-9, no. 23; TR 51A, p. 567, no. 186; AR 20, p. 24.*

Sept. 3[2] 763. From Nawwab Khiradmand Khan (of Farrukhabad). Refers to the news regarding addressee's departure towards *maghrib* (Europe) and expresses sorrow that he (the writer) is unable to see the addressee at the time of departure.

OR 541,[3] *WS, f 1; CR 23, pp. 209-10, no. 24; TR 51A, pp. 609-10, no. 235; AR 20, p. 20.*

Sept. 3 764. From Muhabbat Khan. Complementary on the arrival of the addressee at Calcutta as Governor-General.

OR 542,[4] *WS, f 1; CR 23, pp. 212-14, no. 26; TR 51A, p. 579, no. 209; AR 20, p. 24.*

Sept. 2[5] 765. From Kunwar Daulat Singh. Complementary on the arrival of the addressee at Calcutta as Governor-General.

OR 543,[6] *WS, f 1; CR 23, pp. 153-54, no. 7; TR 51A, p. 580, no. 216; AR 20, p. 21.*

Sept. 3 766. From Amat al-Zahra (Bahu Begam) daughter of Ishaaq Khan. Complementary on the arrival of the addressee at Calcutta as Governor-General.

OR[7] *544, WS, f 1; CR 23, pp. 203-05, no. 21; TR 51A, p. 604, no. 227; AR 20, p. 5.*

Sept. 5 767. From the Nizam.[8] Acknowledges addressee's letter informing the reliving of the addressee and appointment of

[1]Enclosed with a letter from the acting Agent at Farrukhabad, dated 22 August 1805.

[2]The date of receipt in TR is 8 September 1805.

[3]Enclosed with a letter from the Acting Agent at Farrukhabad, dated 30 August 1805.

[4]Enclosed with a letter from the Resident at Lucknow, dated 25 August 1805.

[5]Date of receipt in English is 4 September.

[6]Enclosed with a letter from the Resident at Lucknow, dated 25 August 1805.

[7]Ibid.

[8]Name of the writer does not come forth from OR.

Lord Cornwallis as Governor-General

OR 545,[1] f 1 CR 23, pp. 217-19, no 28; TR 51A, pp. 605-6, no. 229; AR 20, p. 27.

Sept. 5 768. From Mir Alam (of Hyderabad). To the same effect as the foregoing OR 545.

OR 546,[2] WS, f 1; CR 23, pp. 214-17, no. 27; TR 51A, p. 606, no. 230; AR 20, p. 21.

Sept. 5 769. From Ahmad Ali (of Bareilly). Complementary on the appointment of the addressee as Governor-General. Assures of his loyalty to the Company's Government in addressee's Governorship. Dated 23 August, 1805.

OR 547,[3] WS, f 1; CR 23, pp. 219-22, no. 29; TR 51A, pp. 604-05, no. 228; AR 20, p. 4.

Sept. 6 770. From Mirza Shigufta Bakht, son of Jahandar Shah. To the same effect as the foregoing OR 547.

OR 548,[4] WS, f 1; CR 23, pp. 222-24, no. 30; TR 51A, p. 66, no. 231; AR 20, p. 25.

Sept. 5 771. Nawwab Nasir al-Mulk to Pattle. Expresses financial difficulties due to non-payment of writer's salary for the previous two months causing further problems in the day-to-day works of *nizamat* affairs. Requests for the early payment of the arrears and regular payment of salary on time in future.

OR 549,[5] f 1; CR 23, pp. 175-76, no. 17; TR 51A, pp. 606-08, no. 232; AR 20, p. 12.

Sept. 6 772. Nawwab Munni Begam to Pattle. To the same effect as the foregoing.

OR 550,[6] f 1; CR 23, pp. 177-78, no. 18; TR 51A, pp. 608-09, no. 232; AR 20, p. 12.

[1]Enclosed with a letter from the Resident at Hyderabad, dated 25 August 1805.

[2]Ibid., dated 20 August 1805.

[3]Enclosed with a letter from Agent at Bareilly, dated 31 August 1805.

[4]Enclosed with a letter from the Acting Agent at Benares, dated 29 August 1805.

[5]Enclosed with a letter from Pattle to the Deputy Persian Secretary, dated 3 September 1805.

[6]Ibid.

Sept. 7 773. Qazi Muhammad Najm al-Din Khan to Persian Secretary. Request for the issue of a *dastak-i-rahdari* (passport) for Maulavi Zia al-Din Khan, etc., the servants of Nawwab Azim al-Daulah to go to Gopaman along with some provisions and weapons essential for travelling.

OR 551, WS, f 1.

Sept. 7 774. Yusuf Khan, son of Muhammad Umar Khan Jang. Requests for the grant of the area of Shergarh and around on perpetual contract basis to enable the writer to maintain his family expenditure.

OR 552,[1] *f 1, CR 23, pp. 259-60, no. 34.*

Sept. 7 775. Sir George Barlow, the Vice-President to Nasir al-Mulk. Acknowledges receipt of a letter from the addressee congratulating on the occasion of his taking charge of the affairs at the Presidency during the absence of the Governor-General.

CI 41, pp. 456-57, no. 193; TI 51, pp. 238-39, no. 164; AI 20, p. 59.

Sept. 7 776. Sir George Barlow, the Vice-President to Munni Begam. To the same effect as the forgoing CI 193.

CI 41, pp. 456-57, no. 193; TI 51, p. 239, no. 165 AI 20, p. 55.

Sept. 7 777. To Raja Mitrajit Singh of Tekri. In reply to the addressee's letter informing about the discharge of the rent in full to the government for the preceding year.

CI 41, pp. 457-58, no. 194; TI 51, pp. 239-40, no. 166; AI 20, p. 62.

Sept. 7 778. Udney, the Vice-President to Muhammad Najm al-Din Khan, the *Qazi al-Quzat*. Grants a *dastak-i-rahdari* in favour of Maulavi Zia al-Din Khan, an employee of Nawwab Azim al-Daulah, the Nawwab of Karnataka, to travel from Madras to Calcutta and from there to Gopa Mau along with his companions and goods.

CI 41, pp. 458-59, no. 195.

Sept. 8 779. From Bishambhar Pandit. Complementary with a present

[1]Copy enclosed with a letter from the agent at Bareilly, dated 26 August 1805.

of sugar and rose water.

OR 553, WS, f 1; TR 51A, p. 609, no. 234; AR 20, p. 6.

Sept. 8 780. Bishambhar Pandit to George Barlow (the Vice-President). Expresses pleasure on the arrival of Governor-General at Calcutta and prays for the growth and prosperity of the Company's government. Sends a present of rose water along with the letter through Hari Bhadra Pandit.

OR 554, WS, f 1; TR 51A, p. 610, no. 236; AR 20, p. 6.

Sept. 9 781. From Raghuji Bhonsla. Complementary on the arrival of the addressee (Lord Cornwallis) at Calcutta as Governor-General. Also expresses his wish to continue the same friendly relation with the Company's government.

OR 555, WS, f 1; CR 23, pp. 262-65, no. 36; TR 51A, p. 610, no. 237; AR 20, p. 33.

Sept. 9 782. Ashraf al-Nisa Begam to Pattle, the superintendent of *nizamat* affairs. Expresses that she had informed about her financial difficulties six months back through a letter to the addressee delivered by Saiyid Muhammad Ali Khan but no action has so far been taken in this regard. Further says that she is now under huge debt and found her in great difficulty to meet her day-to-day expenses. Requests for sufficient pecuniary help to come out of debts and meet the day-to-day expenses.

OR 556,[1] *f 1; CR 23, pp. 260-62, no. 35; TR 51A, pp. 610-12, no. 238; AR 20, p. 12.*

Sept. 10 783. From Nasr Allah Khan (of Rampur). Complementary on the arrival of Lord Cornwallis at Calcutta as Governor-General.

OR 557, WS, f 1; CR 23, pp. 269-72, no. 38; TR 51A, pp. 612-13, no. 239; AR 20, p. 29.

Sept. 10 784. Nawwab Nusrat Jang to Hillero Barlow, the Vice-President. Complementary on the addressee's appointment as the Vice-President.

OR 558,[2] *WS, f 1; CR 23, pp. 290-92, no. 45; TR 51A, p. 613, no. 240; AR 20, p. 26.*

[1]Copy enclosed with a letter from the Superintendent of *nizamat* affairs to the Deputy Persian Secretary, dated 5 September 1805.

[2]Enclosed with a letter from Pattle, dated 4 September 1805.

Sept. 10 785. From Nawwab Nusrat Jang to Sir George Barlow, the Vice-President. Requests for the release of Nawwab Shams al-Daulah as per the decision taken by Lord Wallesley during his Governorship. Also asks for the continuation of Shams al-Daulah's monthly allowance of Rs. 750 and his wife's allowance of Rs. 500 monthly.

OR 559,[1] *WS, f 1; CR 23, pp. 284-90, no. 44; TR 51A, pp. 616-19, no. 242A; AR 20, p. 26.*

Sept. 10 786. From King Shah Alam II. Expresses deep concern over the departure of the addressee to *Vilayat* (England).

OR 560,[2] *WS, f 1; CR 23, pp. 277-79, no. 41; TR 51A, p. 616, no. 242B; AR 20, p. 19.*

Sept. 10 787. The Nizam to the Resident at Hyderabad. States that the friendly relation existing between the two governments will be maintained and the terms of the treaty concluded between the writer and Pandit Pardhan will also be maintained to protect the interests of the public and states.

OR 562,[3] *f 1; CR 23, pp. 282-84, no. 44.*

Sept. 10 788. From Nawwab Nusrat Jang of Dacca. Solicits Vice-President's order in regard to Shams al-Daulah's attending to *Eid* and *Muharram* festivals and welcoming and seeing off the English gentlemen visiting Dacca.

TR 51A, pp. 613-15, no. 241; AR 20, p. 26.

Sept. 10 789. To Bishambhar Pandit. To the same effect as the foregoing CI 193 and TI 164.

CI 41, pp. 459-60, no. 196; TI 51, p. 240, no. 167; AI 20, p. 46.

Sept. 11 790. Col. Kirkpatrick, the Resident at Hyderabad to the Nizam. Informs the addressee about his taking leave from his (addressee's) court to be replaced by Russel as the new Resident. Dated 25 August 1805.

OR 561,[4] *f 1; CR 23, pp. 281-82, no. 43.*

[1]Enclosed with a letter from Crips, the Deputy Persian Secretary, dated 4 September 1805.

[2]Enclosed with a letter from the Resident at Delhi, dated 24 August 1805.

[3]Enclosed with a letter from the Resident at Hyderabad, dated 27 August 1805.

[4]Ibid.

Sept.[1] 15 791. From Daulat Rao Sindhia. Complements on the arrival of the addressee at Calcutta as Governor-General. Says that Jenkins have been relieved by the writer from his court and requests the addressee to appoint anyone else in his (writer's) court to execute the duties.

OR 563(1),[2] f 1; CR 23, pp. 401-04, no. 70(1).

Sept. 15 792. Daulat Rao Sindhia to Lord Lake. Refers to the case in regard to Lala Gopal Kishan and says that each and every point will be made known to the addressee by Kanwal Nain Munshi and may help remove the clouds of suspicion and misunderstanding caused due to some ill wishers of the two states.

OR 563(2),[3] f 1; CR 23, pp. 404-06, no. 70(2).

Sept. 15 793. Daulat Rao Sindhia to Lt. Col. Malcolm. To the same effect as the forgoing OR 563 (2).

OR 563(3), f 1, CR 23, pp. 406-08, no. 70(3).

Sept. 15 794. Col. John Malcolm to Daulat Rao Sindhia. Reconfirms the friendly relations between the two governments. Expresses displeasure on the count that the addressee has not relieved Jenkins from his court even after repeated requests from the writer. Asks the addressee to relieve Jenkins at the earliest from his court.

OR 563(4),[4] f 1; CR 23, pp. 408-10, no. 70(4).

Sept. 15 795. Ambaji Ingle to Col. Malcolm. To the same effect as OR 563(2).

OR 563(5),[5] f 1; CR 23, pp. 410-12, no. 70(5).

Sept. 15 796. General Lake to Daulat Rao Sindhia. Expresses annoyance over not relieving Jenkins from his (addressee's) court and adds that detention of Jenkins in his court would serve no purpose as he has not been authorized by the Company's government to enter into any negotiation.

OR 563(6),[6] f 1; CR 23, pp. 412-14, no. 70(6).

[1]Date of receipt on the folder is 11 September 1805. However, the date of the receipt of this collection (OR 563) is 15 September 1805 on OR 563/7.

[2]Copy enclosed with a letter from Lt. Colonel Malcolm.

[3]Ibid.

[4]Ibid.

[5]Ibid.

[6]Ibid.

Sept. 15 797. Col. John Malcolm to Ambaji Rao Ingle. Complains that Jenkins has not been relieved from the court of the addressee that is against the norm of friendship. Asks for his early relieving and says that no further negotiation would be possible unless Jenkins is relieved from his court.

OR 563(7),[1] f 1; CR 23, pp. 414-16, no. 70(7).

Sept. 15 798. Daulat Rao Sindhia to Munshi Kanwal Nain. Asks the addressee to see Holkar if he desires so and explain the actual position. Also asks him (the addressee) to see General Lake and Col. Malcolm and assure his (writer) loyalty to Company's government. The rest may be made clear from his (writer's) letter delivered by Lala Gopal Kishan.

OR[2] 563(8), f 1; CR 23, pp. 416-17, no. 70(8).

Sept. 15 799. Lala Gopal Kishan to Munshi Kanwal Nain. Complains that ten letters have been sent to the addressee earlier but no reply has so far been received. Says that the detail regarding the case of Gauri Shankar has already been sent. Also informs about the departure of Mir Khan, his separation from Holkar and his misery due to shortage of money. Further says that the said Khan is stationing at a distance of 5-6 *karohs* from Ajmer and asks the addressee to see him and give essential help.

OR 563(9),[3] f 1; CR 23, pp. 418-23, no. 70(9).

Sept. 12 800. From Nawwab Ahmad Ali Khan (of Rampur). Expresses deep concern on the departure of the addressee to Europe.

OR 564,[4] f 1, WS; CR 23, pp. 303-06, no. 48; TR 51A, p. 619, no. 243; AR 20, p. 4.

Sept. 12 801. From Nawwab Nasr Allah Khan (of Rampur). Expresses deep concern on the departure of the addressee (Lord Wellesley) from Calcutta to Europe.

OR 565, WS, f 1; CR 23, pp. 306-09, no. 49; TR 51A, p. 20, no. 244; AR 20, p. 29.

Sept. 12 802. From Mir Alam (of Hyderabad). Complements and expresses pleasure on the arrival of the addressee (Lord Cornwallis) at Calcutta and his taking the charge of Governor-General of India. Further assures his (writer's) loyalty and

[1]Copy enclosed with a letter from Col. Malcolm.

[2]Ibid.

[3]Ibid.

[4]Enclosed with a letter from the agent at Bareilly to the Deputy Persian Secretary to Government, dated 27 August 1805.

friendship to the Company's government and anticipates a growth of prosperity of the two states under his Governor-Generalship. Says that Col. Kirkpatrick, Resident at Hyderabad will soon pay his respect to the addressee and explain the affairs of friendship and cooperation between the two states.

OR 566,[1] *WS, ff 2, CR 23, pp. 316-20, no. 52; TR 51A, p. 623, no. 246; AR 20, p. 27.*

Sept. 12 803. From Nizam (of Hyderabad). Complements and expresses pleasure on the arrival of the addressee as Governor-General at Calcutta. Reassures his friendship, cooperation and loyalty towards the Company's government and anticipates a further development and prosperity of the two states under the Governor-Generalship of the addressee. Sends a *khilat* and Jewels to the addressee as presents through Col. Kirkpatrick, the Resident at his (writer's) court.

OR 568,[2] *WS, ff 2; CR 23, pp. 312-16, no. 51; TR 51A, pp. 620-22, no. 245; AR 20, p. 27.*

Sept. 13 804. From Amanat Khan. States that he has been serving Alamas Ali Khan but got terminated following the said Khan's joining the Company's service. Thereafter he joined Holkar's Service but left it due to his indisposition and now he is jobless. Requests for favour from the Governor-General.

OR 569,[3] *f 1; CR 23, pp. 325-26, no. 54.*

Sept. 11[4] 805. From Amanat Khan. To the same effect as foregoing OR 569.

OR 570,[5] *f 1; CR 23, pp. 326-27, no. 54.*

Sept. 13 806. From Jangi Khan. Requests for the grant of *pargana* Shergarh or some other adjoining district to Rampur yielding an annual income of Rs. 12,000 on *istamrar-e-theka* (perpetual

[1]Enclosed with a letter from the Resident at Hyderabad, dated 27 August 1805.

[2]Ibid.

[3]Copy Enclosed with a letter from the Agent at Farrukhabad, dated 31 August 1805.

[4]The, dated of receipt on the reverse of the document in Persian is 11 September 1805, but the folder bears 13 September 1805.

[5]Regional letter enclosed with a letter from the Agent at Farrukhabad, dated 31 August 1805.

contract) enabling him to keep his family with him. Dated 23 August 1805.

OR 571,[1] f 1; CR 23, pp. 327-29, no. 55.

Sept. 14 807. From Mirza Muzaffar Bakht (of Farrukhabad). Requests for cooperation from the addressee to maintain his (writer's) status. Also encloses a memorandum to explain his position more clearly. Dated 4 September 1805.

OR 572,[2] WS, ff 2; CR 23, pp. 331-35, no. 57; TR 51A, pp. 624-27, no. 248; AR 20, p. 25.

Sept. 15 808. From Raja Madho Singh, *zamindar* of Tirhut. Complementary on the arrival of the addressee at Patna. Sends an amount of 5 *asharfi* and Rs. 10 to be presented by Lala Chhagan Lal as *nazr.* Regrets for his inability to pay his respect due to his illness.

OR 573, WS, ff 2; TR 51A, p. 627, no. 249; AR 20, p. 36.

Sept. 15 809. From Ashraf al-Nisa Begam. Recounts the services of her father and grandfather to the Company and reciprocate salaries and allowances granted to them thereof. Puts forth her claim of succession on the properties and facilities of her forefathers. Requests for the recognition of her rights over the properties of her late father Rooh al-Din Khan and continuation of his pension in her name so as to look after her old-aged mother properly.

OR 574, WS, f 1; CR 23, pp. 363-68, no. 62; TR 51A, pp. 627-34, no. 250.

Sept. 15 810. From Sinkandar Shukoh. Expresses pleasure on the return of the addressee to India and explains his (writer's) difficulties. Also refers to his application to addressee's predecessor Lord Wellesley regarding his pecuniary problems. Anticipates that the addressee may spare some time to look into his (writer's) problems and resolve to solve them.

OR 575,[3] WS f 1; CR 23, pp. 335-38, no. 58; TR 51A, pp. 634-36, no. 251; AR 20, p. 24.

Sept. 16 811. A *Taliqa-e-Naqd-o-Jins* (list of articles) with Raja Balbhadra

[1]Copy enclosed with a letter from the Agent at Bareilly, dated 31 August 1805.

[2]Enclosed with a letter from the Agent at Farrukhabad, dated 7 September 1805.

[3]Enclosed with a letter from the Resident at Lucknow, dated 10 September 1805.

Bhuj prepared and compared in presence of Shivgram, *subedar* of the said Raja.

OR 576,[1] *ff 4; CR 23, pp. 339-55.*

Sept. 17 812. From Raja Udit Narayan. Informs about the sad demise of his grandmother Rani Gulab Kanwar.

OR 577,[2] *WS, f 1; CR 23, pp. 355-57, no. 60; TR 51A, p. 637, no. 252; AR 20, p. 33.*

Sept. 18 813. To Raghuji Bhonsla of Nagpur. Recalls and expresses pleasure on the establishment of a cordial friendly relation with the addressee's government based on the principles of justice and equality during the writer's previous administration. Further expresses concern over the loss that, the addressee sustained due to some unscrupulous circumstances. Warns the addressee to abstain from joining any confederation against the British government otherwise he will himself be responsible for any adverse result.

CI 41, pp. 260-64, no. 85; TI 50, pp. 240-45, no. 168; AI 20, p. 62.

Sept. 18 814. To Daulat Rao Sindhia. Expresses displeasure for not relieving Jenkins from the addressee's court in spite of repeated requests from the British government further says that the British government will enter into any negotiation with the addressee to settle certain pending points only after the release of Jenkins.

CI, 41, pp. 264-70, no. 85; TI 51, pp. 245-52, no. 169; AR 20, p. 49.

Sept. 20 815. From Sir George Barlow, the Vice President to Nasir al-Mulk. Informs the addressee that a monthly pension of Rs. 500 has been approved for Gauhar Ara Begam, the daughter of the Nawwab Mahdi Ali Khan for her support with effect from the demise of the said Nawwab. Refers to Pattle for further communication.

CI 41, pp. 271-72, no. 86; TI 51, pp. 253-55, no. 170; AI 20, p. 59.

[1]Enclosed with a letter from the Magistrate at Midnapur to the Chief Secretary to Government, dated 13 September 1805.

[2]Copy enclosed with a letter from the Agent at Benares, dated 14 September 1805.

Sept. 20 816. To Munni Begam. To the same effect as the foregoing CI 868 and TI 170.

CI 41, pp. 271-72, no. 86; TI 51, p. 255, no. 171; AI 20, p. 55.

Sept. 22 817. From Kishan Raj Wodiar, Raja of Mysore. Complementary on arrival of the addressee (Lord Cornwallis) at Calcutta as Governor-General and anticipates a day by day growth in the prosperity of the two states and further strengthening of the friendly relations.

OR 578,[1] WS, f 1; CR 23, pp. 380-83, no. 65; TR 51A, pp. 637-39, no. 253; AR 20, p. 36.

Sept. 22 818. From Kishan Raj Wodiar, Raja of Mysore. To the same effect as the OR 578.

OR 579,[2] f 1; CR 23, pp. 383-85, no. 66; TR 51A, pp. 637-39, no. 253; AR 20, p. 36.

Sept. 22 819. From Purnaiya, the minister of Raja of Mysore. Complementary on the arrival of the addressee in India. Dated 30 August 1805.

OR 580,[3] WS, f 1; CR 23, pp. 385-89, no. 67; TR 51A, pp. 639-41, no. 254.

Sept. 22 820. From Purnaiya, the minister of Raja of Mysore. To the same effect to the previous OR 580.

OR 581,[4] f 1; CR 23, pp. 377-80, no. 64; TR 51A, pp. 639-41, no. 254.

Sept. 22 821. Sir George Barlow, the Vice-President to Nawwab Nusrat Jang of Dacca. Acknowledges the addressee's letter and says that the British government has no objection to Shams al-Daulah's (addressee's brother) attending ceremonies of *Eid* and *Muharram* but does not permit the exchange of visits between Shams al-Daulah and the European gentlemen residing in Dacca.

CI 41, pp. 272-75, no. 87; TI 51, pp. 255-57, no. 172; AI 20, p. 58.

[1]Enclosed with a letter from the Resident at Mysore to the secretary to the government, dated 1 September 1805.

[2]Ibid.

[3]Ibid.

[4]Ibid.

Sept 23 822. Saiyid Ali Khan Nusrat Jang (of Dacca) to Sir George Barlow. Expresses deep concern on the ill health of the addressee and requests to be informed of the improvement in his health.

OR 582, f 1; TR 51A, p. 641, no. 255; AR 20, p. 26.

Sept. 23 823. From Raja Udit Narayan. To the same effect as OR 577.

OR 583, f 1, WS; TR 51A, pp. 642-43, no. 256; AR 20, p. 33.

Sept. 24 824. Gauhar Ara Begum to Pattle. Puts forth her claim of succession to the property of her late father and complains against the illegal claims of Bunni Begam for the same. Demands justice from the British government. Also complains about the unkind behaviour of her brother Dilawar Jang.

OR 584, f 1; CR 23, pp. 391-97, no. 67; TR 51A, pp. 643-50, no. 257; AR 20, p. 16.

Sept. 24 825. Nawwab Dilawar Jang to Pattle. States that a stipend of Rs. 11,200 was granted to the writer by the Company's government for the support of the relatives and adherents of his late father. The writer has allocated Rs. 2,000 monthly for his sister Gauhar Ara Begam for her maintenance and promised to keep it continued till the said amount is reimbursed by the Company. But her sister denounced it. Hence she has no rightful claim on it.

OR 585, f 1; CR 23, pp. 397-99, no. 69; TR 51A, pp. 651-52, no. 258; AR 20, p. 9.

Sept. 25 826. Gauhar Ara Begam to Nawwab Dilawar Jang. Renounces her claims to all her shares in her father's property in favour of the addressee (her brother). Dated 30 January 1793.

OR 586,[1] f 1; TR 51A, pp. 653-56, no. 259; AR 20, p. 9.

Sept. 24 827. Saiyid Muhammad Hashim and Saiyid Muhammad Jafar (Sons of Gauhar Ara Begam) to Pattle. Complains against the bad behaviour of their maternal uncle Nawwab Dilawar Jang and requests for assistance.

OR 587, WS, f 1; CR 23, pp. 399-401, no. 69; TR 51A, pp. 656-58, no. 260; AR 20, p. 25.

Sept. 25 828. From Shambhu Bharti. Refers to his previous letter containing the detailed accounts outstanding with the

[1]Copy.

British government. Further dispatches the same as asked by Elphinstone from Nagpur. Requests for an early audience with the addressee to explain his position.

OR 588, WS, f 1; CR 23, pp. 441-44, no. 71; TR 51A, pp. 659-62, no. 261; AR 20, p. 38.

Sept. 25 829. From Shambhu Bharati. Expresses desire to proceed to Calcutta and have an audience with the addressee as soon as permission is granted. Requests to issue an order to Elphinstone to arrange for an appropriate number of troops to escort the writer up to Calcutta. Also complains that Elphinstone has misinformed the addressee regarding assignment of *jagir* to the writer. Further says that he has already sent a detailed account to Elphinstone to forward it to addressee but the latter has again demanded the same. Requests that the *jagirs* of Daryapur, Kolhapur and Anjangaon be granted to the writer and orders issued to the local officers to manage for its transfer and possession to the writer at the time when Berar is separated from Hyderabad.

OR 589, f 1; TR 51A, pp. 662-65, no. 262; AR 20, p. 39.

Sept. 25 830. Nawwab Wazir to Col. Collins. Expresses his (writer) disappointment on the issuing of a summon to Priya Das *tahsildar* of Qannauj a resident of the writer's territory by the court of Kanpur while a petition has already been submitted to the said court that Priya Das is presently sick and will appear before the court as soon as he recovers from sickness. Further warns that occurrences of such acts are unusual and out of established convention. Dated 8 September 1805.

OR 590(1),[1] f 1.

Sept. 25 831. Copy of OR 590(1).

OR 590(2), f 1.

Sept. 25 832. Nawwab Wazir to Col. Collins. States that anybody taking refuge in the writer's territory after committing crime in British territory will be extradited immediately. But asks that summons should not be issued and served in such cases.

OR 590(3),[2] f 1.

[1]Copy enclosed with a letter from the Resident at Lucknow, dated 14 September 1805.

[2]Ibid., dated 15 September 1805.

Sept. 25 833. Nawwab Wazir to Col. Collins. To the same effect as the foregoing. OR 590(3).

OR 590(4),[1] *f 1.*

Sept. 25 834. Col. Collins to Nawwab Wazir. Acknowledges receipt of addressee's letters dated 13 and 14 *Jumada II* (1220 AH) = (8 and 9 September 1805) regarding the case of extradition of one Priya Das, *tahsildar* of Qannauj taking refuge in the addressee's territory. Explains the urgency of Priya Das's presence before the court at Kanpur and says that the issuing of summon in the name of the said person was not aimed at creating any problem for the addressee and hence it should not be taken otherwise. Expect that the addressee will not help and defend the accused Priya Das.

OR 590(5),[2] *f 1.*

Sept. 25 835. Col. Collins to Nawwab Wazir. To the same effect as the foregoing OR 590(5).

OR 590(6),[3] *f 1.*

Sept. 25 836. Col. Collins to Nawwab Wazir. Refers to his previous letter regarding serving of summon to Priya Das, the *tahsildar* of Qannauj issued by the court of Kanpur. Also reminds that the addressee has informed that Priya Das is sick and staying at Lucknow. But information has been given by Munshi Muhammad Baqar that Priya Das has set out on a journey from Lucknow to some other place. Requests the addressee to serve the summon issued by the court of Kanpur to Priya Das.

OR 590(7),[4] *f 1.*

Sept. 25 837. Nawwab Wazir to Col. Collins. Acknowledges receipt of addressee's letter regarding appearance of Priya Das before the court at Kanpur. Says that the writer has accordingly enquired the matter from Kishori Das, who informed that Priya Das may appear before the said court when he is physically fit and has the permission to be away from the court during his treatment.

OR 590(8),[5] *f 1.*

[1]Copy enclosed with a letter from the Resident at Lucknow, dated 14 September 1805.

[2]Ibid., dated 15 September 1805.

[3]Ibid., dated 15 September 1805.

[4]Ibid., dated 15 September 1805.

[5]Enclosed with a letter from the Resident at Lucknow, dated 14 September 1805.

Sept. 25 838. Sir George Barlow, the Vice-President to Raja Udit Narayan Singh of Benares. Condoles on the death of addressee's grandmother Rani Gulab Kanwar.

CI 41, pp. 460-61, no. 197; TI 51, p. 257, no. 173; AI 20, p. 64.

Sept. 25 839. Sir George Barlow, the Vice-President to Nawwab Nusrat Jang of Dacca. Thanks the addressee for his letter sent at the time of the writer's indisposition.

CI 41, pp. 461-62, no. 198; TI 51, p. 257, no. 174; AI 20, p. 58.

Sept. 26 840. Sir George Barlow, the Vice-President to Nawwab Nusrat Jang of Dacca. Informs the addressee that the pensions enjoyed by late Mir Saiyid Ali and late Mirza Ghulam Haider have been transferred to their respective heirs on the recommendation of the addressee.

CI 41, pp. 275-76, no. 88; TI 51, pp. 257-58, no. 175; AI 20, p. 58.

Sept. 27 841. From Raja of Nepal. Complements the addressee on his arrival at Calcutta as Governor-General. Recounts the old and strong relation of friendship between the two governments. Further says that some ill-will persons have tried to create misunderstanding between the two governments but could not succeed due to a positive and encouraging effort of Brooke who promptly reported the truth to the addressee in time. Further informs that Guru Pandit Rajkishan Pandit a confident person is sent to Calcutta to pay homage to the addressee and give some confidential information. Anticipates a hearty and warm welcome of the said Guru at Calcutta.

OR 591, f 1; TR 51, pp. 665-68, no. 263; AR 20, p. 32.

Sept. 28 842. From Nawwab Nusrat Jang (of Dacca). Informs about the safe arrival of writer's brother Nawwab Shams al-Daulah at Dacca from Calcutta and expresses gratitude for making proper arrangement for his journey. Dated 23 September, 1805.

OR 592, WS, WC, f 1; pp. 452-57; no. 73; AR 51A, pp. 676-81, no. 265; AR 20, p. 26.

Sept. 28 843. Jafar Khan to Edmonston, the Persian Secretary. Denies the charges of having ever given any information to Raja Sansar Chand about the preparation of British forces to be mobilized towards Lahore and surroundings, stresses upon his loyalty to British government. Acknowledges the payment of Rs. 412 only out of Rs. 800. Further says that an amount of Rs. 6,420 is also due to payment out of his salary. Requests for its early payment. Further suggests that the *sardars* of this region should be rewarded with *khilat* to win their confidence.

OR 593, WS, WC, f 1; CR 23, pp. 357-63, no. 61; TR 51A, pp. 669-76, no. 264; AR 20, p. 39.

Sept. 29 844. Raja Ranjit Singh of Lahore to A. Seton. Expresses his desire to establish a friendly relation between the two governments.

OR 594,[1] f 1; CR 23, pp. 457-61, no. 74; TR 51A, pp. 681-85, no. 266; AR 20, p. 13.

Sept. 30 845. Nawwab Muin al-Mulk (Dilawar Jang) to Sir George Barlow. Complementary on the addressee's appointment as Vice-President in the absence of the Governor-General.

OR 595, WS, f 1; TR 51A, pp. 685-86, no. 267; AR 20, p. 9.

Sept. 13 846. Zaib al-Nisa Begam. Congratulatory with reassurance of her loyalty to British government.

OR 596,[2] WS, WC, f 1; TR 51A, pp. 623-24, no. 247; AR 20, p. 42.

Sept. -- 847. From the Agent. Says that the letter from Lord Lake to (George) Guthrie regarding reconfirmation of the territory in Doab region to Zaib al-Nisa Begum for her lifelong period on the condition of loyalty and military assistance to British government. Further informs that Guthrie has properly informed the Begam and got the deal signed by her. Dated 21 August 1805.

OR 597,[3] f 1; CR 23, pp. 139-41, no. 1.

Sept. -- 848. From Lal Israj Singh, *zamindar* of Kheragarh. Complains against the wicked plans of some mischief mongers in the writer's *zamindari* and requests that his case may be presented

[1]Copy enclosed with a letter from the agent in ceded province, dated 10 September 1805.

[2]Enclosed with a letter from the Resident at Delhi, dated 13 September 1805.

[3]Copy enclosed with a letter from Malcolm, dated 1 September 1805.

to the government and also requests that the writer may be permitted to hold his *zamindari* according to the old *jama* figure.

OR 598/1,[1] WS, f 1.

Sept. -- 849. From Lal Israj Singh, *zamindar* of Kheragarh. Complains against Babu Deoki Nandan and Kashi Parsad who have imprisoned the writer without any fault. Requests for his release. Also requests for the recovery of the losses inflicted to him due to his taking surity of a few *zamindars* for the payment of *malguzari* (revenue), due over them, from his own pocket.

OR 598/2,[2] WS, f 1.

Sept. -- 850. From Lal Israj Singh, the *zamindar* of Kheragarh. Requests the addressee to transmit writer's petition to the government and wishes to direct the Collector of Allahabad not to attend to the misrepresentation of the writer's enemies on the subject of writer's *zamindari*.

OR 598/3,[3] WS, f 1.

Sept. -- 851. *Sanad* (copy) issued under the seal of Lt. Governor Henry dated 11 January 1803, regarding assignment of *taluqa* Manda of Kheragarh to Lal Israj Singh for his lifetime at the *jama* of Rs. 24,000 in lieu of the services and loyalty to the British government and remit the surplus amount to the treasury.

OR 598/4,[4] f 1.

Sept. -- 852. *Sanad* (copy) under the seal of Ahmuty, Collector of Allahabad. To the same effect as the foregoing.

OR 598/5,[5] f 1.

Sept. -- 853. Hastings to Lala Udit Singh. Communicates the addressee regarding flight of Raja Chait Singh after killing three British and creating panic. Asks the addressee to look after the affairs of the Raj of *sarkar* Benares and Ghazipur, etc., until a permanent arrangement is made in this regard. Further asks the addressee to obey and follow the orders of Babu Ausan Singh in the affairs of Raj and pay the revenue to *khazana-i-mahal*.

OR 598/6,[6] f 1.

[1]Enclosed with a letter from the Judge at Allahabad.

[2]Ibid.

[3]Ibid.

[4]Ibid.

[5]Ibid.

[6]Ibid.

Sept. -- 854. Nawwab Wazir to Lala Israj Singh. Notifies the writer's accession to the *masnad* of the state. Also notifies the appointment of the addressee along Husain Raza Khan and Maharaja Tikait Rai to look after the affairs of revenue and administration of the writer's government.

OR 598/7,[1] f 1.

Sept. -- 855. Nawwab Wazir to Lala Udit Singh confirms the assignment of *pargana* Kheragarh to the addressee and directs him to look after the affairs of the *pargana* and submit the instalments of the revenue to John Bristow regularly and agreeably.

OR 598/8,[2] f 1.

Sept. -- 856. John Bristow to Lala Udit Singh. Informs that *pargana* of Kheragah assigned earlier to Raja Mahip Narayan Singh is now assigned to the addressee by Nawwab Wazir. Further asks the addressee to remit the amount of revenue regularly and submit the amount of the months of Kanwar and Kartik immediately.

OR 598/9,[3] f 1.

Sept. -- 857. Nawwab Wazir to Col. John Collins. Requests for reinforcement to suppress the commotion prevailing in the area (Bahraich). Dated 26 August 1805.

OR 599(1),[4] f 1; CR 23, pp. 224-25, no. 31(1).

Sept. -- 858. Mahdi Ali Khan to Nawwab Wazir. Acknowledges receipt of addressee's letter regarding reinforcement to suppress the commotion in the region of Bahraich by Guman Singh of Gondah who has collected a force of about 20,000 men and 10-12 infantry, etc. Requests the addressee to direct Col. Milton, the officer of Sakrurah Chhawani to send 4-5 companies of army to assist the *amil* in order to suppress the rebellion.

OR 599(2),[5] f 1; CR 23, pp. 225-27, no. 31(2).

Sept. -- 859. Col. Collins to Nawwab Wazir. Acknowledges receipt of addressee's letter along with an application of Mahdi Ali Khan regarding military assistance for the suppression of Guman

[1]Enclosed with a letter from the Judge at Allahabad.

[2]Ibid.

[3]Ibid.

[4]Copy enclosed with a letter from the Resident at Lucknow, dated 1 September 1805.

[5]Ibid.

Singh Raja of Gondah who has created commotion in region of Bahraich with the help of Kishan Parsad and Raja of Khagol (?). Informs the address that sufficient number of troops and artillery pieces would be made available to Mahdi Ali Khan for opening a front against the rebellious.

OR 599(3),[1] f 1; CR 23, pp. 227-29, no. 31(3).

Sept. -- 860. Col. Collins to Nawwab Wazir. Informs the addressee about the receipt of a letter from Capt. Barris at Sakrurah and a copy of the letter of Husain Ali Khan to the Captain regarding statement of Mahdi Ali Khan *amil* of Bahraich in respect of so-called rebellion of Guman Singh in Bahraich. States that according to the above letters the statement given by Mahdi Ali Khan regarding collection of 20,000 troops and 10-12 artillery pieces by Guman Singh of Gondah for creating disturbance in the area of Bahraich is totally false. Further asks that the addressee should himself investigate the affair and bring Mahdi Ali Khan to book.

OR 599(4),[2] f 1; CR 23, pp. 229-31, no. 31(4).

Sept. -- 861. Col. Collins to Nawwab Wazir. To the same effect as the foregoing OR 599(4).

OR 599(5),[3] f 1; CR 23, pp. 231-33, no. 31(5).

Sept. -- 862. Mirza Husain Ali Khan to Capt. Mason. Acknowledges receipt of addressee's letter regarding suppression of Raja Guman Singh and says that the writer is willing to set out tomorrow and stay in the vicinity of Bahraich. States that the information regarding movement of Guman singh would be dispatched as soon as the same is received from the intelligence.

OR 599(6),[4] f 1; CR 23, pp. 233-34, no. 31(6).

Sept. -- 863. Mirza Husain Ali Khan to Capt. Mason. To the same effect as the foregoing OR 599(6).

OR 599(7),[5] f 1; CR 23, pp. 235-36, no. 31(7).

[1]Enclosed with a letter from the Resident at Lucknow, dated 1 September 1805.

[2]Ibid., dated 6 September 1805.

[3]Ibid., dated 8 September 1805.

[4]Ibid., dated 6 September 1805.

[5]Ibid.

Sept. -- 864. Raja Amrit Rao to Governor-General Lord Cornwallis. Assures of the writer's loyalty to Company's government and hopes a strong friendly relation under the rule of the addressee.
OR 601,[1] *f 1.*

Sept. -- 865. From Amrit Rao. Acknowledges receipt of addressee's letter regarding his (addressee's) journey towards Benares. Expresses his eagerness to welcome and see the Governor-General in Benares.
OR 603,[2] *f 1, CR 23, pp. 257-58, no. 33(2).*

Sept. -- 866. Nawwab Wazir to Col. Collins. Requests for the return of Rs. 5 lakh that the writer has advanced for a period of 6 months. Dated 10 *Jumada II*, 1220 AH (5 September 1805).
OR 604(1),[3] *f 1; CR 23, pp. 265-66, no. 37(1).*

Sept. -- 867. Col. Collins to Nawwab Wazir. Acknowledges receipt of addressee's letter regarding repayment of Rs. 5 lakh to the addressee. Further apologizes for the delay occurred in repayment of the said amount in due time. States that his letter will be forwarded to the Governor-General for the early payment of the said amount. Dated 5 September 1805.
OR 604(2),[4] *f 1; CR 23, pp. 266-68, no. 37(2).*

Sept. -- 868. To Col. Collins. Acknowledges receipt of addressee's letter. States that the amount of Rs. 5 lakh due on the Company will soon be paid to Nawwab Wazir. Dated 8 September 1805.
OR 604(3), f 1; CR 23, pp. 268-69, no. 37(3).

Sept. -- 869. From King Shah Alam II. Congratulatory on the addressee's appointment as Governor-General of India.
OR 605,[5] *WS, f 1; CR 23, pp. 272-75, no. 39.*

Sept. -- 870. From King Shah Alam II. Intimates the addressee about granting permission to his son Sulaiman Shukoh for an audience.
OR 606, ff 2, CR 23, pp. 275-77, no. 40.

Sept. -- 871. Saiyid Jafar Khan to Lala Lakhpat Rai *wakil* of Raja Sansar Chand (of Nadaun). Informs the address about his

[1]The document is badly worm eaten.
[2]Enclosed with a letter from Brook, dated 15 October 1805.
[3]Copy enclosed with a letter from Col. Collins.
[4]Ibid.
[5]Enclosed with a letter from resident at Delhi, dated 29 August 1805.

arrival at Lucknow and meeting with the Resident Col. Collins for discussing various issues in order to strengthen the friendly relation between the two governments.

OR 607,[1] f 1; CR 23, pp. 292-97, no. 46.

Sept. -- 872. Saiyid Jafar Khan to Raja Sansar Chand (of Nadaun). States that Company's government does not want to aggrandize the addressee's territory but want to maintain peaceful and friendly relations with the neighbouring chiefs. Further adds that the troops stationed in the vicinity of addressee's territory are only to check the mischievous Sikh *sardars*. Dated 10 September 1805.

OR 608,[2] f 1; CR 23, pp. 298-302, no. 47.

Sept. -- 873. From Khiradmand Khan (of Farrukhabad). States that the doubts developed against the addressee's actions at the time of Holkar's arrival in the region of Doaba has now been removed after the latter's arrival in Bengal. Further says that the information received so far has proven false and now he (the writer) is relieved of all doubts. Thanks for the friendly gestures of the addressee.

OR 609,[3] f 1, WS, WC; CR 23, pp. 329-31, no. 56.

Sept. -- 874. From Amrit Rao. Congratulates the addressee for his appointment as Governor-General and his subsequent arrival in Calcutta. Discusses and explains the long friendly relations of the two states and expresses hope that the same relation would continue under the Governorship of the addressee. Further explains the differences between Baji Rao and the writer. Also explains the reasons of his (writers) visit to Benares. Finally says that his agent Pandit Balal will explain the whole affair in detail who is supposed to visit the addressee after the winter season and expect a warm welcome for the said Pandit at addressee's Court as he is a very close and confident man of the writer.

OR 610,[4] WS, WC, f 1; CR 23, pp 368-77, no. 63.

Sept. -- 875. From Ram Raj Bahadur (Raja of Travancore). Congratulates the addressee on his appointment as Governor-

[1]Enclosed with a letter from the Resident at Lucknow, dated 12 September 1805.

[2]Ibid.

[3]Enclosed with a letter from the Acting Agent at Farrukhabad, dated 15 September 1805.

[4]Enclosed with a letter from the Agent at Benares, dated 1 September 1805.

General. Expresses that the friendly relation between the two governments may be further strengthen under the addressee's rule. Further assures of his loyalty to the Company's government.

OR 611,[1] *WS, WC, f 1; CR 23, pp. 389-91, no. 68.*

Sept. -- 876. Nawwab Wazir to Col. Collins. Acknowledges addressee's letter regarding appearance of Priya Das before the court of Kanpur. Says that Priya Das has no problem in appearing before the court at Kanpur but seeks that much time that may be sufficient for his treatment and recovery from the sickness. Dated 20 August 1805.

OR 612(1), [2] *f 2; CR 23, pp. 444, 45, no. 72(1).*

Sept. -- 877. Order of the *faujdari* court at Kanpur regarding issuance of a summon to Priya Das, the *tahsildar* of Qannauj to appear before the court and settle the accounts. Further orders to issue a letter to Nawwab Wazir to terminate Priya Das from his present duty and impose a fine of Rs. 1,500 for violating the court orders.

OR 612(2),[3] *f 1; CR 23, pp. 445-47, no. 72(2).*

Sept. -- 878. Court order from the *faujdari* court of Kanpur allowing the *zamindar* of Qannauj to appear before the court after his recovery from his illness. The court also orders to issue a notice to the said *zamindar* to deposit a penalty of Rs. 1,500 for his absence from duties without having prior permission. Dated 31 August 1805.

OR 612(3),[4] *f 1; CR 23, pp. 445-47, no. 72(2).*

Sept. -- 879. A show-cause notice to Priya Das, *tahsildar* of Qannauj issued by *faujdari adalat*, Kanpur for his absence from duties without prior permission. Dated 14 August 1805.

OR 612(4),[5] *f 1; CR 23, pp. 447-48, no. 72(3).*

[1]Enclosed with a letter from the Resident at Tranvancore, dated 23 September 1805.

[2]Enclosed with a letter from the Resident at Lucknow, dated 14 September 1805.

[3]Ibid., dated 15 September 1805.

[4]Copy received along with a letter from the Resident at Lucknow, dated 15 September 1805.

[5]Ibid.

Sept. -- 880. Show-cause notice from *faujdari adalat*, Kanpur to Priya Das, *tahsildar* of Qannauj regarding his absence from duties without prior permission.

OR 612(5),[1] f 1; CR 23, pp. 447-48, no. 72(3).

Sept. -- 881. Col. Collins to Nawwab Wazir. Informs about the absence of Priya Das, the *tahsildar* of Qannauj without prior permission from the *faujdari adalat* of Kanpur. Further requests the addressee to ask the said *tahsildar* to appear before the court and explain the reasons for his absence. Dated 18 August 1805.

OR 612(6),[2] f 1; CR 23, pp. 448-49, no. 72(4).

Sept. -- 882. Same as previous letter OR 612(6).[3]

OR 612(7), f 1, CR 23, pp. 448-49, no. 72(4).

Sept. -- 883. Col. Collins to Nawwab Wazir. Complains that the summon issued by the *faujdari* court of Kanpur to Priya Das, the *tahsildar* of Qannauj asking him to appear before the said court and explain the causes for his unauthorized absence from the duties and his going to Lucknow was unlawfully delivered to the father of the said *tahsildar*. Further asks the addressee to check such irregularities and arrange for the appearance of the said *tahsildar* before the court.

OR 612(8),[4] f 1, CR 23, pp. 449-52, no. 72(5).

Sept. -- 884. Hakim Mahdi Ali Khan to Col. Collins, the Resident at Lucknow. Informs that Mir Kazim Ali son of Mir Zain al-Abedin is absconding from Pratapgarh and Scott has already issued order to the army officers of the Company's forces stationed in the region of Pratapgarh and Sultanpur, etc. But so far no sign of his presence has been found anywhere. Further says that it has come to notice that the said Kazim Ali has taken shelter in *qasba* Banda, adjacent to Bundelkhand. Requests to direct Baillei to arrest Kazim Ali and send him safely to Nawwab Wazir.

OR 613 (1),[5] f 1; CR 23, pp. 461-62, no. 75(1).

Sept. -- 885. Copy of the previous OR 613 (1).

OR 613(2), f 1; CR 23, pp. 461-62, no. 75(1).

[1]Copy received along with a letter from the Resident at Lucknow, dated 15 September 1805.

[2]Ibid.

[3]Ibid.

[4]Ibid.

[5]Ibid.

Sept. -- 886. Col. Collins to Nawwab Wazir. Informs that mother of Baqar Ali Khan who was previously not allowed to go to Fatehpur on the complaint of Hakim Mahdi Khan and was given permission on the addressee's recommendation is presently staying at Lucknow. Requests the addressee to allow her again to go to Fatehpur by issuing a travel passport, etc. Dated 11 June 1805.

OR 613(3),[1] f 1; CR 23, pp. 463-64, no. 75(2).

Sept. -- 887. Col. Collins to Nawwab Wazir. To the same effect as the foregoing OR 613(3).

OR 613(4),[2] f 1; CR 23, pp. 467-69, no. 75(5).

Sept. -- 888. Nawwab Wazir to Col. Collins. The writer expresses his inability to let the mother of Mir Baqar Ali Khan go to Fatehpur as her son Mir Kazim Ali has borrowed a substantial amount of money and has not returned till now. Hence there is no way but to detain his mother for the recovery of the said money from Mir Kazim Ali. Dated 12 *Rabi I*, 1220 AH (10 June 1805).

OR 613(5),[3] f 1; CR 23, pp. 464-66, no. 75(3).

Sept. -- 889. Nawwab Wazir to Col. Collins. To the same effect as the foregoing OR 613(5).

OR 613(6), [4] f 1; CR 23, pp. 466-67, no. 75(4).

Sept. -- 890. Nawwab Wazir to Col. Collins. Informs that mother of Mir Baqar Ali may be allowed to go to Fatehpur as soon as the debt due on Mir Kazim Ali is recovered.

OR 613(7),[5] f 1; CR 23, pp. 469-70, no. 75(6).

Sept. -- 891. Nawwab Wazir to Col. Collins. To the same effect as the foregoing (OR 613(7)).

OR 613(8),[6] f 1; CR 23, pp. 469-70, no. 75(6).

Sept. -- 892. Col. Collins to Nawwab Wazir. Informs that the writer agrees to the addressee's proposal regarding grant of permission to mother of Mir Baqar Ali to go to Fatehpur. Further says

[1]Copy received along with a letter from the Resident at Lucknow, dated 3 September 1805.

[2]Ibid.

[3]Ibid.

[4]Ibid.

[5]Ibid.

[6]Ibid.

that he has also informs Brook Smith and Ahmuty regarding addressee's proposal. Requests the addressee to abide by the justice and traditions while granting permission to the mother of Mir Baqar Ali to leave Lucknow. Dated 13 April 1805.

OR 613(9), f 1; CR 23, pp. 470-72, no. 75(7).

Sept. -- 893. Col. Collins to Nawwab Wazir. To the same effect as the foregoing OR 613(9).

OR 613(10),[1] f 1; CR 23, pp. 470-72, no. 75(7).

Sept. -- 894. Nawwab Wazir to Col. Collins. Acknowledges receipt of addressee's letter and explains that the matter of debt due on Mir Kazim Ali was not known to the writer hence her mother was allowed to go to Fatehpur but now the matter regarding borrowing of money by her son Mir Kazim Ali has been explored and proven, thus she could be allowed to go to Fatehpur only after the recovery of the money from Mir Kazim Ali. Dated 10 *Muharram* 1220 AH (11 April 1805).

OR 613(11),[2] f 1; CR 23, pp. 472-74, no. 75(8).

Sept. -- 895. Nawwab Wazir to Col. Collins. To the same effect as the foregoing OR 613(11).

OR 613(12),[3] f 1; CR 23, pp. 472-74, no. 75(8).

Sept. -- 896. Intelligence report from Kabul sent by Mirza Abbas Quli Khan. Reports about his meeting with the king Shah Shuja al-Mulk, his (king's) departure for Peshawar and grant of Rs. 8,000 to Ghulam Muhammad Khan, the *haakim* of Peshawar for the repair of the fort of Attock, etc.

Further reports about arrival of Abd Allah Khan, the *wakil* of Holkar. Dated 13 September 1805.

OR 614(a), f 1; TR 51A, pp. 293-95, no. 93, AR 20, p. 10.

Sept. -- 897. Intelligence report from Rai Ratan Lal and Rai Shambhu Nath. Reports regarding activities going on among Jaswant Rao, Ranjit Singh, Bir Bhoj and Daulat Rao and General Lord Lake, etc. Dated 10 September 1805.

OR 614(b), f 1.

[1]Copy received along with a letter from the Resident at Lucknow, dated 3 September 1805.

[2]Ibid.

[3]Ibid.

Sept. -- 898. Public notification issued under the seal of Nawwab Wazir asking the residents and inhabitants of the Ceded Provinces to abstain from accepting any service under any *sardar* (chief) (*Rayees-e-Beruni*) who are at war with the Company's government. Also asks the persons who are in service of such chiefs prior to this notification to take a leave from their duties. Any person found violating this order shall be punished and his properties may be confiscated. Dated 12 *Jumada II*, 1220 AH (7 September 1805)

OR 615,[1] *f 1.*

Oct. 2 899. From Gulab Rai, *wakil* of Peshwa. Recounts the 14 years service of his father Sevak Ram to the Peshwa and the Company followed by his own service for nearly thirty years with all loyalties. Expresses grief over the appointment of Hari Pandit Udhu as *wakil* of Peshwa in the place of the writer. Requests the addressee to bestow some pension for the livelihood of the petitioner and his dependents or allow him to retire to any holy place along with his dependents where he can spend rest of his life and pray for the welfare of Company's government.

OR 616, f 1; TR 51A, pp. 686-88, no. 268; AR 20, p. 17.

Oct. 2 900. To Daulat Rao Sindhia. To the same effect as the foregoing CI 85 and TI 169, placed at slip no. 815.

OR 617, f 1; CR 23, pp. 501-8, no. 3.

Oct. 2 901. Sir George Barlow, the Vice-President to Nawwab Dilawar Jang. Complementary in reply to addressee's congratulatory letter on the occasion of writer's appointment as the Vice-President and Deputy Governor.

CI 41, pp. 462-63, no. 199; TI 51, p. 259, no. 176; AI 20, p. 49.

Oct. 3 902. From Raja Ranjit Singh of Bharatpur. Expresses happiness over the Governor-General's proposed journey to upper province (Allahabad) and expresses his desire to have the honour of waiting upon the addressee.

OR 618, WS, f 1; CR 23, pp. 508-9, no. 4; TR 51A, p. 689, no. 269; AR 20, p. 36, no. 269.

[1]Copy enclosed with a letter from the Resident at Delhi, dated 27 August 1805.

Oct 7 903. Nawwab Nusrat Jang (of Daccca) to Sir G.H. Barlow, the Vice-President. Acknowledges receipt of addressee's letter dated 23 September 1805. Seeks permission for Shams al-Daulah's visit to Dacca during the festivities of *Eid* and visiting some religious places there on the eve of *Muharram*.

OR 619, f 1; CR 23, pp. 513-15, no. 6; TR 51A, pp. 689-91, no. 270; AR 20, p. 26.

Oct. 9 904. Daulat Rao Sindhia to Lord Lake. Acknowledges receipt of two letters from the addressee and enumerates the aged old friendly relation between the writer and the Company's government. Argues and clarifies that the disappointment of the Governor-General finds no merit in regard to not relieving of Jenkins, the Agent (*wakil*) of the Company as it has been old practice that until a new person is appointed to the said position and received charges of the office, the old one could not leave. Further says that his *wakil* Kanwal Nain would explain in detail the state of affairs.

OR 620(1),[1] f 1.

Oct. 9 905. Daulat Rao Sindhia to Munshi Kanwal Nain. Asks the addressee to represent the case on behalf of the writer before the Governor-General in respect of the misunderstanding created due to the delay in relieving of Jenkins.

OR 620(2),[2] f 1.

Oct. 9 906. Daulat Rao Sindhia to Munshi Kanwal Nain. Informs the addressee regarding his deputation as writer's *wakil* to represent him before the Governor-General in respect of explanation for the delay in relieving of Jenkins.

OR 620(3),[3] f 1.

Oct. 9 907. Daulat Rao Sindhia to Munshi Kanwal Nain. To the same effect as the foregoing.

OR 620(4),[4] f 1.

Oct. 9 908. Krishna Gopal Sahai to Col. John Malcolm. Acknowledges receipt of addressee's letter and expresses his pleasure and thanks for the generosity shown by Lord Lake. Assures the addressee of the continuation of the old friendly relation between the two governments and there is nothing to be suspicious of. Informs about the relieving of the Company's agent with all respect and

[1]Copy enclosed with a letter from Malcolm, dated 25 September 1805.
[2]Ibid.
[3]Ibid.
[4]Ibid.

regards. Further says that others matters of interests between the two governments is addressee's concerns and express pleasure that the addressee's visit to the region would create an atmosphere of pleasure and confidence as the writer may be able to see the addressee and discuss various matters in detail.

OR 620(5),[1] f 1.

Oct. 9 909. Ambaji Rao Ingle to Col. John Malcolm. Acknowledges receipt of addressee's letter. Expresses pleasure that the suspicion that was grew between the two governments could well be removed by Lord Lake. Informs about the departure of Jenkins and says that Munshi Kanwal Nain, the writer's *wakil* may be sent back with all regards.

OR 620(6),[2] f 1.

Oct. 9 910. Altaf Ali Khan to Mangal Khan. Acknowledges receipt of his letter along with the correspondence made between Surji Rao Ghatke and Bharatpur and its perusal by John Malcolm. Says that being the agent of Maharaja Holkar the addressee should make efforts to restore the mutual understanding and confidence between the two governments.

OR 620(7),[3] f 1.

Oct. 9 911. Rana Kirat Singh to Lord Lake. Expresses his problems regarding collection of revenue due to the presence of some miscreants in his region. Informs that he has deposited Rs. 85,000 to Col. Boer after collecting a little as revenue and rest raised as loan and advances. Further says that he has also paid an amount of Rs. 7,000 out of a demand of Rs. 1 lakh and expresses that the rest amount would be deposited as soon as it is arranged.

OR 621,[4] f 1; CR 23, pp. 475-76, no. 76(1).

Oct. 16 912. Rana Kirat Singh to John Malcolm. Expresses his helplessness in payment of the amount of revenue, etc., and maintenance of army due to disturbances created by some miscreants. Seeks help from the addressee to make the affairs sound and peaceful.

OR 622,[5] f 1, CR 23, pp. 478-81, no. 76(2).

[1]Copy enclosed with a letter from Malcolm, dated 25 September 1805.
[2]Ibid.
[3]Ibid.
[4]Ibid.
[5]Ibid.

Oct. 16 913. General Lake to Maharaja Jagat Singh (of Jaipur). Complains that the officials of the addressee are not following the terms of the treaty concluded between the two governments. Expresses his fear that the Governor-General may put this treaty in abeyance if the writer failed to check his men and made them follow the terms of the treaty. Further asks the writer to mobilize his forces against Jaswant Rao Holkar and supply essential provisions to the British army moving behind the said rebel. Dated 1 October 1805.

OR 623,[1] f 1; CR 23, pp. 494-501, no. 2.

Oct. 19 914. To the King (Shah Alam II). Informs the addressee that the writer (Sir George Barlow) has been appointed as Governor-General following the sudden demise of Lord Cornwallis and his immediate visit to the upper provinces for making necessary arrangements.

CI 41, pp. 284-87, no. 92; TI 51, pp. 259-61, no. 177; AI 20, p. 52.

Oct. 19 915. To Mirza Sulaiman Shukoh. To the same effect as the foregoing CI 92 and TI 177. Adds that the writer could not visit the addressee's house as he had to proceed to Benares without delay.

CI 41, pp. 289-91, no. 94; TI 51, pp. 259-61, no. 178, AI 20, p. 67.

Oct. 19 916. To Qutluq Sultan Begam. To the same effect as the foregoing CI 92 and TI 177.

CI 41, pp. 287-89, no. 93; TI 51, p. 261, no. 179.

Oct. 19 917. To Mirza Shigufta Bakht. To the same effect as the foregoing CI 92 and TI 177.

CI 41, pp. 287-89, no 93; TI 51, p. 261, no. 180; AI 20, p. 52.

Oct. 19 918. To Nawwab Wazir. To the same effect as the foregoing TI 177. Adds that the writer would see the addressee on his return from the tour.

CI 41, pp. 291-93, no. 95; TI 51, pp. 261-64, no. 181; AI 20, p. 69.

[1]Copy enclosed with a letter from Malcolm, dated 2 Ocatober 1805.

Oct. 19 919. To Bahu Begam. To the same effect as the foregoing CI 92 and TI 177.

CI 41, pp. 294-96, no. 96; TI 51, pp. 262-64, no. 182; AI 20, p. 46.

Oct. 19 920. To Shams al-Nisa Begam. To the same effect as the foregoing CI 92 and TI 177.

CI 41, pp. 294-96, no. 96; TI 51, pp. 262-64, no. 183; AI 20, p. 66.

Oct. 19 921. To the Peshwa. To the same effect as the foregoing CI 92 and TI 177.

CI 41, pp. 320-21, no. 106; TI 51, p. 264, no. 184; AI 20, p. 60.

Oct. 19 922. To the Raja of Mysore. To the same effect as CI 92 and TI 177.

CI 41, pp. 322-24, no. 107; TI 51, p. 264, no. 185; AI 20, p. 64.

Oct. 19 923. To Purnaiya, *diwan* of the Raja of Mysore. To the same effect as the foregoing CI 92 and TI 177.

CI 41, pp. 322-24, no. 107; TI 51, p. 264, no. 186; AI 20, p. 60.

Oct. 19 924. To Nawwab Azim al-Daulah of Carnatic. To the same effect as the foregoing C I 92 and TI 177.

CI 41, pp. 317-19, no 105A; TI 51, p. 264, no. 187; AI 20, p. 43.

Oct. 19 925. To the Raja of Nepal. To the same effect as the foregoing CI 92 and TI 177.

CI 41, pp. 314-15, no. 104; TI 51, p. 264, no. 180; AI 20, p. 63.

Oct. 19 926. To Raja Raghuji Bhonsla. To the same effect as the foregoing CI 92 and TI 177. Adds and assures that no change will occasion in the disposition of the British government towards the addressee.

CI 41, pp. 279-82, no. 90; TI 51, pp. 264-66, no. 189; AI 20, p. 62.

Oct. 19 927. To the Nizam. To the same effect as the foregoing CI 92 and TI 177.

CI 41, pp. 282-84, no. 91; TI 51, p. 266, no. 190; AI 20, p. 57.

Oct. 19 928. To Mir Alam. To the same effect as the foregoing CI 92 and TI 177.

CI 41, pp. 282-84, no. 91, TI 51, p. 266, no. 191.

Oct. 19 929. To Imdad Husain Khan. To the same effect as the foregoing CI no. 92 and TI 177.

CI 41, pp. 296-98. No. 97; TI 51, pp. 266-67, no. 192; AI 20, p. 50.

Oct. 19 930. To Umrao Begam. To the same effect as the CI 92 and TI 177.

CI 41, pp. 296-98, no. 97; TI 51, p. 267, no. 193; AI 20, p. 59.

Oct. 19 931. To Khiradmand Khan. To the same effect as the CI 92 and TI 177.

CI 41, pp. 296-98, no. 97; TI 51, p. 267, no. 194; AI 20, p. 53.

Oct. 19 932. To Nawwab Ahmad Ali Khan. To the same effect as the foregoing CI 92 and TI 177.

CI 41, pp. 296-98, no. 97; TI 51, p. 267, no. 195; AI 20, p. 45.

Oct. 19 933. To Nawwab Nasr Allah Khan (of Rampur). To the same effect as the foregoing CI 92 and TI 177.

CI 41, pp. 296-98, no. 97; TI 51, p. 267, no. 196; AI 20, p. 57.

Oct. 19 934. To Raja Udit Narayan Singh of Benares. To the same effect as the foregoing CI 92 and TI 177.

CI 41, pp. 305-08, no. 101; TI 51, p. 268, no. 197; AI 20, p. 64.

Oct. 19 935. To Bishambhar Pundit. To the same effect as the foregoing CI 92 and TI 177.

CI 41, pp. 306-08, no. 101; TI 50, p. 168, no. 198; AI 20, p. 47.

Oct. 19 936. To Zaib al-Nisa Begam (Begam Samru). To the same effect as the foregoing CI 92 and TI 177. Further says that the addressee's request for the permanent *jagir* presented before the late Governor-General will be considered with a higher degree of sincerity. Appreciates addressee's exertions for the preservation of peace and tranquillity in the Doab. Expect the same degree of fidelity from the addressee.

CI 41, pp. 311-13, no. 103; TI 51, pp. 268-70, no. 199; AI 20, p. 70.

Oct. 19 937. To Raja Ramraj of Travancore. To the same effect as the CI 92 and TI 177.

CI. 41, pp. 315-17, no. 105; TI 51, pp. 270-71, no. 200; AI 20, p. 63.

Oct. 19 938. To Daulat Rao Sindhia. Informs the addressee of the writer's having been appointed to the office of Governor-General following the death of Lord Cornwallis and also having full information of ongoing engagements between the addressee and Lord Lake for the settlement of some long depending issues. Assures to continue the said negotiation on the same principles as they have been started. Refers to Lord Lake for further communication.

CI 41, pp. 276-79, no. 89; TI 51, pp. 271-73, no. 201; AI 20, p. 49.

Oct. 19 939. To Nawwab Nasir al-Mulk (of Murshidabad). Informs the addressee of the writer's having been appointed Governor-General and his tour to Upper Provinces to settle the administration. Empowers Udney to look after the affairs at Presidency and to attend to the *nizamat* affairs during writer's absence.

CI 41, pp. 298-302, no. 98; TI 51, pp. 273-75, no. 202; AI 20, p. 59.

Oct. 19 940. To Munni Begam. To the same effect as the foregoing CI 98 and TI 202.

CI 41, pp. 298-302, no. 98; TI 51, p. 276, no. 203; AI 20, p. 55.

Oct. 19 941. To Babbu Begum. Informs that the writer has been appointed as Governor-General in place of the late Lord Cornwallis. Assures to promote the interest and prosperity of the *nizamat*.

CI 41, pp. 302-04, no. 99; TI 51, p. 276, no. 204; AI 20, p. 47.

Oct. 19 942. To Nawwab Nusrat Jang of Dacca. To the same effect as the foregoing CI 99 and TI 204.

CI 41, pp. 304-06, no. 100; TI 51, p. 276, no. 205; AI 20, p. 58.

Oct. 19 943. To Nawwab Dilawar Jang. To the same effect as the foregoing CI 99 and TI 205.

CI 41, pp. 304-06, no. 100; TI 51, p. 277, no. 206; AI 20, p. 49.

Oct. 19 944. To Amrit Rao. Informs the addressee that the writer has been appointed as Governor-General following the death of Lord Cornwallis. Further informs of the writer's intention to visit the Upper Provinces and his stay in Benares.

CI 41, pp. 308-10, no. 102.

Oct. 19 945. *Dastak-e-rahdari* issued by George Udney to Maulavi Sharafat Allah granting permission to the said *maulavi* to go to Anup Shahar from Calcutta along with some boxes of goods.

CI 41, pp. 463-64, no. 200.

Oct. 19 946. From the Nizam (of Hyderabad). Acknowledges receipt of the Governor-General's letter and the proposals regarding the plan of a *silahdar*, his establishment and his full approbation.

OR 624,[1] *ff 2; TR 51A, pp. 700-03, no. 273; CR 23, pp. 527-30, no. 12; AR 20, p. 27.*

Oct. 22 947. From Mir Alam. To the same effect as the foregoing OR 624.

OR 625[2]*, ff 2, WS; CR 23, pp. 530-33, no. 13; TR 51A, p. 703, no. 274; AR 20, p. 22.*

Oct. 23 948. Raja Ranjit Singh to Lord Lake. Expresses thanks for the grant of the fort of Deig to the writer.

OR 626/1,[3] *f 1; CR 23, pp. 518-19, no. 8.*

Oct. 23 949. Raja Ranjit Singh to Col. Malcolm. To the same effect as the foregoing OR 626/1.

OR 626/2,[4] *f 1; CR 23, pp. 520-21, no. 9.*

Oct. 25 950. Nawwab Ahmad Bakhsh Khan (of Alwar) to the Company's government. Agrees to pay a *peshkash* of Rs. 1 lakh

[1]Enclosed with a letter from the Acting Resident at Hyderabad, dated 28 September 1805.

[2]Ibid.

[3]Enclosed with a letter from Col. Malcolm, dated 15 October 1805.

[4]Ibid.

in return of the grant of Qila Kishangarh with some more *pargana* and *talluqas* in the vicinity. Dated 21 *Rajab,* 1220 AH (3 October 1805).

OR 627, f 1; CR 23, pp. 521-22, no. 10.

Oct. 25 951. *Dastak-i-rahdari* issued by George Udney to Mirza Ramazan Ali Khan to go to Lucknow from Calcutta along with his attendants and goods.

CI 41, p. 464, no. 201).

Oct. 25 952. *Dastak-i-Rahdari* issued by Udney to Bhagwant Rao, *wakil* of Daulat Rao Sindhia granting permission to the said *wakil* to go to Benares from Calcutta.

CI 41, p. 464, no. 202.

Oct. 25 953. Nawwab Wazir of Awadh to George Barlow. Expresses grief on the sad demise of Lord Cornwallis. Dated 7 October 1805.

OR 628,[1] *f 1, WS; CR 23, pp. 533-35, no. 14; TR 51A, p. 704, no. 275; AR 20, p. 41.*

Oct. 26 954. From Muin al-Mulk Dilawar Jang. Expresses anxiety over the Governor-General's ill health and prays for his quick recovery. Dated 9 October 1805.

OR 629, f 1, WS; CR 23, pp. 517-18, no. 8; TR 51A, p. 704, no. 276; AR 20, p. 9.

Oct. 26 955. Muin al-Mulk Dilawar Jang to Udney. Complementary on the addressee's appointment as Vice-President-in-Council. Dated 26 October 1805.

OR 630, f 1, WS; TR 51A, pp. 704-05, no. 277; AR 20, p. 9.

Oct. 28 956. Nawwab Khan Jahan Khan to Udney. Complements the addressee on his appointment as Vice-President-in-Council. Dated 25 October 1805.

OR 631, f 1; TR 51A, p. 705, no. 278; AR 20, p. 19.

Oct. 28 957. From the Peshwa. Communicating the appointment of Hari Udhav as writer's *wakil* in the addressee's Presidency.

OR 632, WS, f 1; TR 51A, pp. 705-07, no. 279; AR 20, p. 30.

[1]Enclosed with a letter from the Agent at Lucknow, dated 20 October 1805.

Oct. 29 958. Birja and Ganga Ram from the camp of Holkar to the Resident at Delhi. Reports about the movement of Narayan Rao, *harkarah* from Kanod to Loharo. Further furnishes information regarding presence of 50 camels loaded with merchandise at Garhi. It is also learnt that the British foreces have diverted attention towards the area in report.

OR 633,[1] f 1.

Oct. 29 959. Newswriter from the court of Shah Shuja al-Mulk (of Kabul) to the Resident at Delhi. Reports about the arrival of Mir Afzal Khan in the camp of Shah Shuja from Khurasan and appointment of Akram Khan as *haakim* (administrator) of Khashmir, etc., etc. Dated 27 *Jumada II*, 1220 AH (22 September 1805).

OR 634,[2] f 1.

Oct. 30 960. Statements of Mirza Ali Beg, Hasan Ali Beg, Mir Abbas, Haider Ali, Niaz Ali, Ahsan Allah, Ghulam Ashraf recorded before A. Seton the Agent to the Governor-General at Bareilly after the arrest of the first four persons mentioned above under the suspicion of being the men of Jaswant Rao Holkar; order of A. Seton to send these papers to Col. Collins at Lucknow for further action and orders.

OR 635, ff 14; CR 23, pp. 541-83, no. 16.

Oct. 30 961. Amir Khan to Rai Ratan Chand, the *wakil* of Nawwab Wazir. Refers to the previous correspondence held between Nawwab Wazir and Jaswant Rao Holkar and suggests resumption of the old friendly relation between the two states as per agreement codified by late Hadi Beg Khan. Dated 21 October 1805.

OR 636/1,[3] f 1; CR 23, pp. 594-96, no. 17(6).

Oct. 30 962. Col. Collins to Nawwab Wazir. Refers to the letter of Amir Khan, the *wakil* of the addressee and expresses his suspicion that there may be some secret design framed by them against the Company's government. Requests the addressee to present Rai Ratan Chand before the Governor-General for clarifications. Dated 25 October 1805.

OR 636/2,[4] f 1; CR 23, pp. 596-97, no. 17(7).

[1]Enclosure to a letter from the Resident at Delhi, dated 25 October 1805.

[2]Ibid.

[3]Ibid.

[4]Enclosure to a letter from the Resident at Lucknow, dated 25 October 1805. (Also see OR 811, 2 folio.)

Oct. 30. 963. Col. Collins to Nawwab Wazir. Acknowledges receipt of addressee's letter dated 27 October 1805. Expresses surprise that how it may be accepted that the relations of the two states are under cloud and opines that such incidents have to be checked in future. Dated 27 October 1805.

OR 636/3,[1] *f 1, CR 23, pp. 597-99, no. 17(8).*

Oct. 30 964. Col. Collins to Nawwab Wazir. To the same effect as the previous OR 636/3.[2]

OR 636/4, f 1; CR 23, pp. 597-99, no. 17(8).

Oct. 30 965. Intelligence from the newswriter at Bareilly. Reports about the imprisonment of Mirza Ali with some others along some objectionable goods and one letter from Amir Khan addressed to Rai Ratan Chand. Further reports that this letter and other relevant papers and reports are supposed to be sent to the Resident at Lucknow for further investigation, etc.

OR 637,[3] *f 1; CR 23, pp. 619-21, no. 1(3); TR 51A, pp. 719-21, no. 284; AR 20, p. 15.*

Oct. 30. 966. Nawwab Wazir to Col. Collins. States that the allegations levelled against Rai Ratan chand are baseless and require proper investigation to unearth the truth. Dated 2 *Shaban*, 1220 AH (29 October 1805).

OR 759, f 1.

Oct. -- 967. Article 8 (of the project between the Company and Daulat Rao Sindhia). It says that during the period of a war the forts of the region of Jaswant Rao Holkar and the region of Tonk and Rampura would come in the control of Daulat Rao Sindhia.

OR 639, f 1; CR 23, pp. 493-94, no. 1.

Oct. -- 968. From Sunder Singh. Expresses his misery and troubles caused due to unemployment. Requests for some favours.

OR 640, f 1.

Oct. -- 969. From Haji Begam, wife of late Mirza Asad Allah. Requests for the continuation of Rs. 75 per month granted to her late husband as pension.

OR 641, f 1, WS.

[1]Enclosure to a letter from the Resident at Lucknow, dated 27 October 1805.

[2]Copy enclosed with a letter from the Resident at Lucknow, dated 27 October 1805.

[3]Ibid. (Also see OR 811, folio 2.)

Oct. -- 970. Alam Bahadur to the Nizam. Expresses his sincerity and loyalty towards Nizam. Dated 1 October, 1805.

OR 642,[1] *f 1; CR 23, pp. 509-11, no. 5(1).*

Oct. -- 971. Munshi Mir Aziz Allah to the Nizam. Expresses his sincerity and loyalty towards Nizam. Dated 1 October 1805.

OR 643,[2] *f 1; CR 23, pp. 511-13, no. 5(2).*

Oct. -- 972. Capt. Dalston to officers of the Company. Directs the *amils*, *ziladars*, *kotwals*, *zamindars,* etc., of the Ceded Provinces to cooperate with the servants and *harkaras* of *huzoor* (?) who are supposed to visit the region in order to purchase goats and sheeps for the use of European army serving under Lord Lake.

OR 644, f 1, WS; CR 23, p. 516, no. 7; TR 51A, pp. 691-92, no. 271; AR 20, p. 9.

Oct. -- 973. Balaji Kanju to General Wallace. Acknowledges receipt of addressee's letter and informs about his (writer) visit of Poona in order to set the relations of the Company with Srimant Peshwa at behest of Sindhia and Holkar. Further the writer wants to see the addressee at Burhanpur to discuss the matter in detail before leaving for Poona.

OR 645(1),[3] *f 1; CR 23, pp. 522-24, no. 11(1).*

Oct. -- 974. General Wallace to Balaji Kanju and Aswant Rao Ghorpade. Asks the addressee not to cross over river Tapti at present and wait for further orders.

OR 645(2),[4] *f 1; CR 23, pp. 524-25, no. 11(2).*

Oct. -- 975. (i) Abbas Quli Khan (the newswriter at Kabul) to the Resident at Delhi. Informs about the receipt of Holkar's letters regarding bearing of all expenditure incurred on the maintenance of the king's army; states that the *munshi* of the king has been asked to dispatch letters to Raja Ranjit Singh, Amir Khan and others after consulting ther *wazir* of Kabul.

[1]Copy enclosure to a letter from the Acting Resident at Hyderabad, dated 4 October 1805.

[2]Ibid., dated 1 October 1805.

[3]Copy enclosure to a letter from the Acting Resident at Poona, dated 17 October 1805.

[4]Ibid., dated 17 October 1805.

Also informs about the tragic death of Jahandad Khan Durrani in prison.

(ii) Furnishes a detailed account of the expenditure of the troops proposed by Holkar and says that if these terms are accepted by him then a force of 50,000 troops will march from here to assist him.

OR 646,[1] *f 1.*

Oct. -- 976. Jangi Khan to A. Seton, Agent to Governor-General, at Bareilly. Requests for the grant of *parganas* Chaumahla, Sitagarh Khas and Midnapur along with three other villages as *jagir-i-istamrari* instead of annual cash salary (*wajh-e-saliana*) which he has been getting from Company's government.

OR 647,[2] *f 1; CR 23, pp. 599-600, no. 18.*

Oct. -- 977. Intelligence from the newswriter at Lahore. Informs about the defeat of Ahmad Khan a *zamindar* at the hands of Raja Ranjit Singh of Lahore. Dated 14 October 1805.

OR 648, f 1.

Oct. -- 978. Intelligence report from Muhammad Abbas Khan, the newswriter at the court of Shah Shuja al-Mulk, the king of Kabul to Nasir al-Daulah. Informs that the *wazir* has set out for Kabul and until he arrives at Kabul no news could be sent. Further says that the *wakil* of Holkar, Abd Allah Khan does not have an influence at the court of Kabul. Also says that letter from Nawwab Wazir in the names of Governor-General and General Lake is essential for maintaining the relations of friendship between the two states. Dated 17 *Jumada II*, 1220 AH (12 September 1805).

OR 649 (1), f 1.

Oct. -- 979. Intelligence from the newswriter at the court of Shah Shuja al-Mulk of Kabul. Informs of the arrival of Sultan Amir Haider of Bukhara and refers to the fabulous *nazr* made to him. Also informs of the arrival of Shah Zaman Khan from Qandhar to Kabul. Dated 17 *Jumada II*, 1220 AH (12 September 1805).

OR 649 (2), f 1.

Oct. -- 980. Intelligence from the newswriter at the court of Raja Sahib Singh.

(i) Informs about the desire of Maharaja Sahib Singh to

[1]Enclosed with a letter from Seton, dated 31 October 1805.

[2]Ibid.

maintain and strengthen friendship relation with the Company and Holkar.

(ii) Gives intelligence about arrival of Holkar at Jind and dispatch of the *wakil* of Maharaja Sahib Singh to meet Holkar in his camp.

(iii) Reports about the arrival of Bhakka Singh from Patiala for a consultation with Rani Khem Kanwar, etc., etc. Dated 9 October 1805.

OR 650,[1] f 1.

Oct. -- 981. Intelligence from the newswriter at the court of Maharaja Sahib Singh of Patiala to Col. Ochterlony.

(i) Reports about the arrival of Jaswant Rao Holkar at the head of 50,000-60,000 troops near Patiala and his endeavours to placate Maharaja of Patiala against the Company's government.

(ii) Reports about the movements of British high officials in various directions to check the Maratha's movements against the Company's government.

Dated 15 *Rajab,* 1220 AH (9 October 1805).

OR 651,[2] f 1.

Oct. -- 982. Shariat Allah to the Deputy Persian Secretary to Government. Requests for a *dastak-i-rahdari* to travel from Calcutta to Anup Shahar along with his provisions and belongings.

OR 652, f 1.

Oct. -- 983. Intelligence from the newswriter at the court of Maharaja Sahib Singh of Patiala to Col. Ochterlony. Reports about the endeavours being done by Jaswant Rao Holkar to win over support of Sikh chiefs against the Company's government. Dated 22 *Rajab*, 1220 AH (16 October 1805).

OR 653,[3] f 1.

Oct. 984. Ramazan Ali Khan to Deputy Persian Secretary to Government. Requests for a *dastak-i-rahdari* to travel from Calcutta to Lucknow along with his belongings. Dated 29 *Rajab* 1220 AH (23 October 1805).

OR 654, WS, f 1.

Oct. -- 985. Intelligence from the newswriter at the court of Raja

[1]Enclosed with a letter from Col. Ochterlony, dated 10 October 1805.

[2]Ibid.

[3]Ibid.

Sahib Singh of Patiala to Col. Ochterlony. Reports about the endeavours of Jaswant Rao Holkar in respect of winning over the Raja of Patiala to his side against the British forces. Gives detailed account of the various meetings and consultations at various levels in this regard. Dated 23 *Rajab*, 1220 AH (17 October 1805).

OR 655,[1] *f 1.*

Oct. -- 986. From . . . (?). Complementary, stresses upon the writer's security and integrity towards the Company's government.

CR 23, pp. 600-05, no. 19.

Nov. 1 987. Nawwab Wazir to Col. Collins. States that all charges levelled against Rai Ratan Chand, the employee of the writer is wrong and baseless. Requests to investigate the matter to find the truth. Dated 26 October 1805.

OR 656,[2] *f 1; CR 23, pp. 591-93, no. 17(5).*

Nov. 1 988. From Nawwab Wazir. Expresses his loyalty towards the Company's government and states that the allegations made against his employee (Rai Ratan Chand) are all wrong and baseless. Requests for a proper investigation in the matter to find out the truth. Dated 26 October 1805.

OR 657,[3] *f 1; CR 23, pp. 621-23, no. 1(4).*

Nov. 1 989. Wazir Mal to John Monkton. Requests for a *dastak-i-rahdari* to travel from Calcutta to Azimabad and Gaya by waterways on the occasion of the marriage of his son along with some goods. Dated 1 November 1805.

OR 658, f 1.

Nov. 1 990. Kunj Lalji, servant of Raja of Jaipur to Monkton. Requests for a *destak-i-rahdari* to travel from Gaya to Jainagar (Jaipur) along with a few men, horses and some goods. Dated 28 October 1805.

OR 659, f 1.

Nov. 1 991. Udney, the Vice-President-in-Council to Kunj Lal, employee of Raja Jai Singh of Jaipur. Grants a *dastak-i-rahdari* to the address to travel from Gaya to Jainagar.

CI 41, p. 467, no. 205.

Nov. 1 992. Udney, the Vice-President-in-Council to Wazir Mal, *wakil*

[1]Enclosed with a letter from Col. Ochterlony, dated 23 October 1805.
[2]Enclosed with a letter from the Resident at Lucknow, dated 27 October 1805.
[3]Ibid.

of Harak Chand Jagat Seth of Murshidabad. Grants a *dastak* to the addressee to travel from Calcutta to Azimabad and Gaya and back.

CI 41, p. 468, no. 206.

Nov. 1 993. To Nawwab Wazir. In reply to the addressee's letter dated 30 October 1805 in respect of an intercepted letter of Amir Khan addressed to Rai Ratan Chand (the employee of the addressee) implicating the addressee in an alleged correspondence with the enemy. Assures that the writer as well as Col. Collins has no longer any doubts for the addressee's integrity.

CI. 42, pp. 324-28, no. 108; TI 51, pp. 277-81, no. 207.

Nov. 1 994. Udney, the Vice-President-in-Council to Nawwab Dilawar Jang of Murshidabad. Complementary in reply to the addressee's congratulatory letter on the writer's appointment as the Vice-President-in-Council and Deputy Governor of Fort William.

CI 42, pp. 320-21, no. 206; TI 51, p. 281, no. 208.

Nov. 1 995. Udney, the Vice-President-in-Council to Nawwab Khan Jahan Khan. Complementary in reply to the addressee's letter of congratulations on the eve of writer's appointment as the Vice-President-in-Council.

CI. 42, pp. 321-22, no. 207; TI 51, p. 281, no. 209.

Nov. 2 996. To Nawwab Wazir. In reply to the addressee's letter of condolence on the death of Marquess Cornwallis.

CI 42, pp. 328-31, no. 109; TI 51, p. 282, no. 210.

Nov. 2 997. From Jasarat Allah, the servant of Maharaja of Nepal. Informs about the proposed pilgrimage of Shri Kishan Pandit, the *guru* of the said Maharaja to Ganges for a holy dip along with 100 attendants and disciples. Requests for permission to carry arms with them due to security reasons during the journey. Further requests for deployment of four or five *chaprasis* for the same as mentioned above.

OR 660, f 1; TR 51A, p. 713, no. 281, AR 20.

Nov. 5 998. From Raja Narendergir. Complementary.

OR 661,[1] f 1; CR 23, pp. 636-37, no. 210; TR 51A, p. 2, no. 285; AR 20, p. 30.

[1]Enclosed with a letter from the Judge at Banda, dated 2 November 1805.

Nov. 5 999. From Kunwar Kanchangir. Complementary.

OR 662,[1] *WS, f 1; CR 23, pp. 637-38, no. 5; TR 51A, p. 722, no. 285; AR 20, p. 30.*

Nov. 5 1000. Intelligence from the newswriter at the *deorhi* of Raja Sahib Singh of Patiala from Saifabad to Col. Ochterlony. Narrates the circumstances responsible for the entry of Jaswant Rao Holkar and explains about the efforts being made by Raja Sabib Singh (of Patiala) his *diwan* and other concerned persons for the evacuation of Holkar from Patiala. Dated 23 October 1805.

OR 663(a),[2] *f 1.*

Nov. 5 1001. Intelligence from the newswriter at the court of Raja Sahib Singh (of Patiala) from Saifabad to Col. Ochterlony. Informs about the meeting held between the representatives of Jaswant Rao Holkar and the Maharaja of Patiala, etc.

OR 663(b),[3] *f 1.*

Nov. 5 1002. Intelligence from the newswriter at the *deorhi* of Maharaja Sabib Singh of Patiala in Saifabad. Describes the meeting held between Maharaja of Patiala and Jaswant Rao Holkar. Dated 1 *Shaban* 1220 AH (25 October 1805).

OR 664,[4] *f 1.*

Nov. 7 1003. Nawwab Amir al-Daulah Amir Khan to Rai Ratan Chand. Refers to the previons correspondence with the addressee and states that Mirza Ali is being sent to see the addressee to discuss the matters referred to by Nawwab *wazir* in order to marginalize the disturbing elements and establish the control of the Nawwab (Wazir) in the region of Bengal.

OR 665(a),[5] *f 1; CR 23, pp. 615-17, no. 1(1).*

Nov. 7 1004. Co. Collins to Nawwab *Wazir al-Mamalik.* States that the copy of the letter of Amir Khan addressed to Rai Ratan Chand, the servant of the addressee is being sent through Mirza Muhammad Baqar Munshi for the addressee's perusal which provides a clear idea of the secret contacts of Amir Khan and Rai Ratan Chand. Further asks the addressee to investigate

[1]Enclosed with a letter from the Judge at Banda, dated 2 November 1805.
[2]Ibid., dated 28 October 1805.
[3]Enclosed with a letter from the Judge at Delhi, dated 28 October 1805.
[4]Ibid.
[5]Enclosure to a letter from the Resident at Lucknow, dated 26 October 1805.

into the matter. Dated 25 October 1805.

OR 665(b),[1] *f 1; CR 23, pp. 617-18, no. 1(2).*

Nov. 7 1005. Aman Beg to Col. Collins. Denies the charges levelled against his sons Madad Ali and Mirza Ali regarding having contacts with Amir Khan and that they had bearing a letter of Amir Khan addressed to Rai Ratan Chand of Lucknow. Requests for the investigation of the matter to find out the reality. Dated 1 November 1805.

OR 665(c), [2] *f 1; CR 23, pp. 626-28, no. 1(6).*

Nov. 7 1006. Aman Beg to Col. Collins. To the same effect as the foregoing OR 665(c).

OR 665[3] *(d), f 1; CR 23, pp. 626-28, no. 1(6).*

Nov. 7 1007. From Raja Sahib Singh of Patiala. Expresses extreme pleasure and satisfaction on the arrival of the Governor-General of Calcutta to assure the charges of the Company's government.

OR 666,[4] *f 1, WS, CR 23, pp. 643-45, no. 7; TR 51A, p. 722, no. 286, AR 20, p. 37).*

Nov. 8 1008. From Nawwab Wazir. In reply to the addressee's letter informing the death of Marquess Cornwallis. Expresses his deep concern on the said melancholy. Further expresses satisfaction on the occasion of sir George Barlow's succession to the government.

OR 667,[5] *ff 2, WS; CR 23, pp. 650-53, no. 9; TR 51A, pp. 724-25, no. 288; AR 20, p. 41.*

Nov. 8 1009. Shams al-Nisa Begam to Sir George Barlow. In reply to the addressee's communication bearing the news of the death of Marquess cornwallis expresses deep concerns on the said melancholy and satisfaction an the succession of the addressee to the government. Dated 6 *Shaban* 1220 AH (30 October 1805).

OR 668,[6] *WS, WC, f 1; CR 23, pp. 653-55, no. 10; TR 51, p. 725, no. 289; AR 20, p. 38.*

[1]Enclosure to a letter from the Resident at Lucknow, dated 26 October 1805.
[2]Ibid., dated 5 November 1805.
[3]Ibid., dated 5 November 1805.
[4]Ibid., dated 2 November 1805.
[5]Ibid., dated 5 November 1805.
[6]Ibid., dated 5 November 1805.

Nov. 8 1010. From Bahu Begam. Expresses deep sorrow over the death of Marquess Cornwallis and satisfaction over the succession of the addressee (Sir George Barlow) to the Governor-Generalship. Dated 6 *Shaban* 1220 AH (30 October 1805).

OR 669,[1] *WS, WC, f 1; CR 23, pp. 655-57, no. 11; TR 51A, pp. 725-26, no. 290; AR 20, p. 5.*

Nov. 8 1011. From Mirza Sikandar Shukoh. States of his being deprived of the replies of his two letters addressed to Marquess Wellesley and Cornwallis. Expresses deep concerns over the demise of Lord Cornwallis. Hopes his distress will be removed by the sincere favour of the addressee.

OR 670,[2] *WS, f 1; CR 23, pp. 645-49, no. 8; TR 51A, pp. 726-28, no. 291; AR 20, p. 24.*

Nov. 9 1012. From Qutluq Sultan Begam. In reply to the addressee's (Sir George Barlow) letter notifying the death of Lord Cornwallis. Expresses deep sorrow of the sad demise of Lord Cornwallis and expresses satisfaction over the succession of the addressee to the Governor-Generalship of the Company's government.

OR 671, WS, f 1; CR 23, pp. 670-74, no. 14; TR 51 A, p. 729, no. 292; AR 20, p. 20.

Nov. 9 1013. From Mirza Shigufta Bakht. In reply to the addressee's (Sir George Barlow) letter notifying the death of Lord Cornwallis. Expresses sorrow on the sad demise of Lord Cornwallis and satisfaction on addressee's succession to the government. Also expresses hopes of meeting the addressee on his return from Hindustan.

OR 672,[3] *WS, f 1; CR 23, pp. 665-70, no. 13; TR 51A, p. 729, no. 293; AR 20, p. 25.*

Nov. 9 1014. From Vir Rajender Vodyar, the Raja of Coorg. Recounts his long services to Company's government under the patronship of Lord Wellesley and the addressee (Lord Cornwallis) particularly in regard to subjugation and crushing of Tipu Sultan and consequently receiving awards and approbations at various occasion. Further expect all favours

[1]Enclosure to a letter from the Resident at Lucknow, dated 31 October 1805.
[2]Ibid.
[3]Enclosed with a letter from the Resident at Benares, dated November 1805.

from the Company's government under the Governor-Generalship of the addressee.

OR 673,[1] WS, f 1; CR 23, pp. 657-65, no. 12; TR 51A, pp. 759-63, no. 308.

Nov. 11 1015. Bishambhar Pandit to Udney, the Vice-President-in-Council. Complementary on the appointment of the addressee to the post of Vice President-in-Council.

OR 674, WS, f 1; TR 51A, pp. 729-30, no. 294; AR 20, p. 6.

Nov. 11 1016. Udney to Mirza Ramazan Ali Khan. Grants exemption from the duty on the goods carried by the addressee for Nawwab Wazir.

CI 41, pp. 469, no. 207.

Nov. 11 1017. The Vice-President-in-Council to Bishambhar Pandit. In reply to the addressee's complementary letter and expresses thanks for the presents of sugar and rose water.

CI 41, p. 70, no. 208; TI 51, p. 282, no. 211; AI 20, p. 47.

Nov. 12 1018. From Mirza Sulaiman Shukoh in reply to the addressee's (Sir George Barlow) letter notifying the death of Lord Cornwallis. Expresses deep grief on the death of Lord Cornwallis and expresses satisfaction on the succession of the addresse to the seat of Governor-General.

OR 675,[2] WS, f 1; CR 23, pp. 674-78, no. 15; TR 51A, pp. 730-32, no. 295; AR 20, p. 23.

Nov. 13 1019. Raja Sahib Singh of Patiala to Col. Collins. Expresses his (writer's) sincerity and faithfulness towards the Company's government and hopes for a favourable treatment from the Company's administration. Also informs about the arrival of Jaswant Rao Holkar along with a force of 50,000-60,000 troops on the frontiers of writer's state but expresses his inability to enquire that on whose behest the said Holkar has mobilized his forces.

OR 676,[3] ff 2; CR 23, pp. 628-35, no. 2 and pp. 680-86, no. 17.

[1]Enclosed with a letter from the Acting Resident at Mysore, dated 7 October 1805 (see OR 690).

[2]Ibid.

[3]Ibid.

Nov. 13 1020. From the Peshwa. Acknowledges the receipt of addressee's letter informing about the intention of the addressee to return to Europe. Also complains against the disobedience of the chiefs of the state and claims that they should be severely administrated and brought back to their duties.

OR 677,[1] f 1; CR 23, pp. 689-92, no. 19; TR 51A, pp. 732-34, no. 296; AR 20, p. 31.

Nov. 13 1021. From the Peshwa. To the same effect as the foregoing OR 677.

OR 678,[2] f 1; CR 23, pp. 693-95, no. 20; TR 51A, pp. 735-37, no. 297; AR 20, p. 31.

Nov. 13 1022. To Raja Sabib Singh of Patiala. Informs the addressee about the sad demise of Lord Cornwallis and assures of the friendly and favourable relation with the addressee and other native states.

CI 41, pp. 331-34, no. 110; TI 51, pp. 284-86, no. 213; AI 20, p. 65.

Nov. 13 1023. To Raja Sahib Singh (of Patiala). In reply to addressee's letter addressed to deceased Lord Cornwallis informs about the sad demise of Lord Cornwallis and succession of the writer to the post of Governor-General. Further assures of the continuation of friendly relation between the two states and appreciates the addressee's sense of loyalty and sincerity towards the Compay's government.

CI 41, pp. 331-34, no. 110; TI 51, pp. 284-86, no. 213; AI 20, p. 65.

Nov. 13 1024. The Vice-President in Council to the Raja of Cooch Behar. In reply to the addressee's letter to Lord Cornwallis regarding a case forwarded to the provincial court of appeal at Murshidabad following a complaint received from one Ojhanand Gusain. Asks the addressee to act according to the decision delivered by the said court. For further details *wakil* Ras Behari may be referred.

CI 41, pp. 334-36, no. 11; TI 51, no. 212; AI 20, p. 65.

Nov. 13 1025. Vice-President George Udney to Raja Hirender Narayan,

[1]Enclosed with a letter from the Acting Resident at Lucknow, dated 8 November 1805.

[2]Enclosed with a letter from the Acting Resident at Poona, dated 11 November 1805.

the Raja of Cooch Behar. In reply to the letter received from the addressee regading a case forwarded to the provincial court of appeal at Murshidabad by a person called Ojhanand Gusain against the addressee.

CI 41, pp. 334-36; no. 111; TI 51, pp. 282-84, no. 212; AR 20, p. 65.

Nov. 14 1026. Daulat al-Nisa Begam to Pattle. Explains her distress and embarrassed situation to which she has been reduced through Nawwab Dilawar Jang in retaining her pension and other claims which was awarded to her by the Company's government.

OR 679,[1] f 1; CR 23, pp. 717-20, no. 22; TR 51A, pp. 737-40, no. 298; AR 20, p. 10.

Nov. 14 1027. To Raja Narindergir (of Sikandra, Kanpur). Assures the addressee of the usual friendly relations between the two states as it has been during the Governor-Generalship of late Cornwallis.

CI 41, pp. 470-71, no. 209.

Nov. 14 1028. To Kunwar Kanchangir (of Sikandra). To the same effect as the foregoing.

CI 41, pp. 471-72, no. 210.

Nov. 14 1029. To Raja Udit Narayan. Expresses concern on the sad demise of Rani Gulab Kanwar, the grandmother of the addressee.

CI 41, pp. 472 73, no. 211.

Nov. 14 1030. To Raja Ranjit Singh (of Bharatpur). Expresses deep concern on the sad demise of Marquess Cornwallis and assures of the continuation of the prevailing friendly relation between the two states under the writer's governance.

CI 41, pp. 273-75, no. 212.

Nov. 14 1031. To Almas Ali Khan. In reply to addressee's letter of condolence on the sad demise of Lord Cornwallis. Assures the addressee of the continuation of the prevailing friendly relation between the two states under the writer's governance.

CI 41, pp. 275-77, no. 213.

Nov. 14 1032. George Udney, the Vice-President-in-Council to Nawwab Nasir al-Mulk. Expresses deep concern on the ill

[1]Enclosed with a letter from the Superintendent of Nizam to the Deputy Persian Secretary, dated 11 November 1805.

health of the addressee and prays for his early recovery.

CI 11, pp. 176-77, no. 214.

Nov. 15 1033. From Amat al-Zahra (Bahu Begam). In reply to Sir George Barlow's letter announcing the death of Marquess Cornwallis. Expresses her satisfaction on Sir George Barlow's succession to the seat of Governor-General.

OR 680,[1] *WS, f 1; CR 23, pp. 743-45, no. 25; TR 51A, p. 740, no. 249; AR 20, p. 5.*

Nov. 15 1034. From Nawwab Muhabbat Khan. Congratulatory on the eve of Sir George Barlow's succession to the government.

OR 681,[2] *WS, f 1; CR 23, pp. 746-48, no. 27; TR 51A, p. 815, no. 344.*

Nov. 15 1035. Maharaja Sahib Singh (of Patiala) to Col. Collins. To the same effect as the foregoing OR 676.

OR 682,[3] *f 1.*

Nov. 15 1036. From Almas Ali Khan (of Lucknow). Congratulatory on Sir George Barlow's appointment to the government.

OR 735,[4] *WS, f 1; CR 23, pp. 748-49, no. 28; TR 51A, p. 815, no. 341; AR 20, p. 4.*

Nov. 15 1037. From Tahsin Ali Khan (of Lucknow). Congratulatory on the occasion of the addressee's appointment to the government.

OR 737, WS, f 1, f 1; CR 23, pp. 745-46, no. 26; TR 51A, p. 515, no. 345; AR 20, p. 40.

Nov. 16 1038. From Imdad Husain Khan (of Farrukhabad). In reply to the letter of Sir George Barlow announcing the death of Marquess Cornwallis. Expresses deep concern on the sad demise and satisfaction on the succession of Sir George Barlow to the government.

OR 683, WS, f 1; CR 23, pp. 750-52, no. 29; TR 51A, pp. 740-41; no. 300; AR 20, p. 11.

Nov. 16 1039. From Bi Sahib Bakhsh (Wife of Wazir Ali). States that the writer is residing at Munger along with her son Mirza

[1]Enclosed with a letter from the Resident at Lucknow, dated 12 November 1805.

[2]Ibid., dated 12 November 1805.

[3]Ibid., dated 2 November 1805.

[4]Ibid., dated 12 November 1805.

Muhammad Ali in accordance with the order of the government. Expresses that the allowance granted to her for maintenance is extremely inadequate. Requests for an augmentation in the amount of allowance commensurate to her expenditure, etc.

OR 684, f 1; CR 23, pp. 752-53, no. 30; TR 51A, pp. 741-42, no. 301; AR 20, p. 39.

Nov. 16 1040. From Madar al-Daulah. Complains that the *amil* of Khairabad is planning to establish a new Ganj and erect his standard (*jhanda*) in the *jagir* of the petitioner which may cause some new problems for the petitioner as the said *jagir* is the only means of subsistence since the time of Nawwab Asaf Jah.

OR 685,[1] WS, f 1; CR 23, pp. 687-89, no. 18; TR 51A, pp. 242-43, no. 302; AR 20, p. 24.

Nov. 16 1041. From Umrao Begam. In reply to Sir George Barlow's letter notifying the death of Marquess Cornwallis. Expresses deep concern on the death of Marquess Cornwallis and satisfaction on the addressee's succession to the government.

OR 686, WS, f 1; CR 23, pp. 753-56; TR 51A, p. 744, no. 303; AR 20, p. 30.

Nov. 17 1042. To Aqa Muhammad Nabi Khan, the *elchi* (ambassador) of the king of Iran (Persia). Expresses pleasure on the intelligence that the addressee has left Bushehr (Bushire) for Calcutta but feels sorry for breaking the journey in Bombay due to oceanic storm. Suggests that the addressee should undertake the rest of the journey through land route to reach Calcutta.

CI 41, pp. 342-46, no 113; AI 20, p. 44.

Nov. 18 1043. From Raja Udit Narayan Singh (of Benares). To the Same effect as the OR 686.

OR 687,[2] f 1; CR 23, pp. 765-67, no. 34; TR 51A, p. 744, no. 304; AR 20, p. 33.

Nov. 18 1044. From Nawwab Wazir. In reply to the addressee's letter in regard to the supposed correspondence between Amir Khan and Rai Ratan Chand at one hand and the addressee and the said Khan on the other.

OR 688, WS, ff 2; CR 23, pp. 768-74, no. 36; TR 51A, pp. 753-58, no. 307; AR 20, p. 41.

[1]Enclosed with a letter from the Resident at Lucknow, dated 12 November 1805.

[2]Enclosed with a letter from the Acting Agent at Benares, 16 November 1805.

Nov. 18 1045. From Nawwab Wazir. To the same effect as the foregoing OR 688.

OR 689,[1] *f 1.*

Nov. 18 1046. From Raja Vir Rajinder Vodyar of Coorg. Expresses joy on the arrival of Marquess Cornwallis in India; recounts his long services rendered to the Hon'ble Company and hopes for favourable treatment from the Governor-General.

OR 690, WS, f 1; CR 23, pp. 756-63, no. 32; TR 51A, pp. 759-763, no. 308; AR 20, p. 34.

Nov. 18 1047. Nasir al-Mulk to George Udney, the Vice-President-in-Council in reply to addressee's letter expressing concern to the writer's indisposition. Informs of the writer's recovery from the illness.

OR 691, WS, f 1; CR 23, pp. 763-65, no. 33; TR 51A, pp. 763-64; no. 309; AR 20, p. 29.

Nov. 18 1048. From Nawwab Nusrat Jang of Dacca. Communicates his thanks to the Governor-General for his letter dated 20 September regarding disposal of the pension enjoyed by late Mir Ali and Mirza Ghulam Haider. Requests that the same may be continued in the name of Saiyid al-Nisa Begam, the sister of the deceased Mir Ali as Khadija Begam, successor of late Mir Ali has gone astray and no trace of her is found.

OR 693, WS, f 1; CR 51A, pp. 749-51, no. 306; AR 20, p. 27.

Nov. 18 1049. From Nawwab Nusrat Jang of Dacca. Informs of the death of Mirza Asad Allah, an old servant of the Company. Requests to continue his pension in the name of his widow. Also encloses an application from her.

OR 694, WS, f 1; TR 51A, pp. 744-47, no. 305; AR 20, p. 27.

Nov. 19 1050. From Raja Ram Ghulam (of Allahabad). Requests for a passport for journey in the name of Raja Gobindjit Singh and his son Babu Jai Singh to go to Bijipur from Rewan in order to conduct writer's daughter to her in-laws over there. Dated 10 November 1805.

OR 695,[2] *WS, f 1; CR 23, pp. 544-45, no. 59; TR 51A, p. 765, no. 310; AR 20, p. 37.*

[1]Copy of OR 688, received on 30 November 1805.

[2]Enclosed with a letter from the Agent to the Governor at Banares, dated 10 November 1805.

Nov. 19 1051. From Amrit Rao Raghunath. Expresses deep sorrow on the death of Marquess Cornwallis. Further feels happy on the succession of Sir George Barlow to the government and expresses satisfaction.

OR 696,[1] *WS, f 1; CR 23, pp. 775-82, no. 37; TR 51A, pp. 766-74, no. 311; AR 20, p. 3.*

Nov. 19 1052. Jangi Khan to A. Seton, the Agent to the Governor at Bareilly. Refers to the petitioner's applications for grant of a *jagir* in Chaumahla that was not accepted by the addressee. Requests for grant of a *jagir* in *pargana* Badaun fetching an amount of Rs. 15,000 (fifteen thousand) for the maintenance of the petitioner.

OR 692, f 1; CR 23, p. 768, no. 35.

Nov. 20 1053. From Baijnath Singh, the *darogha* of Police. Reports that Bodhi Khadka an *amil* of Nepal government is in practice of collecting revenue from Dhulia Bhundar and other *tappas* for the year 1213 *Fasli* and demands two installments. Seeks orders for proper action as may be fit.

OR 698/a,[2] *WS, f 1; CR 23, pp. 799-800, no. 41(1); TR 51A, pp. 774-75, no. 312.*

Nov. 20 1054. Magistrate of Gorakhpur to Baijnath Singh, *darogha* of police at Dhulia Bhundar. Asks the addressee to demand the authorization letter from Bodhi Khadka for collecting revenue from Dhulia Bhundar and other *tappas* and transmit it to the writer.

OR 698[3]*/b, WS, f 1; CR 23, pp. 800-01, no. 41(2); TR 51A, pp. 775-77, no. 313.*

Nov. 20 1055. A. Seton to Nawwab Nasr Allah Khan of Rampur. Says that the addressee may do justice in the case of Imam al-Din of Meerut whose nose had been cut by a *zamindar* Shakir of Bhamrauli in the domain of Rampur.

OR 699,[4] *f 1.*

Nov. 20 1056. From Farzand Ali, *mukhtar-e-kar* of Sambhalpur.

[1]Enclosed with a letter from the Agent to the Governor at Banares, dated 17 November 1805.

[2]Enclosed with a letter from the Magistrate at Gorakhpur, dated 11 November 1805.

[3]Ibid.

[4]Enclosed with a letter from A. Seton, dated 15 November 1805.

Reports about the arrival of Nana Sahib at Chanda and intention of Khandaji to destroy Khirhar. Forwards the request of the residents of Khirhar for help. Waits for an order from the addressee. Dated 15 October 1805.

OR 700, f 1; CR 23, pp. 638-43, no. 6.

Nov. 20 1057. From Nawwab Nusrat Jang of Dacca. Requests for permission to proceed to Patna through river up to Munger for a change of climate as prescribed by the doctor. Awaits a speedy reply.

OR 702, f 1, WS; CR 23. TR 51A, pp. 777-79, no. 314; AR 20, p. 27.

Nov. 20 1058. From the newswriter (at Rampur). Intelligence reports of the *deorhis* of Nawwab Ahmad Ali Khan, Nawwab Nasr Allah Khan, Inayat Allah Khan, Karim Allah Khan and Hasan Ali Khan for the date 2 November 1805.

OR 703/1, f 1.

Nov. 20 1059. From the newswriter (at Rampur). Intelligence report of the *deorhis* of Nawwab Ahmad Ali Khan, Nawwab Nasr Allah Khan, Inayat Allah Khan and Karim Allah Khan and Hasan Ali Khan for the date 11 November 1805.

OR 703/2, f 1.

Nov. 20 1060. From newswriter (at Rampur). Intelligence reports of the *deorhis* of Nawwab Ahmad Ali Khan, Nawwab Nasr Allah Khan, Inayat Allah Khan, Nawwab Karim Allah Khan and Hasan Ali Khan for the date 3 November 1805.

OR 703/3, f 1.

Nov. 20 1061. From the newswriter (at Rampur). Intelligence reports of the *deorhis* of Nawwab Ahmad Ali Khan, Nawwab Nasr Allah Khan, Inayat Allah Khan, Karim Allah Khan and Hasan Ali Khan for the date 12 November 1805.

OR 703/4, f 1.

Nov. 20 1062. From the newswriter (at Rampur). Intelligence reports of the *deorhis* of Nawwab Ahmad Ali Khan, Nawwab Nasr Allah Khan, Inayat Allah Khan, Karim Allah Khan and Hasan Ali Khan for the date 23 October 1805.

OR 703/5, f 1.

Nov. 20 1063. From the newswriter (at Rampur). Intelligence reports of the *deorhis* of Nawwab Ahmad Ali Khan, Nawwab Nasr Allah Khan, Inayat Allah Khan, Karim Allah Khan and Hasan

Ali Khan for the date 4 October, 1805.

OR 703/6, f 1.

Nov. 22 1064. From Nawwab Madar al-Daulah. States that the *amil* of Kairabad has forcibly erected his *jhanda* and commenced the establishment of a new Ganj in village Majhar Hatta. Seeks protection from the British government and hopes that the aspersion of the *amil* will be removed.

OR 704,[1] f 1; CR 23, TR 51A, pp. 779-81, no. 315, AR 20, p. 25.

Nov. 22 1065. From Jani Begam. Expresses pleasure and satisfaction on George Barlow's succession to the government. Requests for a respectable provision for the subsistence.

OR 705,[2] f 1; CR 23, pp. 801-04, no. 42; CR 51A, pp. 781-82, no. 316; AR 20, p. 18.

Nov. 23 1066. From Amanat Khan. States that he has been arrested and put into prison on false charges. Requests for his release from the prison and some proper provision for the subsistence of him and his dependents.

OR 706,[3] f 1; CR 23, pp. 817-18, no. 48.

Nov. 23. 1067. From King Shah Alam II. Expresses deep sorrow on the sad demise of Marquess Cornwallis and pleasure on the appointment of Sir George Barlow as Governor-General. Requests the addressee to issue satisfactory instructions to Col. Ochterlony on the subjects confirmed by the late Governor-General.

OR 707,[4] f 1, WS; CR 23, pp. 810-14, no. 46; TR 51A, pp. 783-85, no. 317; AR 20, p. 19.

Nov. 23 1068. From the Nizam of Hyderabad. Expresses deep sorrow over the sad demise of Marquess Cornwallis and Col. Kirkpatrick. Concedes to the appointment of Russel as new Resident at Hyderabd.

OR 708, f 1, WS; CR 23, pp. 824-25, no. 50; TR 51A, pp. 785-87, no. 318; AR 20, p. 28.

[1]Enclosed with a letter from the Resident at Lucknow, dated 13 November 1805.

[2]Ibid., dated 19 November 1805.

[3]Enclosed with a letter from the Agent to government at Farrukhabad, dated 16 November 1805.

[4]Enclosed with a letter from the Resident at Delhi, dated 16 November 1805.

Nov. 23 1069. Nasir al-Mulk to Udney, the Vice-President-in-Council. Complementary on the appointment of the addressee as officiating Governor-General in absence of Sir George Barlow. Anticipates the continuance of the same favourable friendly relations as happened in the past regimes.

OR 709,[1] *WS, f 1; CR 23 pp. 830-31, no. 54; TR 51A, pp. 787-88, no. 319; AR 20, p. 28.*

Nov. 23 1070. Nasir al-Mulk to Udney (the Vice-President-in-Council and incharge of government). Informs the addressee of the writer's severe indisposition. Dated 19 November 1805.

Nov. 23 1071. From the Nizam (of Hyderabad). In reply to Sir George Barlow's letter notifying the death of Marquess Cornwallis. Expresses deep concern over the sad demise and satisfaction on the addressee's appointment as Governor-General.

OR 711,[2] *WS, f 1; CR 23, pp. 827-29, no. 52; TR 51A, p. 805, no. 328; AR 20, p. 28.*

Nov. 23 1072. Udney, the Vice-President-in-Council to Nawwab Nasir al-Mulk. Acknowledges the receipt of addressee's letter of congratulation sent on the occasion of the writer's appointment as Vice-President.

CI 41, pp. 479-80, no. 216; AI 20, p. 59, no. 223.

Nov. 23 1073. Udney to Munni Begam. Acknowledges receipt of the addressee's congratulatory letter on the occasion of writer's appointment as Governor-General (incharge). Expresses concern over the indisposition of Nawwab Nasir al-Mulk and pray for his quick recovery.

CI 41, pp. 480-82, no. 217; AI 20, p. 55, no. 224.

Nov. 23 1074. To Nawwab Nasir al-Mulk. Expresses concern on the intelligence of addressee's indisposition and prays for his quick recovery.

CI 41, pp. 482-83, no. 218; AI 20, p. 59, no. 225.

Nov. 23 1075. To Capt. Thomas Sydenham. Informs the addressee about his appointment as Resident at Hyderabad following the death of Col. Kirkpatrick.

CI 41, pp. 346-48, no. 114; AI 20, p. 67.

Nov. 23 1076. To the Nizam (Hyderabad). Conveys the news of the

[1]Enclosed with a letter from Pattle, dated 20 November 1805.

[2]Enclosed with a letter from the Resident at Hyderabd, dated 13 November 1805.

death of Col. Kirkpatrick, the Resident at Hyderabad and nomination of Capt. Sydenham to succeed the late Colonel.

CI 41, pp. 348-52, no. 115; AI 20, p. 57.

Nov. 24 1077. To Sulaiman Agha, the envoy of Pasha of Baghdad. Expresses satisfaction over the news of addressee's safe arrival at Basra after having been exposed to the inconvenience from shipwreck and from the atrocities of the barbarous inhabitants of the coast on which the addressee landed. Also expresses concern over the unwarrantable behaviour of Capt. Reed, the Commander of the ship. Assures of an enquiry against these complaints. Encloses a letter addressed to the Pasha to be delivered to him through the Resident at Baghdad.

CI 41, pp. 353-55, no. 116; TI 51, pp. 287-89, no. 230; AI 20, p. 44.

Nov. 24 1078. To the Pasha of Baghdad. Expresses sorrow for the trouble experienced by the addressee's envoy Sulaiman Agha during his journey towards Bushire particularly for the misbehaviour of the Captain of the ship, Capt. Reed. Assures that enquiry will be conducted and action taken against the said Captain.

CI 41, pp. 355-58, no. 117; AI 20, p. 60.

Nov. 24 1079. To the Viceroy of Pegu, the Governor of the city of Rangoon and 32 Provinces of Hinzawiddy and southern ports. Expresses disappointment over the news that the government of Rangoon has put into confinement the British nationals in Rangoon and has also unhooked the British ships of rudders consequent upon capture of a vessel in the colour of Burmese Navy coming from the isles of France without any formal papers of identification of the nation to which it belonged by the British Navy.

Asks the addressee to release the British people from confinement and restore the hanging of rudders immediately. Assures of the settlement of the matters regarding capture of the said vessel. Further suggests that the persisting relations between the two governments may be fruitful if the addressee complies with the requests.

TI 51, pp. 290-95, no. 231; AI 20, p. 70.

Nov. 25 1080. From Nawwab Dilawar Jang (of Bengal). In reply to Sir George Barlow's letter notifying the death of Marquess Cornwallis. Expresses deep sorrow on that occasion and satisfaction at the succession of Sir George Barlow to the seat of Governor-General.

OR 712,[1] *WS, f 1; CR 23, pp. 838-44, no. 58; TR 51A, p. 793, no. 322; AR 20, p. 9.*

Nov. 25 1081. Nawwab Nasr Allah Khan (of Rampur) to A. Seton, agent to Governor-General at Bareilly. Informs that the recommendation of the *mufti* in regard to conducting the father and relatives of the assassinated had already been sent with Munshi Gopal Chand Das. Further the assassin Afghan *turksawar* along Imam Ali, the father of assassinated, are now being sent for the judgement.

OR 726(a),[2] *f 1; CR 23, pp. 834-36, no. 57(1).*

Nov. 26 1082. From Zaib al-Nisa Begam. Mourns on the demise of Marquess Cornwallis; informs about her financial and military help rendered to the Company's government. Dated 17 November 1808.

OR 714,[3] *WS f 1; CR 23, pp. 847-52, no. 62; TR 51A, pp. 793-97, no. 323; AR 20, p. 42.*

Nov. 26 1083. A. Seton to Nawwab Nasr Allah Khan. Says that since the assassination of the native resident has taken place in the Company's territory, the parties concerned should be sent to the Company's court for judgment.

OR 726(b),[4] *f 1; CR 23, pp. 836-38, no. 57(2).*

Nov. 27 1084. Pattle to Gauhar Ara Begam. Informs the addressee regarding the position taken by the Vice-President-in-Council regarding allowances to her, the widow of late Nawwab Bande Ali Khan. Accordingly she has been asked to receive Rs. 400 per month and the rest amount will be distributed among sons and daughters of the late Nawwab. If not, the *Sharia* law will decide the case.

OR 715,[5] *f 1; CR 23, pp. 852-56, no. 62; TR 51A pp. 799-803, no. 325; AR 20, p. 12.*

Nov. 27 1085. Gauhar Ara Begam to Pattle. Asserts her claim on the

[1]Enclosed with a letter from the Deputy Persian Secretary, dated 18 November 1905.

[2]Copy enclosed with a letter from the Resident at Bareilly, dated 15 November 1805.

[3]Enclosed with a letter from the Resident at Delhi, dated 19 November 1805.

[4]Copy enclosed with a letter from the resident at Bareilly, dated 15 November 1805.

[5]Enclosed with a letter from Pattle, 3 November 1805.

allowances enjoyed by late Nawwab Bande Ali Khan during his lifetime. Further states that the late Khan had been enjoying the said allowances of Rs. 800 on her behalf from the hereditary property left by her father late Nawwab Murtaza Khan. Expresses her misery and complains against her brother's ill behaves. Hopes for a favourable and quick solution of the dispute.

OR 716,[1] f 1; CR 23, pp. 852-56, no. 62; TR 51A, pp. 799-803, no. 32; AR 20, p. 12.

Nov. 27 1086. Nawwab Nasr Allah Kahn to A. Seton. Copy of the OR 726(a).

OR 726[2] (c), f 1; CR 23, pp. 834-36, no. 57(1).

Nov. 28 1087. Babbu Begum to Udney. Complementary letter on the eve of Udney being invested with the charge of Vice-President, dated 30 *Shaban*, 1220 AH (23 November 1805).

OR 717,[3] WS, f 1; CR 23, pp. 861-62, no. 64; TR 51A, pp. 803-4, no. 326; AR 20, p. 6.

Nov. 28 1088. From Nawwab Nusrat Jang (of Dacca). Seeks permission to go to westward for a climatic change as prescribed by the physician attending to the writer following his severe illness due to high fever. Dated 23 November 1805.

OR 718,[4] WS, f 1; CR 23, pp. 635-36, no. 3; TR 51A, pp. 804-5, no. 327; AR 20, p. 27.

Nov. 28 1089. From Nawwab Nusrat Jang (of Dacca). Acknowledges receipt of the addressee's letter informing death of Marquess Cornwallis and his (addressee's) succession to the seat of Governor-General. Expresses deep concern on the death of Marquess Cornwallis and satisfaction over addressee's succession as Governor-General.

OR 720,[5] WS, f 1; CR 23, pp. 856-61, no. 63; TR 51A, pp. 789-93, no. 321; AR 20, p. 27.

[1]Enclosed with a letter from Pattle, dated 23 November 1805.

[2]Copy enclosed with a letter from the Resident at Bareilly, dated 15 November 1805.

[3]Enclosed with a letter from the Superintendent of *nizamat* affairs to the Deputy Persian Secretary, dated 25 November 1805.

[4]Enclosed with a letter from in judge at Dacca to the Deputy Secretary, dated 24 November 1805.

[5]Enclosed with a letter from the judge at Dacca to the Persian Secretary, dated 24 November 1805.

Nov. 29 1090. Udai Chand Dutt to the Deputy Secretary. Requests for the grant of a *dastak-i-rahdari* (Passport) in favour of the writer to travel from Calcutta to Benares along with provisions to accord his father to Calcutta.

OR 721, f 1.

Nov. 29 1091. Nawwab Nasir al-Mulk (of Dacca) to Pattle. To the same effect as the foregoing OR 719.

OR 722,[1] f 1; CR 23, pp. 866-70, no. 68; TR 51A, pp. 811-12, no. 335; AR 20, p. 12.

Nov. 29 1092. From Ashraf al-Nisa Begam (of Lucknow). Describes her miserable condition due to lack of income following the death of his father. Requests the addressee to consider her case and make a proper enhancement in the allowance so that she could meet her daily expenses comfortably.

OR 723,[2] f 1; CR 23, pp. 864-66, no. 66; TR 51A, pp. 812-13, no. 336; AR 20, p. 12.

Nov. 29 1093. George Udney to Udai Chand Dutt. Grants a *dastak-i-rahdari* (Passport) to travel between Calcutta to Benares along with the listed provisions without paying duties.

CI 41, pp. 483-84, no. 219.

Nov. 29 1094. To the Wazir. Acknowledges receipt of the gifts with thanks sent through Gokul Chand Chaubey.

CI 42, pp. 484-85, no. 220; TI 51, pp. 295-96, no. 232; AI 20, p. 69.

Nov. 30 1095. Col. Malcolm to Munshi Kanwal Nain (*wakil* of Raja Daulat Rao Sindhia). Informs the addressee regarding grant of *jagirs* to Daulat Rao Sindhia and his *sardars* who played important role in serving the Company in establishing friendly relation between the Company and the Indian rulers. Gives a detailed account of the grants confirmed on individuals. Dated 22 November 1805.

OR 724[3], ff 2; CR 23, pp. 883-84, no. 74.

Nov. 30[4] 1096. Nawwab Munni Begam to George Udney. Comple-

[1]Enclosed with a letter from Pattle, dated 26 November 1805).

[2]Enclosed with a letter from the Superintendent of *nizamat* affairs to the Deputy Secretary, dated 26 November 1805.

[3]Enclosed with a letter from Col. Malcolm, dated 28 November 1805.

[4]The date of receipt writer in Persian is 30 November while in English it is 23 November.

mentary on the succession of Sir George Barlow to the seat of Governor-General. Expresses hope that the old friendly relations between the two states would further be strengthened.

OR 725,[1] WS, f 1; CR 23, pp. 831-33, no. 55).

Nov. 30 1097. A. Seton to Nawwab Nasr Allah Khan. Copy of the OR 726(b).[2]

OR 726(d); f 1; CR 23, pp. 836-38, no. 57(2).

Nov. 30 1098. From Munni Begam (of Bengal). Expresses grief over the death of Lord Cornwallis and satisfaction at Sir George Barlow's succession to the government. Dated 26 *Shaban* 1220 AH (19 November 1805).

OR 727, WS, f 1; CR 23, pp. 871-76, no. 71; TR 51A, p. 806, no. 331; AR 20, p. 23.

Nov. 30 1099. From Nawwab Nasir al-Mulk. Expresses deep concern over the death of Lord Cornwallis and satisfaction on the succession of sir George Barlow as Governor-General, dated 26 *Shaban* 1220 AH (19 November 1805).

OR 728,[3] WS, f 1; CR 23, pp. 819-24, no. 49; TR 51A, p. 805, no. 329; AR 20, p. 29.

Nov. 30 1100. Nawwab Nasir al-Mulk to Udney. Informs the Governor-General regarding his (writer's) recovery from illness. Dated 26 November 1805.

OR 729,[4] WS, f 1; CR 23, pp. 876-78, no. 71; TR 51A, pp. 809-11, no. 334; AR 20, p. 29).

Nov. 30 1101. From Nawwab Wazir. Congratulatory on Sir George barlow's arrival at Allahabad. Informs that a present of two elephants, two *palakis* and one seasonal *libada* (woollen cloak) has been sent through Gokul Chand for the addressee's personal use.

OR 731, WS, f 1; CR 23, pp. 870-71, no. 69; TR 51A, p. 814, no. 337; AR 20, p. 41.

[1]Enclosed with a letter from Pattle, dated 20 November 1805.

[2]Copy enclosed with a letter from the Resident at Bareilly, dated 15 November 1805.

[3]Enclosed with a letter from Pattle, dated 20 November 1805.

[4]Enclosed with a letter from Pattle to the Persian Secretary to Government, dated 27 November 1805.

Nov. 30 1102. From the Nizam (of Hyderabad). Expresses grief at the death of Lord Cornwallis and satisfaction on the appointment of Sir George Barlow to the government.

OR 732,[1] *WS, f 1; CR 23, pp. 862-64, no. 65; TR 51A, p. 814, no. 338; AR 20, p. 29.*

Nov. 30 1103. From Mir Alam (of Hyderabad). To the same effect as the foregoing OR 732.

OR 733, WS, f 1; CR 23, pp. 890-92, no. 76; TR 51A, p.814, no. 339; AR 20, p. 22.

Nov. 30 1104. From Mir Alam (of Hyderabad). Expresses deep concern over the death of Marquess Cornwallis and Col. Kirkpatrick; shows willingness that Russel may be appointed as the Resident at Hyderabad.

OR 734,[2] *f 1; CR 23, pp. 825-27, no. 51; TR 51A, p. 815, no. 340; AR 20, p. 22.*

Nov. 30 1105. From Sharaf Ali Khan (of Lucknow). Congratulatory on the occasion of addressee's appointment to the government.

OR 736,[3] *WS, f 1; CR 23, pp. 894-95, no. 78; TR 51A, p. 815, no. 342; AR 20, p. 39.*

Nov. 30 1106. From Nawwab Madar al-Daulah (of Lucknow). Congratulatory on the occasion of addressee's appointment to the government.

OR 738, WS, f 1; CR 23, pp. 678-80, 16; TR 51A, p. 815, no. 346; AR 20, p. 25.

Nov. 30 1107. Raja Bhawani Din (of Lucknow). Congratulatory on the occasion of addressee's appointment to the government.

OR 739,[4] *WS, f 1; CR 23, pp. 895-97, no. 79; TR 51A, p. 815, no. 347; AR 20, p. 7.*

Nov. 30 1108. From Nawwab Kiradmand Khan (of Farrukhabad). Expresses deep concern at the death of Lord Cornwallis and

[1]Enclosed with a letter from the Acting Resident at Hyderabad, dated 29 November 1805.

[2]Ibid., dated 23 November 1805.

[3]Enclosed with a letter from the Resident at Lucknow, dated 9 November 1805.

[4]Ibid., dated 13 November 1805.

satisfaction on the succession of Sir George Barlow to the government.

OR 740,[1] *WS, f 1; CR 23, pp. 880-82, no. 73; TR 51A, p. 816, no. 348; AR 20, 23.*

Nov. 30. 1109. Nawwab Munni Begam. Informs about the indisposition of writer's son Nawwab Nasir al-Mulk. Dated 19 November 1805.

OR 741 WS, f 1; CR 23, pp. 892-93, no. 77; TR 51A, p. 817, no. 349; AR 20, p. 23).

Nov. 30 1110. Ram Sewak Thakur and others from Bodh Gaya. States that they had inherited 4009 *bighas* of land as *madad-e-maash* granted to their forefathers by Emperor Shah Alam II duly endorsed and verified subsequently by the *wazir* Qamar al-Din Khan and the *zamindar* Babu Tribhuwan Singh the grandfather of Raja Mitrajit Singh. Some times back under the instigation from Ram Hitkar Gosain the said *zamindar* (Mitrajit Singh) made a complaint in order to capture the said land and dislodged the petitioners. The case was investigated and a decree issued by Thomas Low in favour of petitioners. But till date the land has not been restored to them. Requests to issue an order to the Collector of Gaya to restore the land and hand over the amount of revenue collected so far by the *amin* appointed by the Collector.

OR 742, f 1; TR 51A, pp. 806-08, no. 332; AR 20, p. 37.

Nov. 30 1111. To Munni Begam. Expresses extreme concern at the intelligence regarding Nawwab Nasir al-Mulk's severe indisposition and hopes more favourable accounts in this connection.

CI 41, pp. 485-86, no. 221; TI 51, p. 296, no. 233; AI 20, p. 55.

Nov. 30 1112. To Nawwab Nasir al-Mulk. Expresses deep concern at the intelligence received from Nawwab Munni Begam regarding addressee's severe indisposition and hopes for his quick recovery.

CI 41, pp. 487-88, no. 222; TI 51, pp. 296-97, no. 234; AI 20, p. 59.

[1]Enclosed with a letter from the Acting Agent to government at Farukhabad, dated 13 November 1805.

Nov. 30 1113. Nawwab Nasir al-Mulk to Udney. In reply to the addressee's letter enquiring of the writer's health. Informs about his recovery from the illness but still feels extreme weakness.

TR 51, p. 806, no. 330; AR 20, p. 29.

Nov. 30 1114. From Maharaja Ranjit Singh (of Bharatpur). Congratulatory on the safe arrival of the addressee at Allahabad and expresses his (writer's) desire to have the honour of waiting upon him.

OR 743, WS, f 1; TR 51A, p. 689, no. 269; AR 20, p. 36.

Nov. 30 1115. Ramazan Ali Khan to John Monkton, the Deputy Persian Secretary to the government. Applies for a *dastak-e-rahdari* (passport) for a duty-free journey from Calcutta to Lucknow along with provisions and goods.

OR 744,[1] *WS, f 1.*

Nov. -- 1116. Intelligence from the newswriter at the court of Shah Shuja al-Mulk of Kabul. Informs about the arrival of Shah Shuja at Chaman and mobilization of his forces towards Kashmir to chastise Abd Allah Khan the *haakim* (administrator) of Kashmir, etc., etc.

OR 745, ff 2.

Nov. -- 1117. From (Nawwab Wazir). Complementary on the arrival of the addressee at Allahabad. Refers to the old friendly relation with the Company and anticipates its continuation under the rule of the addressee.

OR 747, f 1; CR 23, pp. 888-89, no. 75.

Nov. -- 1118. From Raja Sahib Singh of Patiala. Expresses joy and satisfaction on the appointment of the addressee (Lord Cornwallis) to the Company's government in India. Hopes that the writer may be enabled to maintain his dominions in peace and repose with the support of addressee.

OR 748, f 1; CR 23, pp. 804-06, no. 43; TR 51A, pp. 723-24; AR 20, p. 37.

Nov. -- 1119. Maharaja Ranjit Singh of Lahore to Col. John Collins. Informs that the writer is stationing at Dal Firoz near Multan where he has been presensted with the gifts of Persian horses

[1]The date of application on the OR is 11 *Shaban* 1220 AH and the date of issue of *dastak* is 11 November 1805.

and other precious items by the *haakim* of Multan through the latter's agents.

OR 749,[1] *f 1; CR 23, pp. 808-10, no. 45.*

Nov. -- 1120. Raja Balbhadra Bhuj, the *zamindar* of fort of Ganga (Orissa) to Adams. Complains against the high handedness of Company's officials in regard to the *jagir* affairs of the petitioner. Also informs about the capture of the petitioner's *haveli* and dishonour meted by the said officials. Request's the addressee to look into the matter and impart justice.

OR 750, f 1; CR 23, pp. 736-42, no. 24.

Nov. -- 1121. From Amrit Rao. Elaborates the situations prevailing in the region and the injustice meted out to him by Baji Rao and others. Requests the addressee to do justice and acknowledge his claims.

OR 751, ff 2; CR 23, pp. 695-702, no. 21(1).

Nov. -- 1122. From Ganpat Singh, *taluqadar* of *pargana* Gopinathpur. Complains about the possession of *pargana* Gopinathpur by Govind Singh and others and also of their evil design against the writer. Requests to direct the District Magistrate of Murshidabad to do the justice towards him.

OR 752, f 1.

Nov. -- 1123. From Pal Singh and Samar Singh of Jhusi (Allahabad). Complains against the oppressions of the *amil* of Jhusi. Requests that justice be imparted to them.

OR 753, f 1.

Nov. -- 1124. From Shiv Parsan Singh and other of *pargana* Suram. Complains against the oppression of Devki Nandan, the *amil* of the said *pargana* and requests that the writers be rescued from the *amil's* oppression and justice be imparted.

OR 754, f 1.

Nov. -- 1125. *Patta-e-Qaul-o-Qarar* executed by Lachhman Singh Chaudhary in favour of Brode (Acting Collector of Bundelkhand) to give 28 *bighas* of land to the latter for an annual rent of Rs. 2 per *bigha* totaling to Rs. 56 per annum for the construction of *bangla*. Dated 15 July 1805.

OR 755, f 1.

[1]Copy enclosed in a letter from the Resident at Lahore, dated 22 November 1805.

Nov. -- 1126. Muhammad Hakim al-Din son of *Qazi al-Quzat* Muhammad Najm al-Din Khan to the Resident at Lucknow. Refers to the written representation of the *Qazi al-Quzat* and his own regarding reprisal of the changes incorporated by Almas Ali Khan in the office of the *Qazi al-Quzat* which have long been maintained and enjoyed by his family since the time of his forefathers. Requests to make proper reprisal of the changes.

OR 756, f 1.

Nov. -- 1127. From . . . (?). Expresses anxiety for not receiving any letter from the addressee. Complements on the success of Company's forces.

OR 757, f 1.

Nov. -- 1128. From Raja Bakhtawar Singh (of Machheri). Refers to writer's previous letter and communications through Raja Randhir Singh on the issue of supply of water from the river Niswari as per the settlement. Requests the addressee to make arrangement for the supply of enough water in the writer's territory from the said river.

OR 758/a, f 1.

Nov. -- 1129. General Lord Lake, Commander-in-Chief to Raja Bakhtawar Singh (of Machheri). Grants the fortress of Kishangarh and other *pattas*, etc., to the said Raja in return of Dadri, Bhawana, etc., in *taluqa* Haryana and a *peshkash* of Rs. 1 lakh. Aslo assures to maintain adequate supply of water from river Niswari. Dated 14 October 1805.

OR 758/b,[1] *f 1.*

Nov. -- 1130. From Raja Bakhtawar Singh (of Machheri). Describes in detail the whole story of the barrage at river Niswari and requests for making proper arrangement for adequate water supply from the said river.

OR 758/c, ff 2.

Nov. -- 1131. Col. John Malcolm to Nawwab Asad Allah Khan. Communicates that grants of Rs. 15,000 per annum for the writer and his dependents, etc., have been recommended and approved. Asks the addressee to accept this grant.

OR 760/a, f 1.

[1]Copy of the *sanad*.

Nov. -- 1132. Lord Lake to Col. Malcolm. Informs him of the grant of Rs.15,000 per annum to Nawwab Najabat Ali Khan in lieu of his joining the Company's army. Dated 6 April 1805.

OR 760/b, f 1.

Nov. -- 1133. Nawwab Wazir to Husaini Begam. Acknowledges receipt of two letters. Asks the addressee not to send Manzoor Ali Khan, *khwajasara* (eunuch) for the service of the writer and his household. Dated 2 November 1805.

OR 761, f 1.

Nov. -- 1134. From . . . to Major (Lennon). Gives an account of a battle between the writer and the miscreants in *mauza* Katra, etc.

CR 23, pp. 731-33, no. 23(2).

Nov. -- 1135. Anjha Ram, *tahsildar* of *pargana* Barh to. . . . Narrates an account of the fight between the enemy's troop and Company's forces. Further says that the enemy's troops are in commanding position and has besieged the Company's forces.

CR 23, pp. 733-34, no. 23(3).

Nov. -- 1136. Followers of Nawwab Wazir Ali Khan to the Company's officials at Allahabad. Demands immediate release of the said Nawwab otherwise they (the writers) would attack the British establishment and kill the British people.

CR 23, pp. 734-35, no. 23(4).

Nov. -- 1137. From Nawwab Qasim Ali Khan. Congratulatory on Sir George Barlow's succession to the government.

TR 51A, p. 815, no. 343; AR 20, p. 7.

Dec. 2 1138. From Nawwab Nusrat Jang. Congratulatory on the occasion of Sir George Barlow's succession to the seat of Governor-General, dated 29 October 1805.

OR 762, WS, f 1.

Dec. 2 1139. Gauhar Ara Begam to Pattle. Expresses her financial difficulties and requests to issue her allowances regularly in time.

OR 763,[1] *f 1; CR 23, pp. 909-10, no. 1;*
TR 51A, pp. 817-18, no. 351; AR 20, p. 12.

[1]Enclosed with a letter from the Superintendent of *nizamat* affairs, dated 28 November 1805.

Dec. 2 1140. From Nawwab Shamsher Bahadur (of Banda). Complementary on the arrival of Governor-General in India. Further seeks permission to wait upon his Lordship while visiting the Upper Provinces.

OR 764, WS, f 1.

Dec. 3 1141. From Maharaja Raj Kishan Bahadur. Requests for a *dastak-e-rahdari* (passport) to visit the holy places of Gaya, Benares and Parag (Allahabad).

OR 765, f 1.

Dec. 3 1142. From Dilawar Jang. Remonstrate against the provision that the government has made to pay an allowance of Rs. 1,000 per annuam to Mir Kazim Ali, the foster son of his father Nawwab Muzaffar Jang from the annual stipend of Rs. 11,200 fixed for the writer since the year 1792 AD. Argues that the said Mir was born from a slave girl serving on his late father and hence he (the Mir) has no right of heritance by any rule. Requests to make an additional amount available to the writer to meet the said extra allowance to the Mir.

OR 766, WS, f 1; TR 51A, pp. 818-25, no. 352; AR 20, p. 9.

Dec. 3 1143. From the Vice President to Babbu Begam. Acknowledges addressee's letter of congratulation on the writer's appointment as Vice-President and Deputy Governor of Fort William.

CI 41, pp. 488-89, no. 223; TI 51, p. 297, no. 235; AI 20, p. 47.

Dec. 3 1144. From the Vice-President to Maharaja Raj Kishan Bahadur. Grants a *dastak-i-rahdari* to the addressee to go to Gaya and Kashi to perform pilgrimage.

CI 41, p. 489, no. 224.

Dec. 4 1145. From Husain Ali Khan of Lucknow. Congratulatory on George Barlow's succession to the government.

OR 697,[1] WS, f 1; CR 23, pp. 981-86, no. 21; TR 51A, p. 829, no. 358; AR 20, p. 17.

Dec. 4 1146. From Raja Narendergir of Sikandra. Acknowledges receipt of the addressee's letter containing assurance of all favours to the writer. Expresses his expectations that the British government would continue to the same friendly and

[1]Enclosed with a letter from the Resident at Lucknow, dated 12 November 1805.

favourable relation with the writer as it has been maintained during last 50 years. Further says that his (writer's) *wakil* would give other details of the affairs verbally.

OR 767, WS, f 1; TR 51A, pp. 825-27, no. 353; AR 20, p. 30.

Dec. 4 1147. From Qutluq Sultan Begam. Complementary with a present of a *libadah*.

OR 768, WS, f 1; CR 23, pp. 1004-05, no. 28; TR 51A, p. 828, no. 534; AR 20, p. 20.

Dec. 4 1148. From Kunwar Kanchangir of Sikandra. Complementary and expressive of his attachment to the British government.

OR 769, WS, f 1; TR 51A, p. 829, no. 357; AR 20, pp. 30 and 37.

Dec. 4 1149. From Nawwab Wazir of Awadh. Complementary with a present of fruits.

OR 770, WS, f 1; CR 23, pp. 915-16, no. 4; TR 51A, p. 829, no. 359; AR 20, p. 41.

Dec. 4 1150. From Munni Begam. Informs the addressee about the recovery of Nawwab Nasir al-Mulk from indisposition. Dated 15 November 1805.

OR 771, WS, f 1; CR 23, pp. 913-15, no. 3; TR 51A, p. 829, no. 360; AR 20, p. 23.

Dec. 4 1151. From Babbu Begam. Expresses grief on the demise of Lord Cornwallis and satisfaction on the appointment of Sir George Barlow to the government. Dated 20 November 1805.

OR 772,[1] *WS, f 1; CR 23, pp. 910-13, no. 2; TR 51A, pp. 829-30, no. 361; AR 20, p. 6.*

Dec. 4 1152. From Sultan Muhammad Shah. Complementary on the succession of Sir George Barlow to the government.

OR 773, WS, f 1, TR 51A, p. 830, no. 363; AR 20, p. 39.

Dec. 4 1153. From Nasir al-Daulah (of Agra). Congratulatory on Sir George Barlow's arrival at Allahabad.

OR 774, WS, f 1; TR 51A, pp. 830-31, no. 364; AR 20, p. 29.

Dec. 4 1154. From Khan Jahan Khan. Congratulatory on the

[1]Enclosed with a letter from the Superintendent *nizamat* affairs, dated 22 November 1805.

succession of the addressee to the government.

TR 51A, p. 830, no. 362; AR 20, p. 19.

Dec. 4 1155. From Shaikh Salar Bakhsh. Congratulatory on the addressee's arrival at Allahabad. Expresses his desire to wait upon him.

TR 51A, p. 831; no. 365; AR 20, p. 39.

Dec. 4 1156. From Muhammad Ali Khan. Expresses his concern on the death of Lord Cornwallis and satisfaction on the accession of the addressee to the seat of Governor-General.

OR 795, WS, f 1; TR 51A, p. 828, no. 355.

Dec. 5 1157. Kunwar Randhir Singh to Mercer. Informs about the death of Maharaja Sahib. Anticipates the same favour from the addressee as it has been during the lifetime of the deceased.

OR 775(i),[1] *f 1.*

Dec. 5 1158. Mercer to Kunwar Randhir Singh. Expresses grief on the sad demise of Maharaja Ranjit Singh and assures the addressee of the same friendly relation as it prevailed during the lifetime of the late Maharaja.

OR 775 (ii),[2] *f 1.*

Dec. 5 1159. Mirza Raza Quli, the king of Persia to Samuel Manesty, the British Resident at Busra. Informs the addressee about the unscrupulous assaults of *taifa-e-Russia* (Russian troops) in the region of Erevan and their subsequent suppression and crushing defeat at the hands of Persian soldiers. Asks the addressee to impress upon the king of England in respect of a joint action of British and Persian governments against the Russian movements.

OR 776/a,[3] *f 1.*

Dec. 5 1160. Samuel Manesty, the Resident at Busra to the King of Persia. Acknowledges the receipt of addressee's letter and expresses pleasure on the success of Persian troops over the Russians. Assures that the writer would present the addressee's proposal for a joint operation of British and Persian governments against the Russians in the best possible way.

OR 776/b,[4] *f 1.*

[1]Copy enclosed with a letter from Mercer, dated 30 November 1805.

[2]Ibid.

[3]Enclosed with a letter from Samuel Manesty, the Resident at Busrah, dated 13 December 1804.

[4]Ibid.

Dec. 5 1161. Mirza Raza Quli, the king of Persian to Samuel Manesty, the British Resident at Busra. Informs the addressee about the nefarious attacks of Russian troops on the territories of Persia and their subsequent defeat at the hands of Persian forces. Also informs about the military help offered by the French government against Russia and its subsequent rejection by the writer in view of the friendly relation of British and Persian governments.

OR 776/c,[1] *f 1.*

Dec.5 1162. Samuel Manesty, the Resident at Busra to Mirza Raza Quli. Expresses pleasure on the victory of the Persian forces over the Russian invaders. States that the Persian government should not depend on the military aid of British government in its warfare against the Russians as England and Russia are united by an amicable ties and friendly treaties; also expresses writer's inability to go to London because of several reasons. Suggests the addressee not to rely even on French government for its false intriguing and dangerous indisposition.

OR 776/d,[2] *f 1.*

Dec. 5 1163. Maho Singh, *Subedar* to. . . . Requests for a *dastak-i-rahdari* (passport) to go to Madras via Cuttack along with his men, beast and provision as detailed in the application. Dated 4 December 1805.

OR 777, f 1.

Dec. 5 1164. Vice-President to Subadar Maho Singh. Grants a *dastak-i-rahdari* (passport) to go to Mandraj (Madras) via Cuttack from Calcutta along his men and provision, etc.

CI 41, pp. 489-90, no. 225.

Dec. 6 1165. Mir Baqar Ali Khan to. . . . Expresses that all his brothers got separated immediately after the death of his father about 12 years back. Since then each of his brothers is individually responsible for their affairs and none has any thing to do with the other. In such a condition any order bereaving his mother to move from Lucknow towards Fatehpur on the charges of Hakim Mahdi *amil* of Nawwab Wazir due to non-payment of any dues by Mir Kazim Ali Khan, one of writer's brothers, is not justified as she has been staying along with the writer for the last 12 years. Requests the addressee to set up enquiry in

[1]Enclosed with a letter from the Resident at Busrah, dated 13 December 1804.
[2]Ibid.

the matter for fact finding and issue order to Col. Collins to allow his mother to go to Fatehpur.

OR 778,[1] f 1.

Dec. 6 1166. From Daulat Rao Sindhia. Acknowledges receipt of addressee's letter notifying the death of Cornwallis. Express deep sorrow over the sad demise and satisfaction on the appointment of the addressee (Sir George Barlow) as the Governor-General.

OR 713,[2] f 1; CR 23, pp. 846-47, no. 60, TR 51A, pp. 836-38, no. 368; AR 20, p. 8.

Dec. 6 1167. From Muhammad Baqar Ali Khan. Appraises the addresse of the situations in connection with the ban on his mother's movement from Lucknow to Fatehpur. Requests to direct the Resident at Lucknow to approach to Nawwab Wazir for allowing his mother to go to Fatehpur.

OR 779, WS, f 1; CR 23, pp. 916-18, no. 5; TR 51A, pp. 831-33, no. 336; AR 20, p. 7.

Dec. 6 1168. From Raja Narendergir. Complementary letter.

OR 780,[3] WS, f 1; CR 23, p. 919, no. 6; TR 51A, p. 828, no. 356; AR 20, p. 30.

Dec. 6 1169. Ilahi Khanam to the Resident at Lucknow. Referring to the objections regarding validity of writer's *nikah* (marriage) to Wazir Ali Khan, furnishes details of her marriage with the said Khan on the testimony of the witnesses along with their seals and signature affixed thereon.

OR 783,[4] WS, f 1; CR 23, pp. 924-25, no. 8; TR 51A, pp. 834-36, no. 367; AR 20, p. 15.

Dec. 7 1170. From Maulavi Zia Allah Khan, an employee of Nawwab Walajah of Karnataka (Carnatic). Informs about the departure of writer with 12 men and other provision to Gopa Mau from Madras.

OR 781, f 1.

[1]The date does not come forth from the document. This case has been comprehensively dealt in letter OR 613.

[2]Enclosed with a letter from Malcolm, dated 26 November 1805.

[3]Enclosed with a letter from Capt. Baillie, dated 4 December 1805.

[4]Enclosed with a letter from the Resident at Lucknow, dated 27 November 1805.

Dec. 7 1171. To Qutluq Sultan Begam. Complementary. Acknowledges the addressee's letter and the gifts.

CI 41, pp. 490-91, no. 226; TI 51, p. 297, no. 236; AI 20, p. 52.

Dec. 8 1172. From Nawwab Muin al-Mulk. Complementary letter along a gift of 20 baskets of Oranges. Dated 7 December 1805.

OR 782, WS, f 1; TR 51A, p. 838, no. 369; AR 20, p. 9.

Dec. 9 1173. From Mirza Muzaffar Bakht. Acknowledges receipt of the addressee's letter and assures that he would stay at Patna according to the terms and conditions agreed upon and receive his usual pension there.

OR 784[1]*, WS, ff 2; CR 23, pp. 920-23, no. 7; TR 51A, pp. 838-43, no. 370; AR 20, p. 25.*

Dec. 9 1174. To Nawwab Dilawar Jang. Acknowledges receipt of addressee's letter along with 20 baskets of oranges.

CI 41, pp. 492-93, no. 227; TI 51, pp. 297-98, no. 237; AI 20, p. 49.

Dec. 9 1175. To Nawwab Shamsher Bahadur. Acknowledges addressee's letter seeking his permission to see to writer while visiting the upper provinces. Expresses his (writer's) inability to give an audience to addressee personally due to various engagements in the upper provinces. Informs about Capt. Baillie's appointment at Bundelkhand to look after the affairs of the provinces.

CI 41, pp. 358-60, no. 118.

Dec. 10 1176. To Raja Narendergir (of Kanpur). Informs the addressee that Capt. Baillie has been sent on a political mission to Bundelkhand who will deliver this letter and other communications to the addressee. The writer has also directed Capt. Baillie to confer a *khilat* on the addressee on the occasion of his father's death.

CI 41, pp. 360-62, no. 119; TI 51, pp. 298-300, no. 238; AI 20, p. 65.

Dec. 10 1177. To Raja Kanchangir (of Kanpur). To the same effect as the foregoing letter.

CI 41, pp. 360-62, no. 119; TI 51, pp. 298-300, no. 239; AI 20, p. 65.

[1]Enclosed with letter from the Acting Agent at Farrukhabad, dated 4 December 1805.

Dec. 11 1178. Muhammad Musharraf, Muhammad Najm al-din and Siraj al-Din, the *qazis* to the *Qazi al-Quzat* and *muftis* of *Adalat-i-Diwani Sadr*. Enquire that who should get the allowance of late Fakhr al-Nisa Begam and how should it be distributed among the heirs.

OR 785,[1] f 1; CR 23, pp. 926-29, no. 9.

Dec. 11 1179. Babuji Kanjar to Col. Close. Expresses his displeasure for not having been allowed an audience by Col. Wallace, however, seeks a meeting with the addressee to discuss some important matter.

OR 786,[2] ff 2, CR 23, pp. 929-36, no. 10.

Dec. 11 1180. To the Nizam Asaf Jah (of Deccan). Acknowledges the receipt of addressee's letter lamenting the death of Lt. Col. Kirkpatrick, the representative of Company's government in the addressee's Court. Informs that Capt. Thomas Sydneham has been appointed to succeed the late Col. Kirkpatrick. Further informs that Russel will continue to assist the new Resident in his duties.

CI 41, pp. 364-66, no. 121; TI 51, pp. 301-03, no. 240; AI 20, p. 57.

Dec. 11 1181. To Mir Alam (of Deccan). To the same effect as the foregoing.

CI 41, pp. 364-66, no. 122; TI 51, pp. 301-03, no. 241; AI 20, p. 54.

Dec. 11 1182. To Amrit Rao. Expresses concern on the delay occurred in the discharge of the addressee's stipend. Suggests the addressee to postpone his journey to Allahabad till proper arrangements are made to accommodate the train of his men and provision.

CI 41, pp. 366-70, no. 123; TI 51, pp. 303-06, no. 242; AI 20, p. 44.

Dec. 11 1183. From Daulat al-Nisa Begam. States her financial difficulties due to non-payment of her regular pension by Nawwab Dilawar Jang for the last 12 years. Further makes a claim of Rs. 23,500 due on the said Nawwab. Requests the addressee to look into the matter and direct Nawwab Dilawar Jang to pay the said amount at once immediately so that she

[1]Enclosed with letter from the Magistrate of Diwani Adalat Sadr to Deputy Persian Secretary, dated 6 December 1805.

[2]Persian translation of original Marathi letter enclosed with a letter from the Resident at Poona, dated 15 November 1805.

can pay back the debts of the bankers and *mahajans* which has threw her life into utter starvation.

OR 787,[1] *WS, f 1; CR 23, pp. 937-42, no. 11; TR 51A, pp. 843-48, no. 371; AR 20, p. 10.*

Dec. 14 1184. Col. Collins to Nawwab Wazir. With reference to the order of the Council asks the addressee to direct Rai Jai Singh Rai to furnish a detailed list of the *rozinadars* (daily pensioners) of the *suba* Allahabad so that the writer can submit the same in time. Dated 29 November 1805.

OR 788(a), f 1; CR 23, pp. 943-44, no. 12(i).

Dec. 14 1185. Nawwab Wazir to Col. Collins. Referring to addressee's letter regarding a detailed list of *rozinadars* of Allahabad *suba* states that the record of any kind asked for by the addressee are not available in his office. Dated 30 November 1805.

OR 788(b),[2] *f 1; CR 23, pp. 944-46, no. 12(2).*

Dec. 15 1186. Munni Begam to Thomas Pattle. Requests that orders be issued in the name of the Collector for the payment of her allowances in time so that she may not fell into problem in the commence month of *Ramazan*.

OR 790, f 1; CR 23, pp. 970-71, no. 18.

Dec. 15 1187. Application of Hari Udhav, Balaji and others regarding refund of *mahasul* deposited at Gaya as per details given therein. Clarifies that due to non-availability of *wasiqa-i-mafi-i-mahsul* they had to pay the toll tax at Gaya.

OR 791, f 1.

Dec. 15 1188. From Amrit Rao. Recapitulates the assurance given by General Wellesley for the allotment of a suitable *jagir*, expresses his apprehension of the evil designs of Baji Rao. Requests to grant him a *jagir* at Poona as the climate at Benares is not favourable to him. Further says that he will be given a sum of Rs. 10 lakh (ten lakh) in addition to his monthly allowances so that he can distribute it as alms, etc., according to his family traditions. Requests to issue orders to the officer posted at Batarhatta to exempt the pilgrims from the taxes in his favour. Dated 8 *Ramazan* 1220 AH (30 November 1805).

OR 792, WS, f 1; CR 23, pp. 1006-11, no. 29; TR 51A, pp. 850-56, no. 372; AR 20, p. 3.

[1]Enclosed with a letter from the Superintendent of *nizamat* affairs.
[2]Enclosed with a letter from the Resident at Lucknow, dated 5 December 1805.

Dec. 15 1189. To Raja Vir Rajinder Vodyar, the Raja of Coorg. Informs the addressee about the sad demise of Marquess Cornwallis and succession of the writer to the seat of Governor-General. States that the writer is fully apprised of the prevailing friendly relations between the two governments and assures of its favourable and amicable continuation in future also.

CI 41, pp. 373-76, no. 126; TI 51, pp. 308-10, no. 244; AI 20, p. 66.

Dec. 16 1190. To Nawwab Wazir. Acknowledges and expresses thanks for addressee's letter received on 15 December 1805 accompanying a present of pomegranates, apples and other fruits.

CI 41, pp. 492-94, no. 228; TI 51, p. 310, no. 245; AI 20, p. 69.

Dec. 16 1191. Nawwab Nasir al-Mulk to Pattle, the superintendent of *nizamat* affairs. Acknowledges receipt of Rs. 1,000 for the month of November. Explains his problems for the non-payment of the arrears and requests the addressee to get a letter issued in the name of the collector for the payment of arrears so that he can meet the expenses on the eve of *Eid*.

OR 789, f 1; CR 23, pp. 968-70, no. 17; TR 51A, pp. 556-57, no. 373; AR 20, p. 12.

Dec. 17 1192. From Saiyid Jafar Khan. Describes the atrocities of the Sikh *sardars* in the leadership of Raja Sansar Chand and Raja Jodh Singh and expresses desire to come under the protection of the Company's government.

OR 793, WS, f 1.

Dec. 17 1193. Order issued to officers posted for the collection of duties asking that they should not demand any duty from Maulavi Zia Allah Khan along with twelve men and other provisions who are supposed to travel from Madras to Calcutta via Gopa Mau.

OR 794; f 1.

Dec. 18 1194. To Daulat Rao Sindhia. Informs about the appointment of Mercer as permanent representative of the British government at the addressee's court who will be proceeding to his camp without delay and will deliver the usual credentials of office upon his arrival there.

CI 41, pp. 376-78, no. 127; TI 51, pp. 311-12, no. 246; AI 20, p. 49.

Dec. 19 1195. To Amrit Rao. Considering the addressee's financial difficulties assures that measures have been taken for the settlement of all his affairs. Acknowledges the intelligence of the addressee's postponing his visit to Allahabad till 1 *Shawwal*, adds that the orders will be issued to the officers concerned to provide the addressee all possible facilities and accommodation during his pilgrimage at Allahabad.

CI 41, pp. 378-81, no. 128; TI 51 pp. 312-14, no. 246A; AI 20, p. 44.

Dec. 20 1196. From Mir Alam. Expresses deep concerns on the death of Lord Cornwallis and satisfaction on the accession of the addressee to seat of Governor-General.

OR 796, WS, ff 2; CR 23, pp. 988-90, no. 23; TR 51A, p. 858, no. 374; AR 20, p. 22.

Dec. 20 1197. From Harak Chand Jagat Seth. Complementary on the accession of the addressee to seat of Governor-General.

OR 797, WS, f 1; TR 51A, p. 859, no. 375; AR 20, p. 17.

Dec. 20 1198. From Harak chand Jagat Seth to the Vice-President-in-Council. Complementary on Sir George Udney's appointment as Vice-President-in-Council.

OR 798, WS, f 1; TR 51A, p. 860, no. 376; AR 20, p. 17.

Dec. 20 1199. From Munshi Aziz Allah. Tenders his resignation from the post of head *munshi* to the Resident at Hyderabad on account of his deteriorating heath and desires to spend his remaining life in Lucknow, his native place.

OR 799, WS, f 1; CR 23, pp. 986-88, no. 22; TR 51, pp. 861-62, no. 377; AR 20, p. 4.

Dec. 21 1200. Mercer to Rana Kirat Singh (of Gohad). Acknowledges addressee's letter regarding settlement of the matter pending in relation to some *parganas.* Asks the addressee to see the writer along with his men while the latter will shortly visit the area. Further assures that the *sanads* regarding aforesaid *parganas* will be executed and handed over to the addressee.

OR 800(1),[1] f 1; CR 23, pp. 1023-26, no. 36(1).

Dec. 21. 1201. Rana Kirat Singh (of Gohad) to Mercer. Solicits grant of *sanads* in perpetuity for the *parganas* Dholpur Bari

[1]Enclosed with a letter from Mercer, dated 21 December 1805.

and Rajakhera comprising his state. Requests that necessary arrangements may be made for his safe arrival at that place, etc., etc.

OR 800 (ii),[1] *f 1; CR 23, pp. 1026-29, no. 36(2).*

Dec. 22 1202. Raja Randhir Singh of Bharatpur to Mercer. Expresses pleasure on the proposed visit of the addressee to Akbarabad and regret that the writer would not be able to see him there due to some other engagements.

OR 800 (ii), f 1; CR 23, pp. 1029-31, no. 36(3).

Dec. 22 1203. To Nawwab Wazir. Expresses deep confidence in the old intimate relationship between the two states and appreciates the proper endeavours of the addressee in favour of the Company. Solicits addressee's consent for a delay in the payment of the amount due over the Company. Further assures that the addressee will be rewarded handsomely.

CI 41, pp. 381-83, no. 129; TI 51, pp. 315-16, no. 247; AI 20, p. 69.

Dec. 23 1204. Nawwab Nusrat Jang to Udney, the Vice-President-in-Council. Informs about the death of Khair al-Nisa Begam. Requests for the continuation of her pension in favour of her husband Mirza Muhammad Ali and son Mirza Ali.

OR 801(i), f 1; TR 51A, pp. 864-66, no. 379; AR 20, p. 27.

Dec. 23 1205. Mirza Muhammad Ali and Mirza Ali, the husband and son of late Khair al-Nisa Begam respectively to Udney, the Vice-President-in-Council. Request for the continuation of the pension granted to late Khair al-Nisa Begam in their names as they do not have any means of subsistence.

OR 801(ii), f 1; TR 51A, pp. 866-67, no. 379; AR 20, p. 27.

Dec. 24 1206. Raja Kirat Singh to Mercer. States that the writer had been having possession of Gohad and other *mahal* as hereditary property according to the settlement made by the Governor-General. Now the Governor-General has assigned these *mahals* to Daulat Rao Sindhia consequent upon the accusation that the writer has violated the terms of agreement. Assures that the writer is a loyal ally of the Company and would follow the orders of the Governor-General as a token of loyalty. Requests

[1]Enclosed with a letter from Mercer, dated 21 December 1805.

that *parganas* of Dholpur Bari and Rajakhera be granted to him perpetually as there is no other means of subsistence for him and his dependents.

OR 802,[1] *f 1; CR 23, pp. 958-60, no. 14.*

Dec. 24 1207. Mercer to Rana Kirat Singh (of Gohad). Agrees to the proposal for the grant of *parganas* Dholpur Bari and Rajakhera to the addressee provided the latter vacates Gohad and takes up his resident at Dholpur and also handover the administration to the Company's government. Dated 17 December 1805.

OR 803, f 1; CR 23, pp. 992-94, no. 25.

Dec. 24 1208. From Ramazan Ali Khan. Requests for a *dastak-i-rahadari* (passport) to undertake a journey from Calcutta to Lucknow along Darogha Aqa Mir and few attendants and the luggage as detailed. Dated 25 *Ramazan* 1220 AH (17 December).

OR 804, WS, f 1.

Dec. 24 1209. The Vice-President-in-Council (Udney) to Jagat Seth (of Murshidabad). Acknowledges addressee's complementary letter sent on the occasion of writer's appointment as the Vice-President and Deputy Governor of Fort William.

CI 41, pp. 494-95, no. 229; TI 51, p. 316, no. 248; AI 20, p. 51.

Dec. 24 1210. Resident at Lucknow to Mirza Ramazan Ali Khan. Grants a *dastak-i-rahdari* to the addressee to undertake a journey from Calcutta to Lucknow along with goods and attendants, etc.

CI 41, p. 495, no. 230.

Dec. 24 1211. To Sultan Muhammad Shah. Acknowledges receipt of addressee's complementary letter on the occasion of writer's appointment as the Governor-General. Requests that the addressee should not expose himself to the inconveniences for visiting Allahabad for the purpose of meeting the Governor-General.

CI 41, pp. 495-97, no. 231; TI 51, p. 317, no. 249; AI 20, p. 56.

Dec. 24 1212. To Muhammad Ali Khan. Acknowledges addressee's letter expressing concern at the death of Marquess Cornwallis and pleasure on the appointment of the writer (Sir George Barlow) as the Governor-General.

CI 41, pp. 497-98, no 232; TI 51, p. 317, no. 250; AI 20, p. 56.

[1]Enclosed with a letter from Mercer, dated 18 December 1805.

Dec. 24 1213. To Mirza Husain Ali Khan (s/o late Nawwab Haider Beg Khan). Acknowledges receipt of addressee's congratulatory letter on the occasion of writer's appointment as the Governor-General.

CI 41, pp. 498-99, no. 233; TI 51, p. 318, no. 252.

Dec. 24 1214. To Nawwab Khiradmand Khan (of Farrukhabad). Acknowledges addressee's letter expressing deep concern on the death of Marquess Cornwallis and satisfaction on the appointment of the writer (Sir George Barlow) as Governor-General.

CI 41, pp. 499-500, no. 234; TI 51, p. 318, no. 251; AI 20, p. 53.

Dec. 24 1215. Nawwab Hafiz al-Mulk Muhabbat Khan. Acknowledges the addressee's complementary letter on the occasion of writer's appointment as Governor-General.

CI 41, pp. 500-01, no. 235; TI 51, p. 318, no. 253; AI 20, p. 56.

Dec. 24 1216. To Nawwab Madar al-Daulah (of Lucknow). Acknowledges the addressee's complementary letter on the occasion of the writer's succession to the seat of Governor-General. Expresses his inability to see the addressee as the writer is expected to depart from Allahabd.

CI 41, pp. 501-02, no. 236; TI 51; p. 319, no. 254; AI 20, p. 55.

Dec. 24 1217. To Maharaja Bahawani Din. Acknowledges receipt of addressee's letter of congratulation on the appointment of the writer as Governor-General and the *nazr* presented on the occasion.

CI 41, pp. 502-03, no. 237; TI 51, p. 319, no. 255; AI 20, p. 66.

Dec. 24 1218. To Alamas Ali Khan. To the same effect as the foregoing CI 237.

CI 41, p. 503, no. 238; TI 51, p. 320, no. 256; AI 20, p. 46.

Dec. 24 1219. To Nawwab Qasim Ali Khan. To the same effect as the foregoing CI 237.

CI 41, pp. 504-05, no. 239; TI 51, p. 320, no. 257; AI 20, p. 47.

Dec. 24 1220. To Nawwab Sharaf Ali Khan. To the same effect as the foregoing CI 237.

CI 41, pp. 504-05, no. 239; TI 51, p. 320, no. 258; AI 20, p. 68.

Dec. 24 1221. To Nawwab Tahsin Ali Khan. To the same effect as the foregoing CI 237.

CI 41, pp. 505-06, no. 240; TI 41, pp. 320-21, no. 259; AI 20, p. 68.

Dec. 26 1222. From Nawwab Nasir al-Mulk. Informs about the writer's recovery from illness. Dated 15 December 1805.

OR 805, WS, f 1; CR 23, pp. 995-98, no. 26; TR 51A, pp. 869-70, no. 381; AR 20, p. 29.

Dec. 28 1223. Udney, the Vice-President-in-Council to the Viceroy (of Pegu). Encloses a copy of Governor-General's letter sent to the addressee on the subject of the hostile measures adopted by the government of Rangoon against the British subjects and British ships there and asks the addressee to see into the matter and manage a quick redressal.

TI 51, pp. 321-23, no. 260, AI 20, p. 70.

Dec. 29 1224. From Raja Raghuji Bhonsla. Acknowledges receipt of the addressee's letter and expresses great grief on the death of Marquess Cornwallis. Also expresses satisfaction on the accession of the addressee to the seat of Governor-General.

OR 638, WS, f 1; CR 23, pp. 1013-17, no. 31; TR 51A, pp. 874-76, no. 385; AR 20, p. 33.

Dec. 29 1225. From Gokul Chand Chaubey. Requests for a *dastak-i-rahdari* for himself and his companions to travel along with a few carts and provision.

OR 806, f 1.

Dec. 29 1226. From Shridhar Laxman. Expresses hope that he will constantly be employed to strengthen the relation of friendship between the two states and that the addressee will manifest his disposition to promote the Raja's interests.

OR 807, WS, f 1; CR 23, pp. 1020-22, no. 34; TR 51A, pp. 870-71, no. 382; AR 20, p. 40.

Dec. 29 1227. From Raghuji Bhonsla. Sends some gifts to the addressee and requests for their acknowledgement, encloses a list of gifts.

OR 808,[1] WS, ff 2; CR 23, pp. 1017-18, no. 32; TR 51A, pp. 872-73, no. 383; AR 20, p. 33.

[1]Enclosed with a letter from the Resident at Nagpur, dated 11 December 1805.

Dec. 29 1228. From Jaswant Rao Ramchandra, *subedar* of Jhansi. Complementary on the assumption of office of the Governor-General by the addressee.

OR 809, WS, f 1; CR 23, pp. 1019-20, no. 33; TR 51A, pp. 873-74, no. 384; AR 20, p. 18.

Dec. 29 1229. From Amrit Rao. Acknowledges receipt of the addressee's letter regarding grant of a *jagir* to the writer against his monthly stipend.

OR 810,[1] WS, f 1; CR 23, pp. 1011-13, no. 30; TR 51A, pp. 876-78, no. 386; AR 20, p. 3.

Dec. 30 1230. From Nawwab Wazir. Refers to the correspondences made with Col. Collins and argues that a comprehensive investigation be made to find out the truth and clear the suspicion caused due to an alleged correspondence made between Amir Khan and Rai Ratan Chand. Further assures the addressee of his (writer's) loyalty to the Company's government. Encloses copy of intelligence report from Bareilly and other few related letters.

OR 811,[2] f 1.

Dec. 30 1231. From Raja Randhir Singh (of Bharatpur). Informs about the sad demise of his (writer's) father. Requesters for the same favourable relation as it happened during his father's life.

OR 812,[3] WS, f 1; CR 23, pp. 1022-23, no. 35; TR 51A, pp. 878-79, no. 387; AR 20, p. 36.

Dec. 30 1232. From Hari Uddhav Kashyap, the employee of *Peshwa*. Requests for a *dastak-i-rahdari* to be issued in the name of Balaji Lachhman to travel from Calcutta to Poona along with a few men and goods. Dated 27 December 1805.

OR 813, f 1.

Dec. 30 1233. To Nawwab Wazir. States that due to various engagements it will not be possible for the writer to see the addressee at Kanpur. Also expresses his gratification for the attention and kindness that the addressee has manifested towards the Company's government.

CI 41, pp. 383-85, no. 130; TI 51, pp. 323-25, no. 261; AI 20, p. 69.

[1]Enclosed with a letter from the Agent at Benares.

[2]See OR 636 and 637.

[3]Enclosed with a letter from Mercer, dated 24 December 1805.

Dec. 30 1234. The Vice-President to Balajai Lachhman. Grants a *dastak-i-rahdari* to the addressee to conduct a travel from Calcutta to Poona along with a few men and goods.

CI 41, pp. 507-08, no. 242.

Dec. 30 1235. The Vice-President to Mahipat Rao. Grants a *dastak-i-rahdari* to travel from Calcutta to Nagpur with goods and other provisions.

CI 41, pp. 508-9, no. 243.

Dec. 31 1236. From Purnaiya. Tenders condolence on the death of Lord Cornwallis. Expresses pleasure that the prosperity of the state has grew properly under the British government. Further gives details of the visit of Olex to survey the region.

OR 814/a, f 1; CR 23, pp. 1031-36, no. 37(1).

Dec. 31 1237. From Kishan Raj, *wazir* of the Raja of Mysore. Expresses grief over the demise of Lord Cornwallis. Anticipates that no changes will occur in the relation of the two states. Expresses pleasure that the state has grew its prosperity under the British government.

OR 814/b, f 1; CR 23, pp. 1036-40, no. 37(2).

Dec. 31 1238. Farzand Ali Khan, *munshi* at Sambalpur to the Magistrate at Cuttack. Refers to his previous letter bearing details of the situation prevailing in the region, says that one Jiwan Singh who had gone up to Nagpur along with Elphinstone had arrived back and has verbally reported that Nana Sahib has arrived at Chanda, started repairing of the fort, plundered a number of laden bullock carts belonging to English gentleman and has blocked the way of the Company and its allies.

OR 215[1]/a, f 1; CR 23, pp. 1040-42, no. 38(1)
TR 51A, pp. 879-82, no. 388; AR 20, p. 16.

Dec. 31 1239. Jujhar Singh, the *zamindar* of Raigarh to Robert. States that in the month of September Babu Markand Saha arrived at Ratanpur at the head of 150 *sawar* and 150 foot-soldiers from Nagpur. Informs that the writer has sent a *harkarah* to Ratanpur to ascertain the affairs there. Assures that the writer will send the report as soon as he receives the same from the *harkarah*.

OR 815/c, f 1; CR 23, pp. 1042-45, no. 38(2);
TR 51A, pp. 882-84, no. 389; AR 20, p. 16.

[1]Enclosed with a letter from the magistrate at Cuttack, dated 25 December 1805.

Dec. -- 1240. The Vice-President to Gokul Chand Chaubey. Grants a *dastak* to the addressee to travel towards Lucknow along with his companions.

CI 41, pp. 506-7, no. 241.

Dec. -- 1241. . . . to Major Lytton (?). States that they have come from Nawwab Wazir Ali Khan and now they are at a distance of two *dhowar* (?) from the fort of Allahabad and they will arrive soon, etc.

OR 792A(i), f 1.

Dec. -- 1242. Anjha Ram *tahsildar* of *pargana* Barh to Major Lytton. Reports about the mobilization of the Tilanga Company to suppress the miscreants and their success over the enemy.

OR 792A(ii), f 1.

Dec. -- 1243. Bhikan Singh, *jamadar* to Major Lytton. Reports about the battle fought between his soldiers and the miscreants. Also gives details of the wounded soldiers.

OR 792A(iii), ff 2.

Dec. -- 1244. *Yaddasht* regarding list of the papers of the case of Wazir Ali and others.

OR 817/i, f 1; CR 23, pp. 946-47, no. 13(i).

Dec. -- 1245. *Zabanbandi* (statement) of Ram Roop Chaubey of Chakra, *pargana* Barh recorded before the Magistrate of Allahabad regarding movement of Wazir Ali in the region along with his forces.

OR 817/ii, f 1; CR 23, pp. 847-50, no. 13(2).

Dec. -- 1246. Hiragir, *qiladar* of Bargarh to Kunwar Kanchangir. Says that one, Jagat Rai has been brought by Wazir Ali to his area; the *amil* of the said area has fled away and the Raja of Rewan has camped across the river Naunis (?). Further says that he is at alert in the *chauki* to check the miscreants. Dated 18 *Shaban* 1220 AH (11 November 1805).

OR 817/iii, f 1; CR 23, pp. 951-52, no. 13(3).

Dec. -- 1247. Magistrate of Bundelkhand to Raja Narendergir. Requests him to instruct his officials to arrest Wazir Ali immediately.

OR 817/iv, f 1; CR 23, pp. 952-53, no. 13(4).

Dec. -- 1248. Raja Narendergir to the Magistrate of Bundelkhand. Informs that Chaugarhi was under the British rule but Bhopal

Singh Baghela, the brother of the Raja of Rewan has captured it sometimes back.

OR 817/v, f 1; CR 23, pp. 953-54, no. 13(5).

Dec. -- 1249. Hiragir, *qaladar* of Bargarh to Kunwar Kanchangir. Acknowledges receipt of the addresee's letter asking the writer to arrest Ghulam Makhdum. States that the said person was wounded in village Sanliha but has now shifted somewhere else. Further says that there is no trace of Wazir Ali in Bargarh.

OR 817/vi, f 1; CR 23, pp. 954, no. 13(6).

Dec. -- 1250. Magistrate of Bundelkhand to Kunwar Kanchangir. Enquires about the location of *mauza* Sanliha. Dated 6 December 1805.

OR 817/vii, f 1; CR 23, pp. 955-56, no. 13(7).

Dec. -- 1251. Kunwar Kanchangir to the Magistrate of Bundelkhand. States that if any trace of Wazir Ali will be reported in Bargarh immediate measures will be adopted for his arrest.

OR 817/vii, f 1; CR 23, pp. 956-57, no. 13 (8).

Dec. -- 1252. Muhammad Abbas Khan to the Resident at Delhi. States that the news about the affairs at Qandhar, condition of Prince Qaisar, arrival of Zaman Shah and Fath Khan has alreadly been reported. Argues that the rumour should not be given attention. Dated 28 *Shaban* 1220 (21 November 1805).

OR 818/a, f 1; CR 23, pp. 997-1000, no. 27(1).

Dec. -- 1253. Intelligence report from the court of Shah Shuja of Kabul to the Resident at Delhi. Informs about the visit of Balahisar by the king of Kabul; informs about the arrival of Jaswant Rao Holkar at Patiala to see Raja Ranjit Singh and other Sikh chieftains to seek their cooperation etc. etc. Dated 23 *Shaban* 1220 AH (16 November 1805).

OR 818[1]/b, f 1; CR 23, pp. 1000-04, no. 27(2).

Dec. -- 1254. Nawwab Wazir to Col. Collins. Acknowledges receipt of addressee's letter enquiring about one, Badr al-Din alias Mir Kallu who has been detained at Akbarabad by the police and who has stated that since the writer has been displeased with him, so he has come to this place. Says that he (the writer) is

[1]Enclosed with a letter from the Resident at Delhi, dated 28 December 1805.

not displeased with the said person and is free to go to anywhere at will. Dated 25 *Ramazan* 1220 AH (17 December 1805).

OR 819,[1] *f 1; CR 23, pp. 991-92, no. 24.*

Dec. -- 1255. Gokul Chand, *darogha* of police in *pargana* Amor to the Magistrate at Gorakhpur. Comprehensively describes that the plundering of the area and kidnapping of Kashi Nath, *patwari* and others by Bhola Nath *patwari*, the rebel. Further says that they are not allowed to maintain more then a few men for security purposes where as there is a need of adequate number of police men to give security to the villages in this area as it is the border of the territory of Nawwab Wazir. Requests to look into the problem and suggest proper remedy.

OR 820/a, ff 2; CR 23, pp. 1065-68, no. 41(i).

Dec.-- 1256. Mirza Nabi Beg, *darogha* of police at *pargana* Amor to the Magistrate at Gorakhpur. Encloses depositions of Kashi Nath *patwari* and others for further enquiry and investigations.

OR 820/b, f 1; CR 23, pp. 1068-69), no. 41(2).

Dec. -- 1257. Mirza Nabi Beg, *darogha* of police at *pargana* Amor to the Magistrate of Gorakhpur. Submits the details of the robbery and kidnapping of Kashi Nath *patwari* and other by Bhola Nath *patwari* and his men.

OR 820/c, ff 3; Cr 23, pp. 1070-75, no. 41(3).

Dec. -- 1258. From Sita Ram and others, the sons of late Mansa Ram. State that *mauza* Phoolpur, Keri, Nonari, Jagdishpur, Mundiari etc. were granted to his late father Mansa Ram by late Nawwab Asaf al-Daulah and they have the possession of the aforesaid *mauzas* till the time the Company established their rule over this area. Thereafter the said grants were confiscated by the *Sarishtadars*. Requests for the restoration of there assignments to them. Encloses the copies of the *sanads*.

OR 821/a, f 1, WS; CR 23, pp. 960-62, no. 15(1).

Dec. -- 1259. Nawwab Asaf al-Daulah of Awadh to the *mutasaddis* etc. of *pargana* Nizamabad, Azamgarh. Notifies the revenue free grant of *mauza* Jagdishpur and Mundiari etc. to Bulaqi Das and Lalji Mal. Enclosed is a copy of *sanad*. Dated 15 *Jumada*

[1]Enclosed with a letter from the Resident at Lucknow, dated 21 December 1805.

II, 1209 AH (7 January 1795).
OR 821/b,[1] f 1; CR 23, pp. 962-63, no. 15(4).

Dec. -- 1260. Nawwab Asaf al-Daulah of Awadh to the *mutasaddis* etc. of *pargana* Mahul. Notifies the revenue free grant of *mauza* Phoolpur etc. w.e.f 1200 *Fasli* to Radha Kishan and Harbhajan Lal sons of Mansa Ram. Dated 1 *Shaban* 1207 AH (14 March 1793).
OR 821[2]/c, f 1; CR 23, pp. 962-63, no. 15(2).

Dec. -- 1261. Nawwab Asaf al-Daulah to the *mutasaddis* etc. of *pargana* Mahul. Notifies the revenue free grant of *mauza* Keri, Darijha and Sonari etc. to Sita Ram w.e.f. 1201 *Fasli*. Dated 7 *Rajab* 1208 AH (8 February 1794).
OR 821/d,[3] f 1; CR 23, pp. 964-66, no. 15(3).

Dec. -- 1262. Kunwar Kanchangir Himmat Bahadur of Sikandra (Bilashpur) to the Magistrate of Bundelkhand. Enlist the officials attached to the officers of the Company.
OR 822, f 1; CR 23, pp. 1047-60, no. 39.

Dec. -- 1263. Shivraj, *faujdar* to the Collector of Gorakhpur. Requests to appoint one or two men of merit to resolve and find out a solution of the dispute on the ownership of *pargana* Dhiru.
OR 823[4]/a, WS, f 1; CR 23, pp. 972-73, no. 19(1).

Dec. -- 1264. *Rubakar-i-adalat-i-faujdari* of John Ahmuty, the Magistrate of District Gorakhpur. States that it has come to light according to a comprehensive investigation that the *talluqa* Dhiru has been in the territory of the Raja of Bansi and the said *talluqa* has been in the Raja's possession up till now. Hence there is no question of any one's claim over the said *talluqa*.
OR 823[5]/b, f 1, WS, CR 23, pp. 974-75, no. 19(2).

[1]Enclosed with a letter from the Resident at Lucknow, dated 15 December. 1805.

[2]Ibid.

[3]Ibid.

[4]Copy enclosed with a letter from the Judge at Gorakhpur, dated 17 December 1805.

[5]Ibid.

Dec. -- 1265. *Kaifiat* (remarks) stated by Tara Chand, Hira Lal, Ram Niwarak Sahai and Kishan Parsad etc. the *qanugos*. Confirms that *Patta* Dhiru has been part of *pargana* Ratpur Bansi since old times and the Raja of of Bansi have his authority over it till date.

OR 823[1]/c, WS, f 1; CR 23, pp. 975-76, no. 19(3).

Dec. -- 1266. Parbhakar Belal, *diwan* of Rao Amrit Rao to Brooke, the Agent of Governor-General at Benaras. Says that a *dastak* (passport) be issued to facilitate Rao Amrit Rao to make a journey to Allahabad for a holy dip along with his servants, attendants and security men. Also asks to issue orders to the official to make proper arrangements for the supply of food and other provisions as well as grass etc.

OR 824[2]/a, f 1; CR 23, pp. 979-80, no. 20(1).

Dec. -- 1267. A *gumashta* of Rao Amrit Rao to Brooke, the Agent to Governor-General at Benaras. Requests to issue a letter to the official to make proper arrangement for a safe and duty free journey of Rao Amrit Rao to Allahabad along with his attendants and security men.

OR 824[3]/b, f 1; CR 23, pp. 980-81, no. 20(2).

Dec. -- 1268. Maharaja Ranjit Singh to Col. John Collins. Assures the addressee of his unquestionable attachment to the Company's government and adds that his welcoming correspondence with Jaswant Rao Holkar is only an outwardly courtesy. Says tht even sending his *wakil* Dahna Singh to the camp of Holkar is nothing but an outward show.

OR 825[4] f 1' CR 23, pp. 966-68, no. 16.

Dec. -- 1269. Moti Lal to John Meakon. Requests that a *dastak-i-rahdari* (Passport) be issued in regard to his taking up journey from Calcutta to Lucknow. Also says tht the officials should be ordered to insure a safe and secure journey along with his attendants and provision. Encloses a list of articles.

OR 826 ff 2.

[1]Copy enclosed with a letter from the Judge at Gorakhpur, dated 17 December 1805.

[2]Copy enclosed with a letter from the Agent to Governor-General at Benares, dated 26 Dec. 1805.

[3]Ibid., dated 17 December 1805.

[4]Copy enclosed with a letter from the Resident at Lucknow, dated 15 December 1805.

Dec. -- 1270. From Mir Muhammad Sadiq Gulsitanah (of Isfahan). Describes the losses incurring in his *jagir* (probably at Bardawan) during the last few years causing regular pecuniary problems. Further informs that Mirza Abu Talib has been appointed *mukhtar-i-kar* to see the affairs and explains the virtual position of the *Jagir* to the addressee. Dated 12 *Rajab* 1220 AH (6 October 1805).

OR 827, WS, f 1.

Dec. -- 1271. Faujdar Bhagatvir to Babu Kanwalkantji. Informs that he (the addressee) has been appointed *amil* of Chautria Butwal and asks that the revenues of various *parganas* under the *tahsil* of Butwal should be submitted to the writer.

OR 829/a, WS, f 1; CR 23, pp. 1064-65, no. 40(2).

Dec. -- 1272. Faujdar Bhagatvir to Kanwalkantji. To the same effect as the foregoing (OR 829/a).

OR 829/b, WS, f 1; CR 23, pp. 1060-62, no. 40 (1).

Dec. -- 1273. Shaikh Muhammad Ghisa, *mukhtar* of Muhammad Timur Shah. Requests for the restoration of certain gardens in Allahabad where there are a number of tombs of great men like Prince Muhammad Jahangir (probably s/o Akbar II).

OR 830, WS, f 1.

Dec. -- 1274. To the Nizam. Acknowledges the addressee's letter expressing concern on the death of Marquess Cornwallis.

CI 41, pp. 362-64, no. 120.

Dec. -- 1275. To Mir Alam. To the same effect as the foregoing.

CI 41, pp. 362-64, no. 120).

ILLUSTRATIONS

هو

نواب صاحب والاقدر عالیشان مظهر لطف و احسان قدر دان نیازمندان دام الطافه

بعد گذارش مراتب عقیدت و اخلاص و مدارج رسوخ مودت و نیاز که خارج از شرح و بیان است

بالتماس می پردازد لله الحمد که نیازمند همواره بدعای استقامت مزاج لطف امتزاج و ازدیاد

مدارج شوکت و اقبال عالیجناب رطب اللسان است و در همین ایام نامه والا که مملو

و محشو بانواع نوازش و قدردانی پرتو عاطفت انداخته بمدد وصول خود دانی محفوره و هم

اغوش طمانیت و انبساط نامحصوره پرداخته معزز و ممتاز سربلند و سرفراز ساخت الله تعالی

این قدردانی ها بانواع عظمت و اجلال و جمعیت و اقبال سلامت باکرامت دارد که همه احوال بهبود

جمیع متوسلان سرکار است چون خیراندیش برسوخ نیازمندی که خود را محض دست گرفته

سرکار و نیکخواه می انگارد و بدین الطاف انجناب بعزت و حرمت چنانکه باید و شاید

ارام یافته است متر صد ارجاع اعطاف و الطاف که نیازمند را از نیازمندان و

مخلصان صمیمی تصور فرموده همواره در گوشه خاطر عاطر فرایاد ضمیر

منیر داشته باصدار عنایت نامجات معزز و مباهی باید فرمود که حضور

همعنی از موهبت عظمی و عطیات کبری جناب ارزو بهمتا و خاصه قدر دانی

انجناب نسبت بحال خود منصور تواند شد افتاب دولت و حشمت از مطلع

جاه و شوکت طالع باد

OR 54

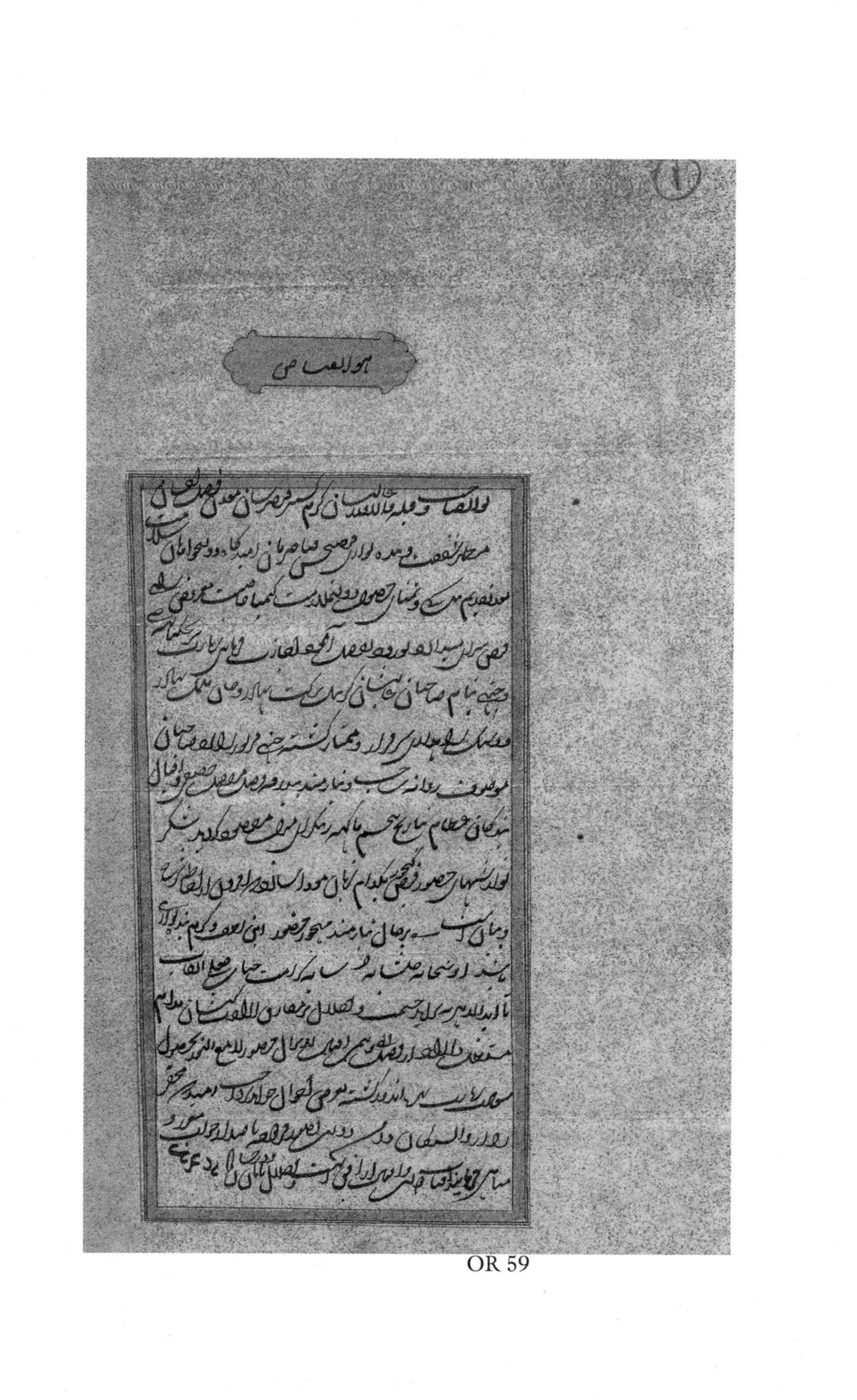

هو العاصی

[illegible]

OR 59

1

Received 2nd Febr 1805

از اسناد

پروانه ارسالیه مقصدوره مطلع است در هفتم ماه دسمبر سنه ۱۸۰۴ عیسوی در باب پاره کرده داد و دو قطعه

یکی سند پرگنه سدهوره بنام عطاء الله و دوم سند پرگنه جونه بنام مظهر شاه متعلقه ضلع گورکهپور که منجمله مرسله

مجوزه بابی حاجب الله فدوی صلکمند بود بسبب گشتن یکی و دو قطعه اسناد مانده بود شرف صدور یافت و در حوالد

حسب الحکم حضور اسناد پرگنه مسمی تا خیر مذکور [illegible] ساخته داخل دفتر حضور نموده شد

معروضه بیست و نهم ماه جنوری سنه ۱۸۰۵ عیسوی مطابق بیست و هفتم شهر شوال سنه ۱۲۱۹ هجری [illegible]

OR 82

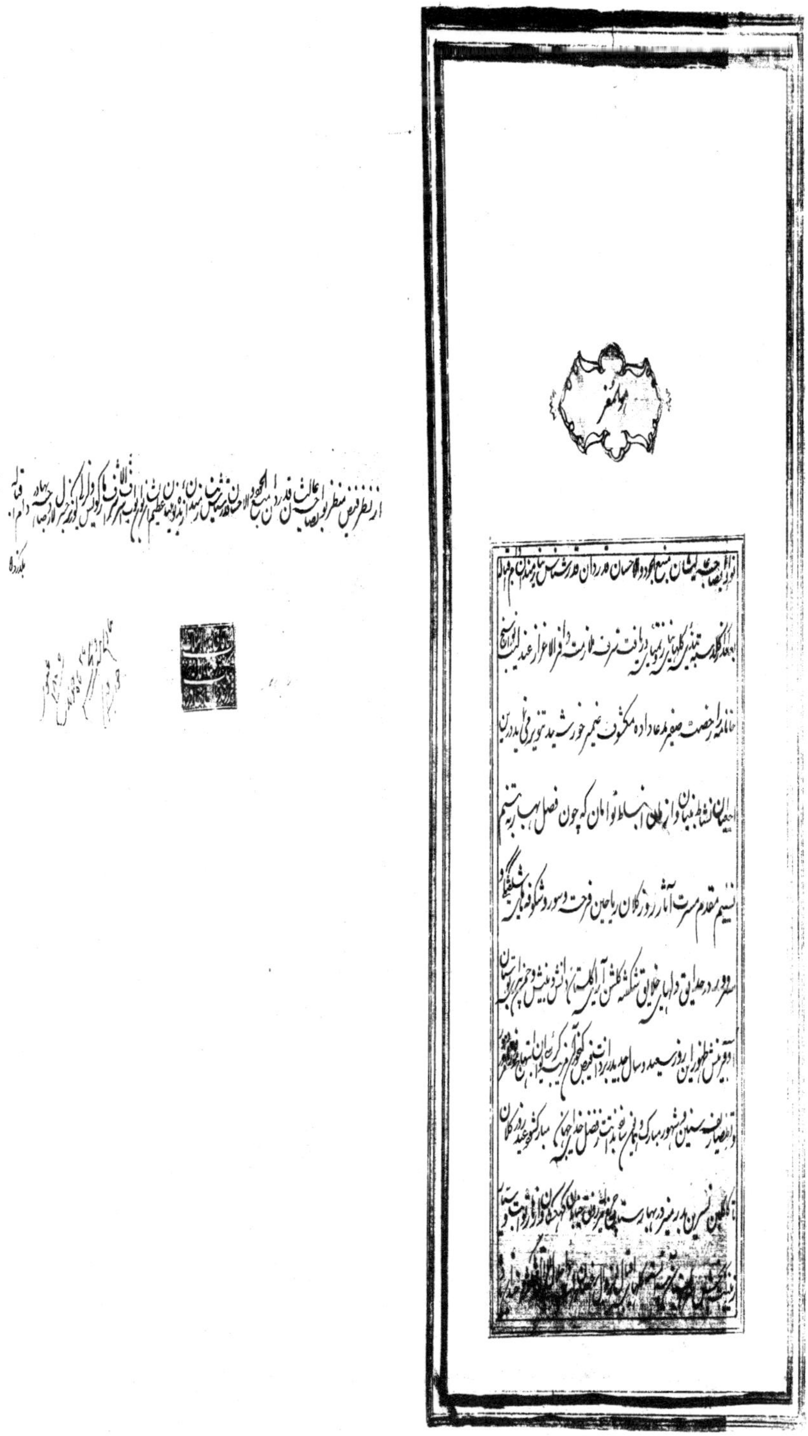

OR 99

الله

نوابصاحب مشفق مهربان کرمفرمای مخلصان سلامت

بعد ابراز مراتب تمنای سامی مواصلت دافی المسرت
والافادت که خلاصه مقاصد دلی است مشهود
خاطر الطاف ذخایر نموده می آید درینولا قدری
میوه ولایت از قسم انار وغیره بمقتضای
محبت واتحاد برای آن کرمفرمای مخلصان
متحف شده خواهد رسید ترصد از الطاف
آن است که خاطر محبت مآثر را پیوسته
منتظر جویای دریافت اخبار بشاشت آثار
انگاشته بتسطیر شفقت نامجات مسرور و شادکام
میساخته باشند ایام جمعیت و شادمانی و بهجت و کامرانی مدام بکام باد

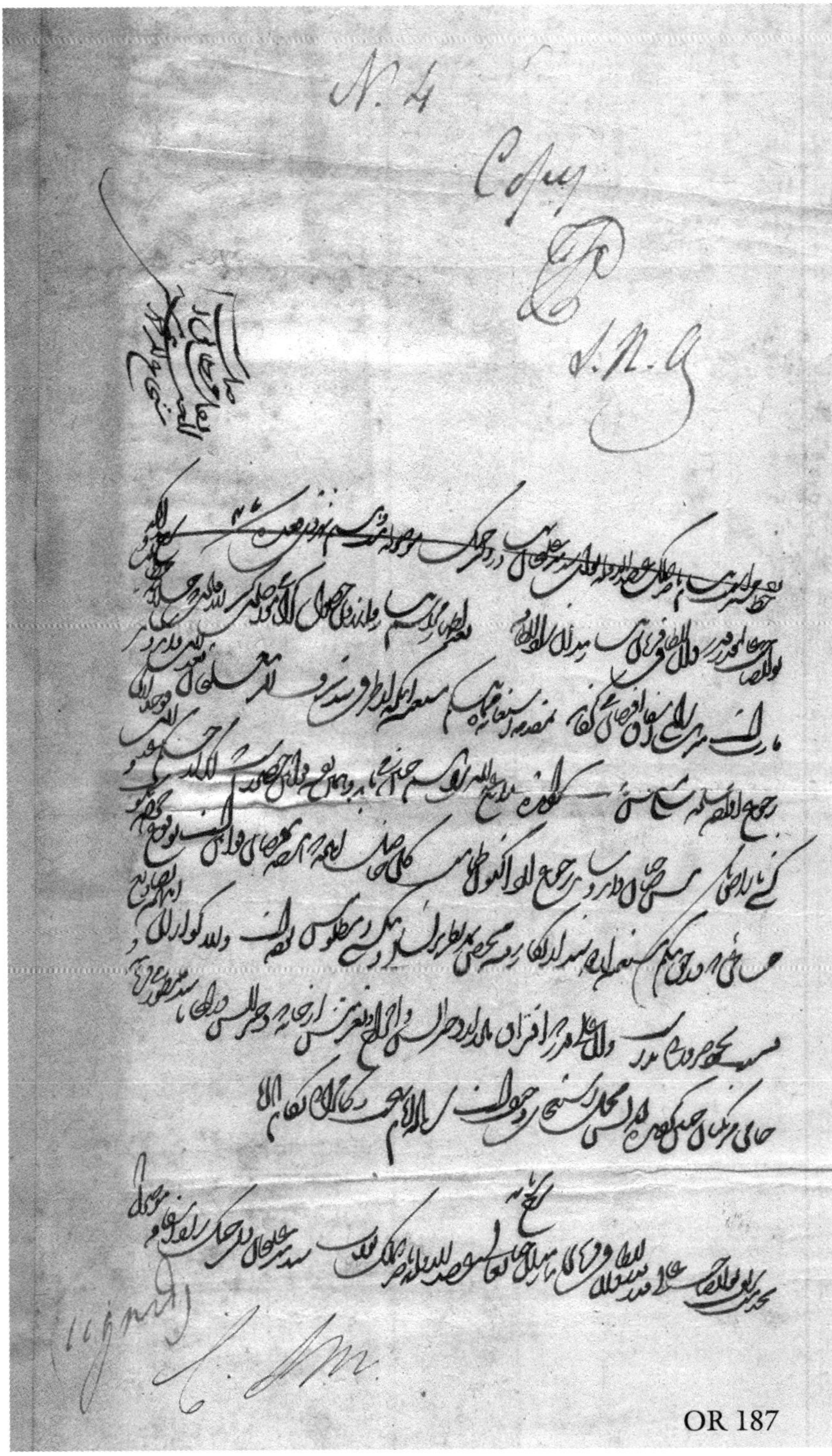

OR 187

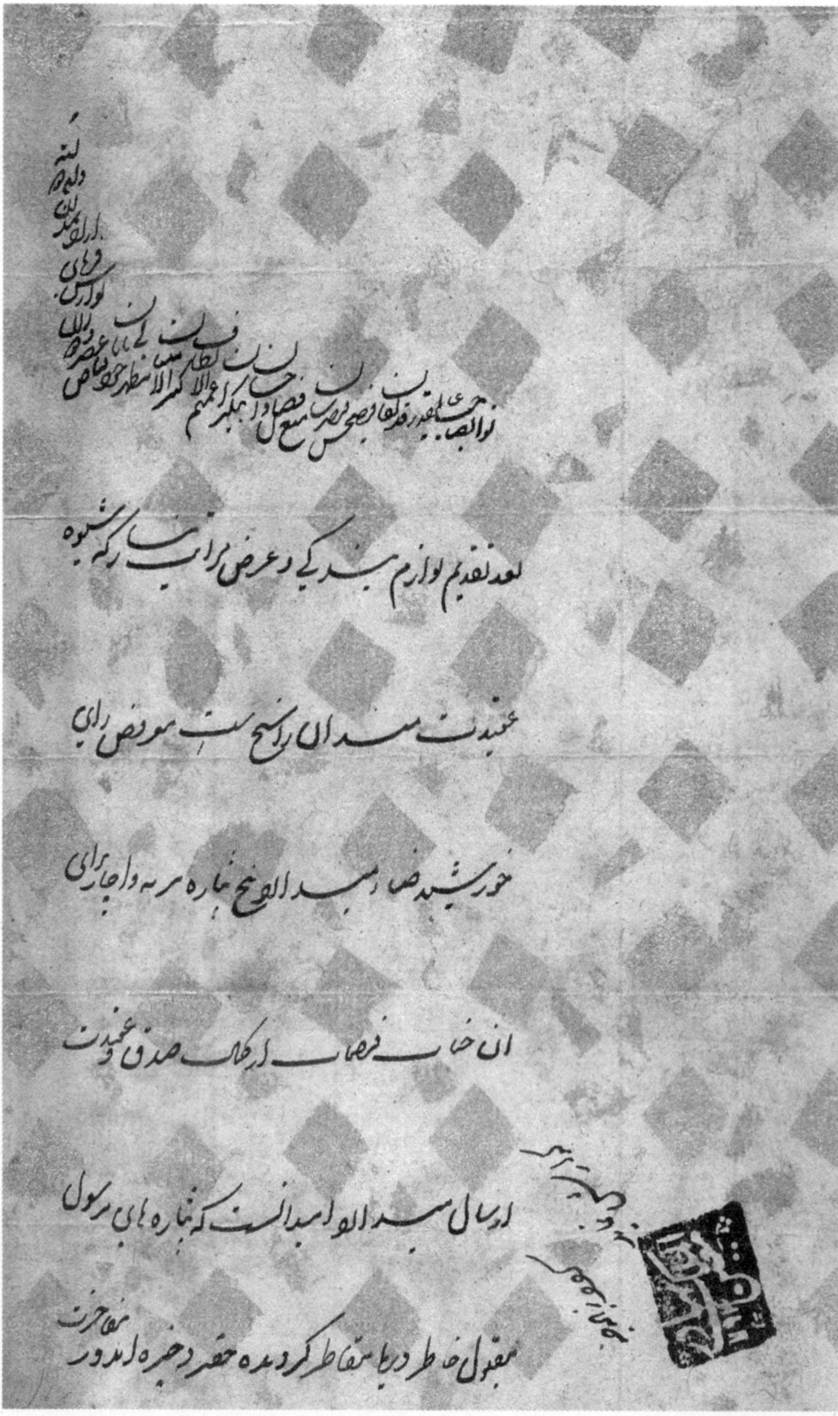

بعد تقدیم لوازم بندگی و عرض مراتب اخلاص که شیوه

عقیدت بنده آن راسخ است معروض رای

خورشید ضیا میسازد الحق پنج پاره مرتبه واجب برای

آن جناب فرصت ازکمال صدق عقیدت

ارسال بنده الوا بند آنست که پنج پاره های مرکول

مقبول خاطر دریا مقاطر کرده حقیر ذخیره اندوز مفاخرت

OR 240

لا يخفى جنابكم العالي

من طرف اليهودي الذي هم ثلاثة انفار واحد منهم برادر الايلچي والاثنين صراريف الكمپني صدر عليهم حوالة من حضرة
افندينا ايده الله تعالى لاجل مساعدة السفر المبارك بمبلغ اربعة عشر الف قرش ولما داعيكم سمع بذلك شفنا هذا
خلاف عهدنامة الذي بين الدولتين العليتين ومن اخلاصنا لحضرة افندينا سلمنا خمسة عشر الف قرش من مالنا
برسم المساعدة لان يظهر خلوص نيتنا بين ايادي حضرة افندينا ثم عطانا جناب خزينه دار اغا تمسك وداعيكم
سلم التمسك لجنابكم العالي لان تاخذون لنا بيورلدي على وجه المذكور وفيما بعد ما ارسلو ويبعثو لنا خبر بان
المبلغ المذكور ما هو لك ومال اليهودي وتعطل هذا الامر ثم حلفو اليهودي على ان وجه المذكور مالكم او مال الباليوز
وصار عندكم معلوم بان ما لنا وما عطينا الوجه المذكور الا بسبب زيادة اخلاصنا والى الان ما نعرف متى
يوصلنا بيورلدي على ذلك وسبب الذي في كل الامور داعيكم يصدع جنابكم العالي وصداقتنا مع جنابكم
من صميم الفواد فالان ايضا اخبرناكم لان جنابكم تبعثون لنا بيورلدي الشريف على وجه المذكور حيث اننا
ما قصرنا بشروط الاخلاص في كل الامور سابقا ولاحقا خصوصا في اعطاء هذا الوجه وبعد ذلك هذا شي
ظاهر الذي داعيكم جالس في الجول والبرية لاكن لما مخلصكم في هذا الطرف ومنصبنا باقي علينا بحسب
اوامر كبارنا واجب علينا بان لا نغفل على امر الذي هو صلاح الدولتين العليتين وهذا قريب سنتين او ازيد
بانه ما كان يصير بينكم وبين شاه الايران بتبليغ المطالب والكتب كان على يد مخلصكم وكذلك هذا
من مدة بان دولت شاه الايران مع دولت شاه الانكليز صاير واحد فلاجل ذلك وجب علينا بان نهتم
على امر الذي صلاح الدولتين وهو هذا الذي جانا خط من جناب ميرزا بزرك وزير حضرة عباس ميرزا
ولي عهد شاه الايران في توصية اكرام الجنازه وجناب محمد حسن خان قاجار والخط المذكور وصل
بلا وقت عندنا ورد نا رسله امين لخدمتكم العالي صار سبب الذي اخرناه والان ارسلناه الى خدمتكم
بان تعرضونه مضمونه بين ايادي حضرة افندينا لان ما نشوف صلاح الدولتين وهكذا ابروديه مع
مترددين من اهل الايران خصوصا مع جناب الايلچي محمد نبي خان الذي هو رايح لدولتنا وجناب المذكور من المقربين
والمعتمدين الشاه الايران وكذلك مخلص لحضرة افندينا وغاية ما يكون خواطره عزيز عندهم كما هنا في الهند سبب الذي كثير
امورات صدر منه من قديم الايام الذي هو صلاح لدولتنا وكذلك في الايران بكل امكان صلاح دولتنا بذل غاية الجهود
بذلك وبعد ذلك ما ندري اذا يجينا من الهند باكيت ويصير لنا لازم تاتار حضرة افندينا يعطينا تاتار ام لا وهذا
السوال وجب علينا سبب ان مستر مني كاتب لنا بعض الحكي من لسان حضرة افندينا الذي ما يختفي في عقل
مخلصكم ونسئل الله سبحانه وتعالى يحصل سفركم المبارك في النصر والظفر وينصركم عز وجل على الاعداء ويرزقنا
ملاقاتكم بالفرح والسرور والدعاء خير ختام

OR 243

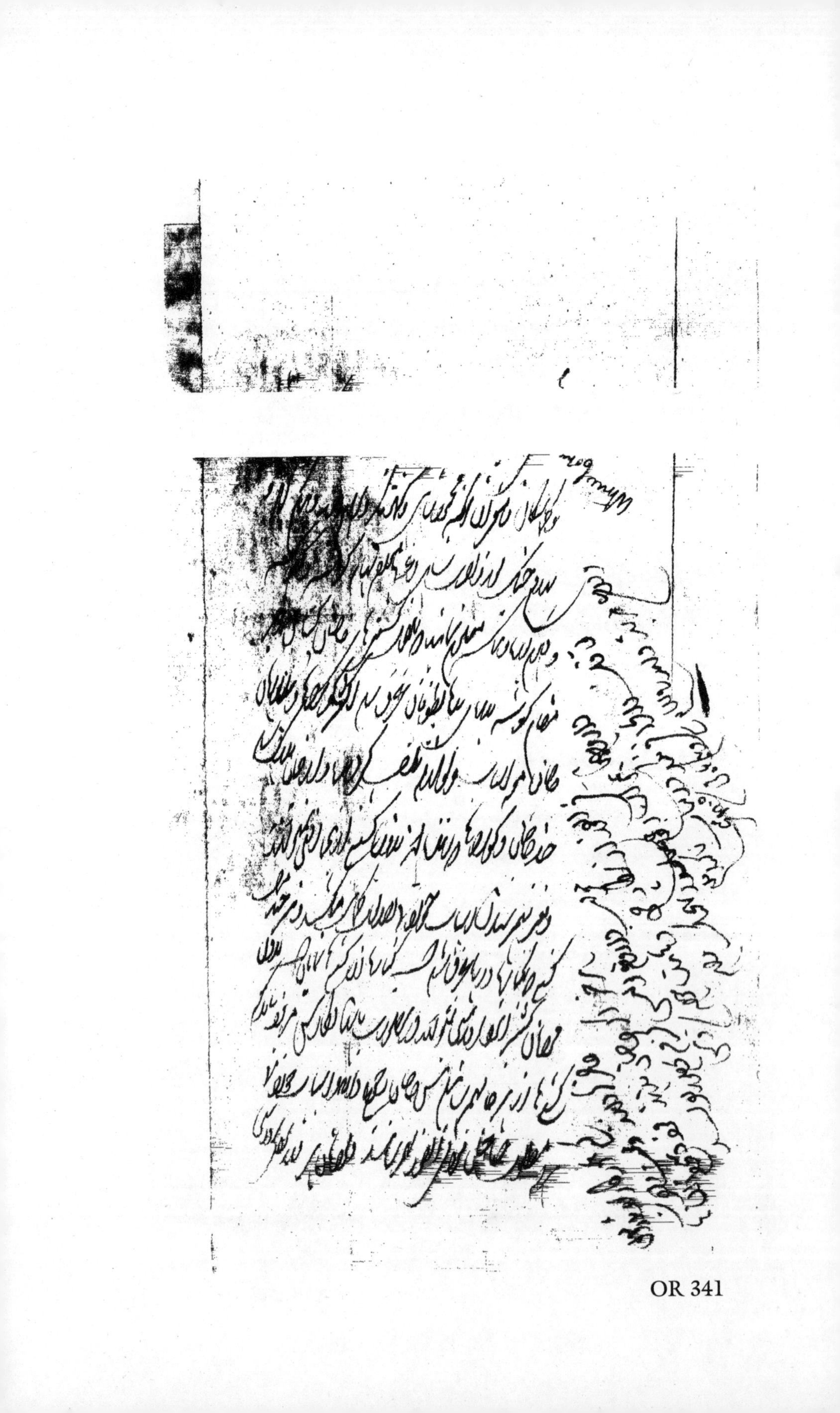

OR 341

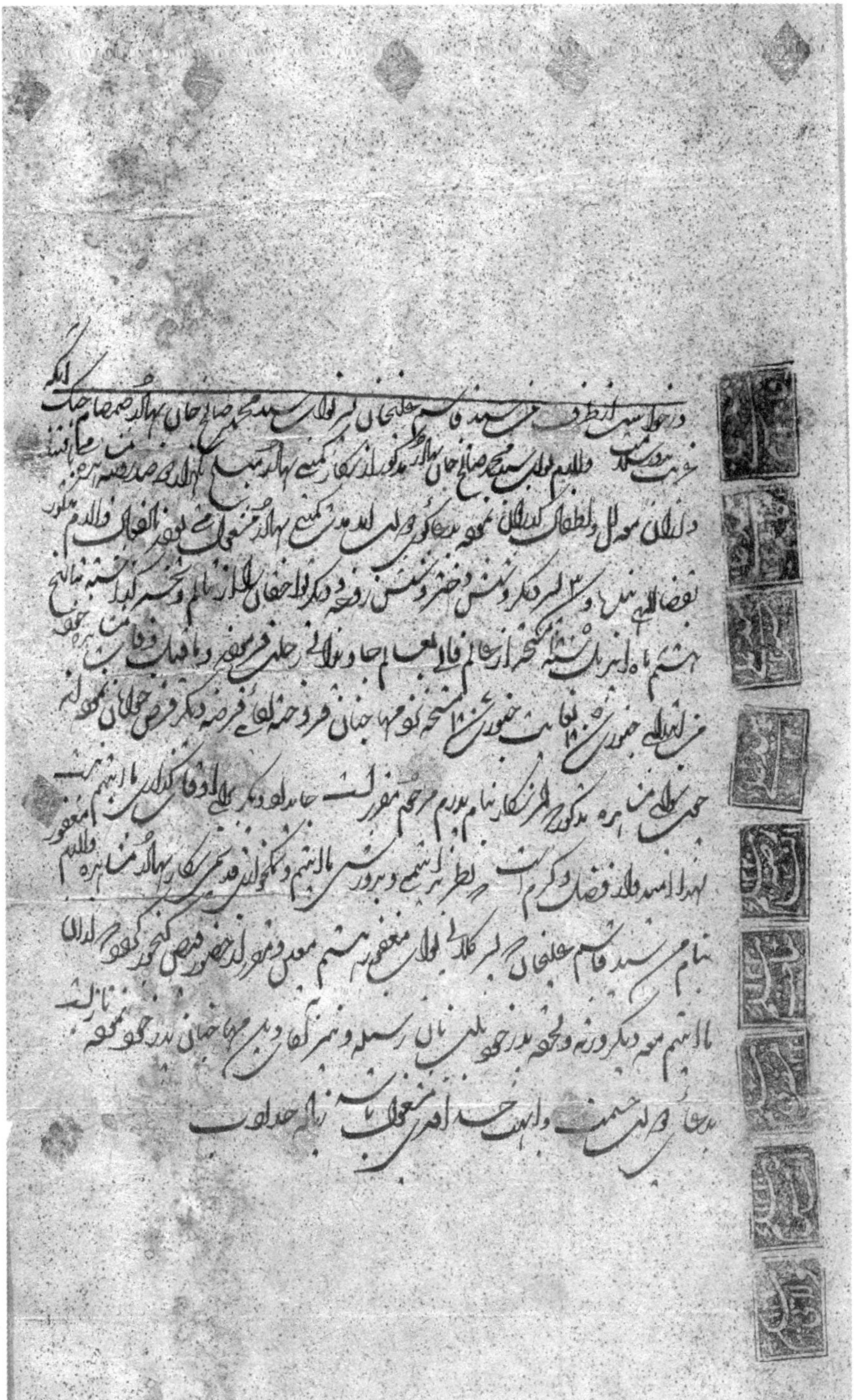

OR 389

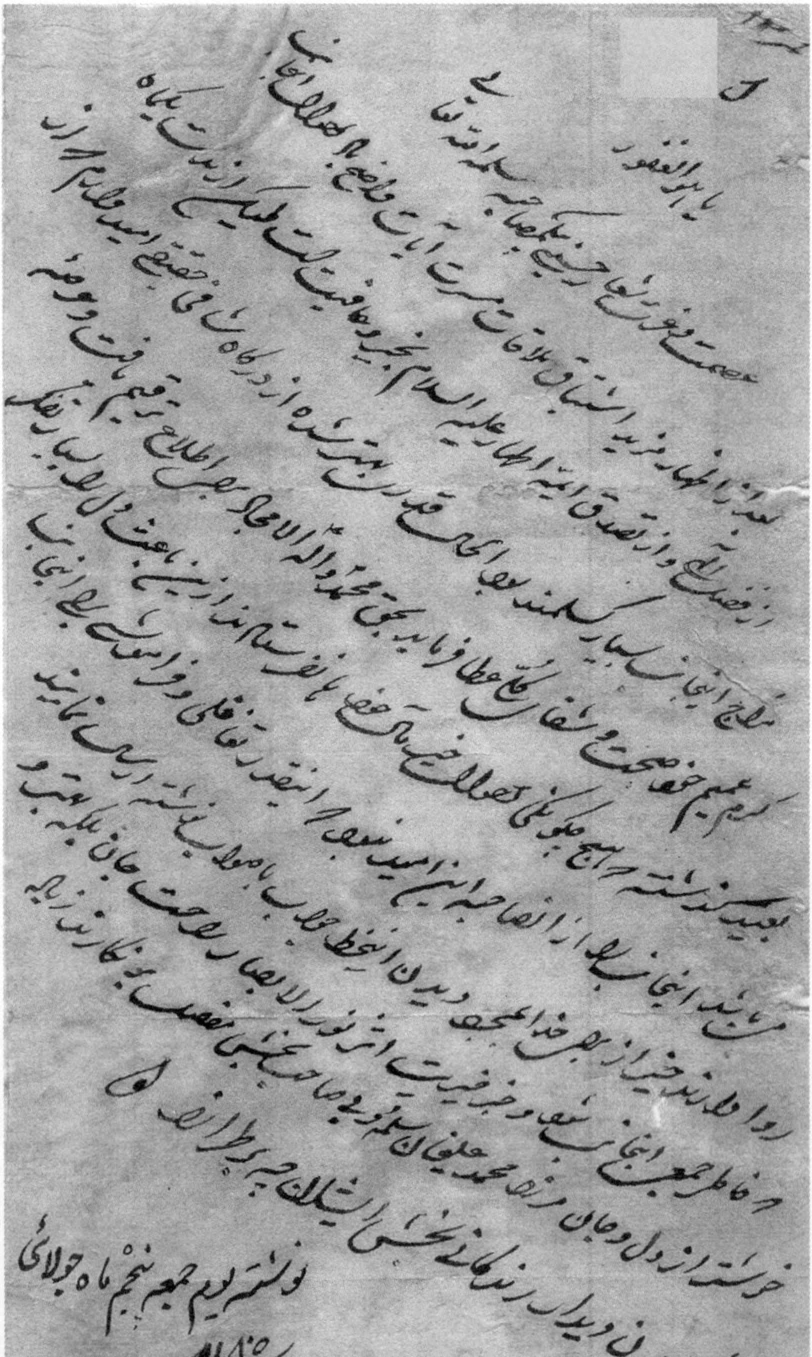
نوشته یوم جمعه پنجم ماه جولائی
سنه ۱۸۰۵

OR 438

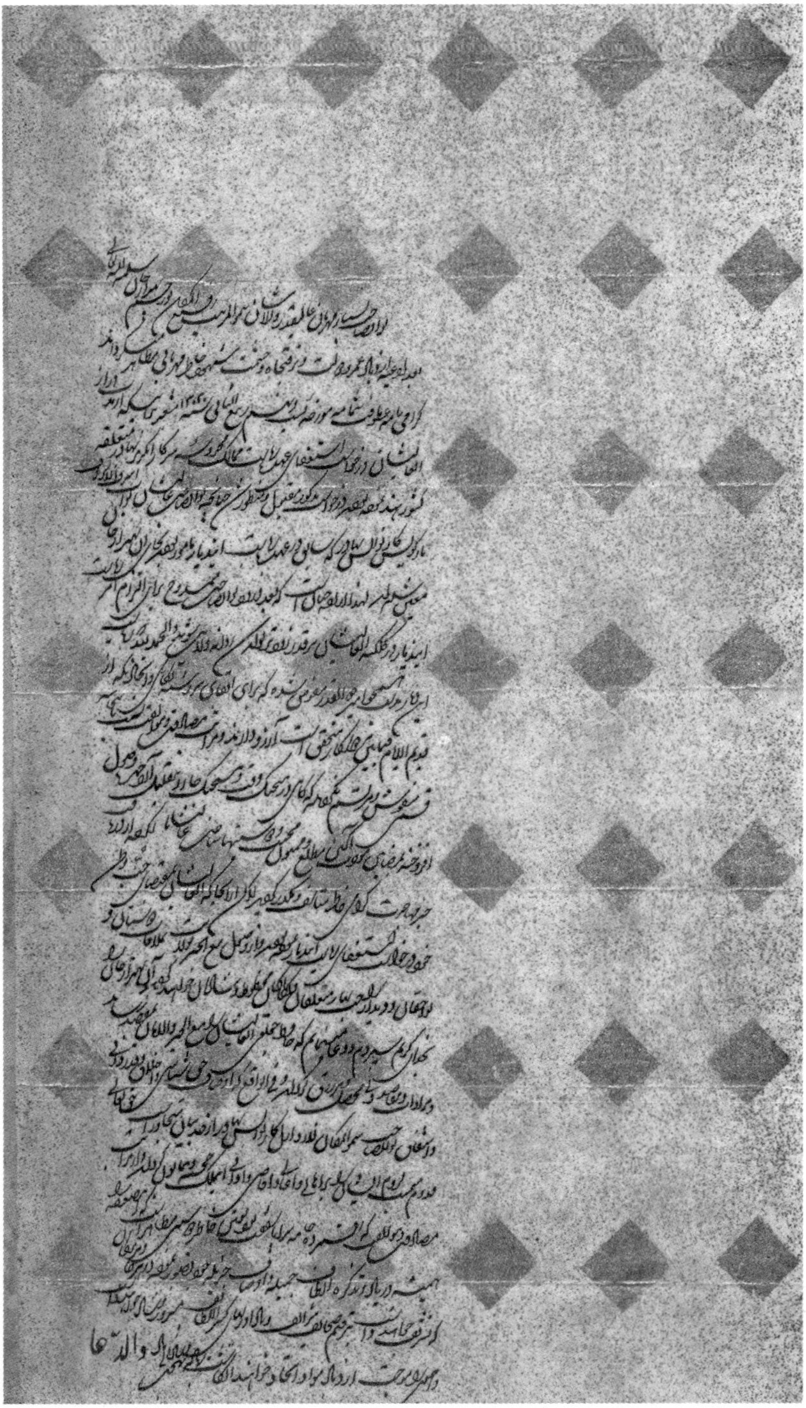

OR 448

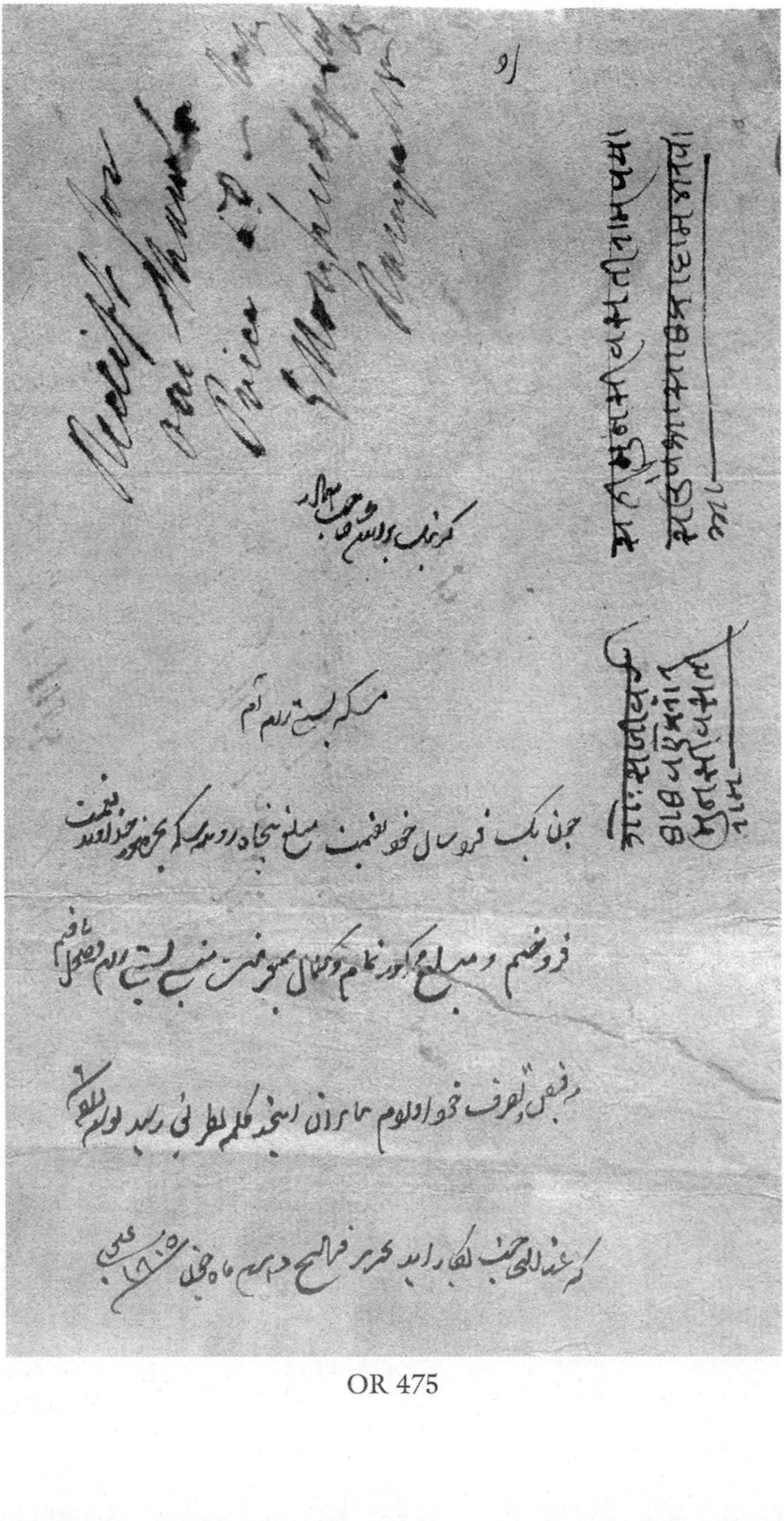

OR 475

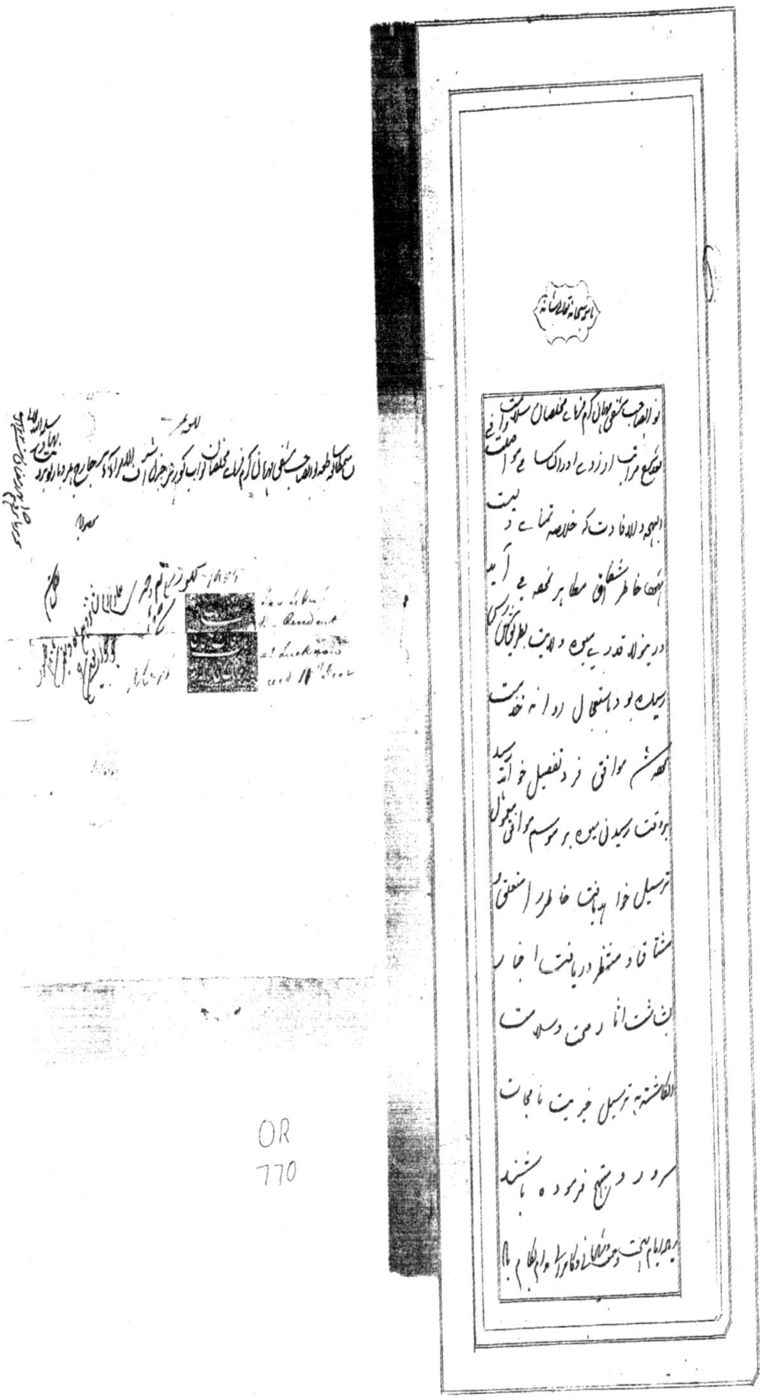

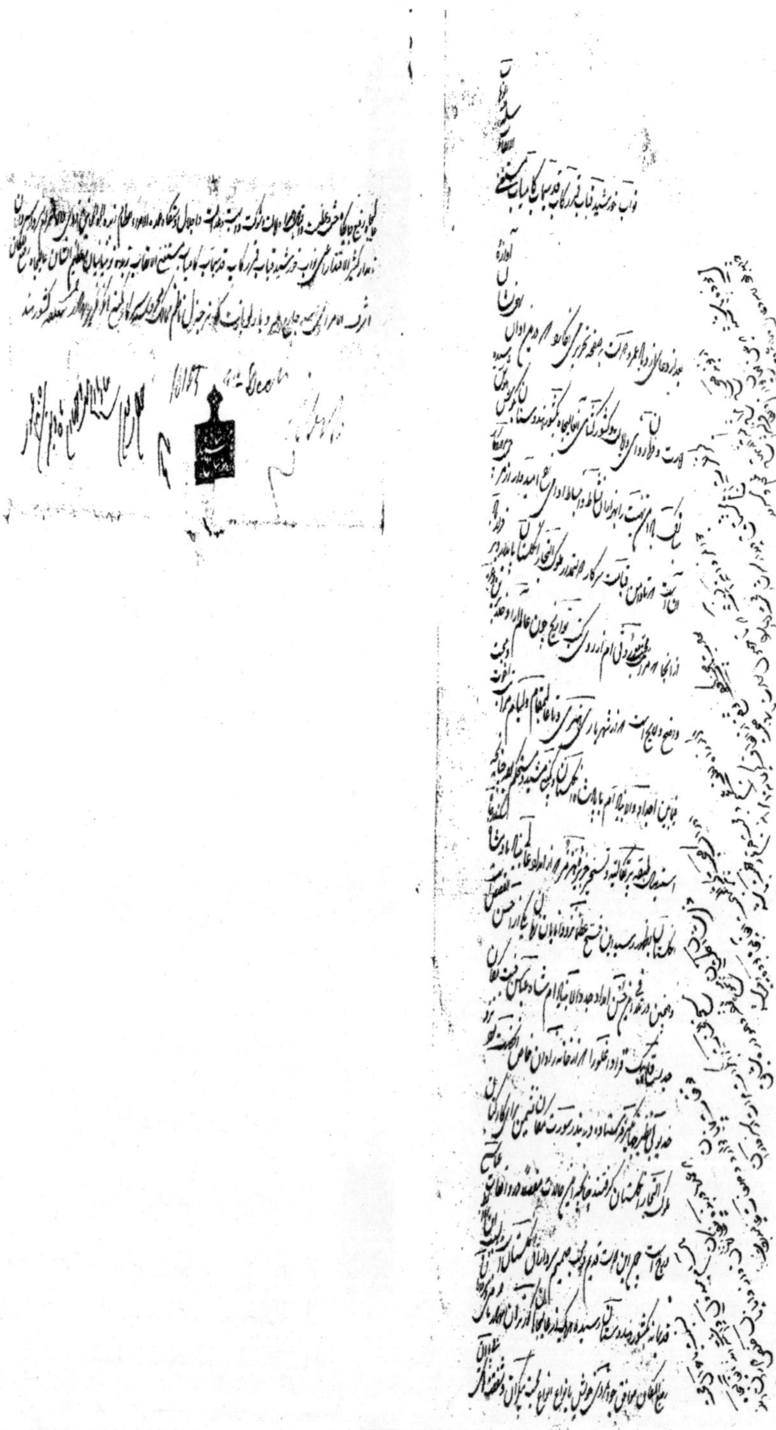

OR 773

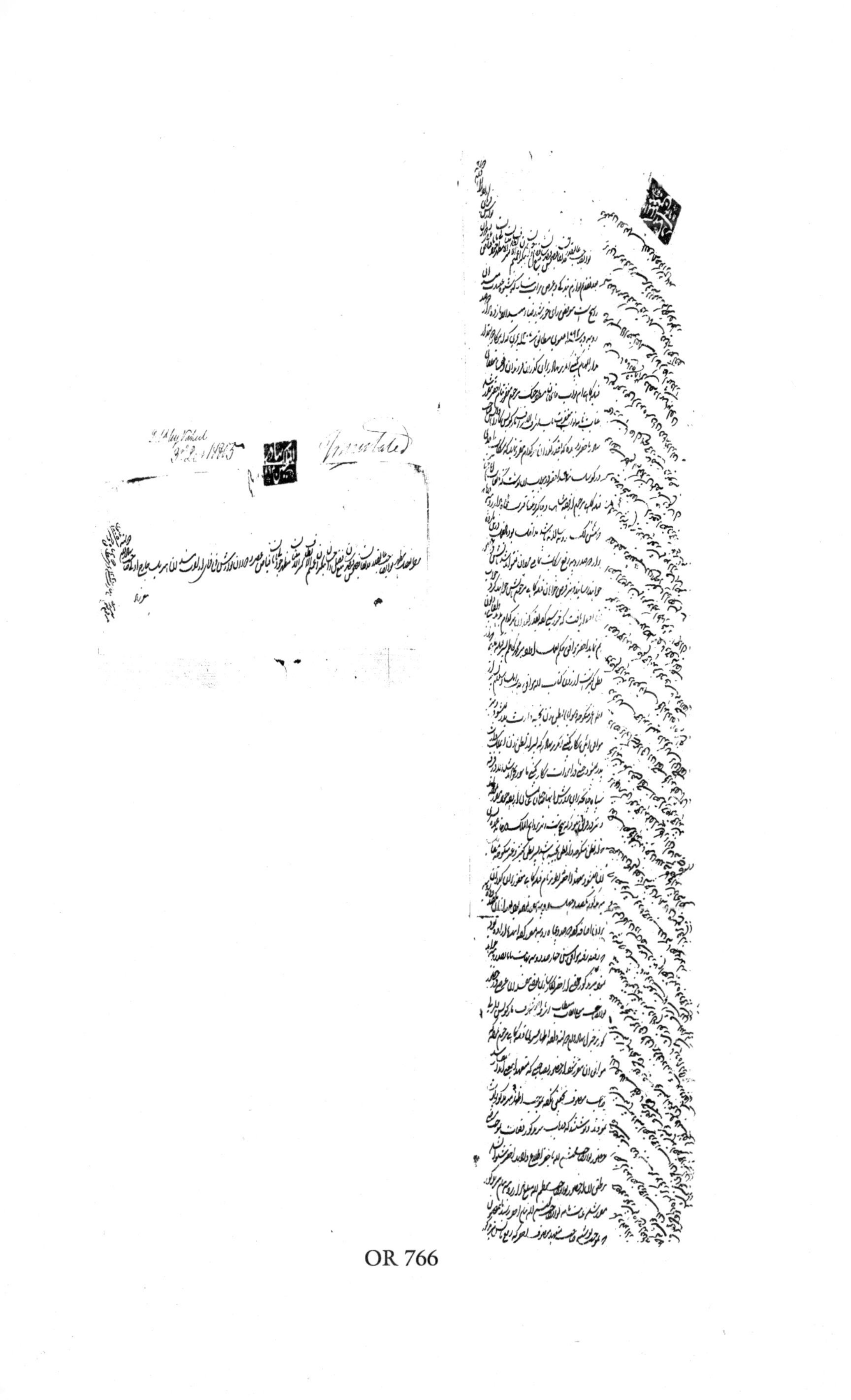

Translated

OR 766

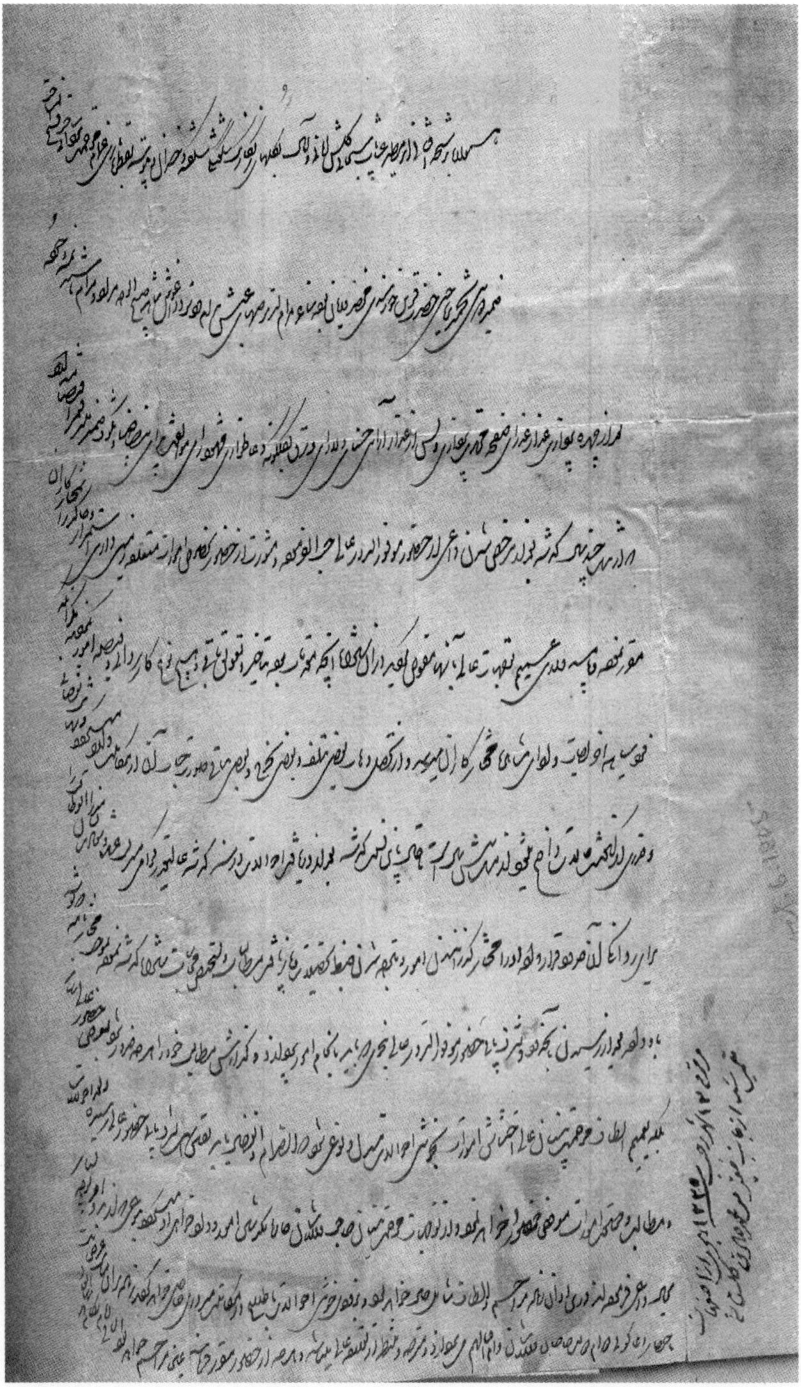

OR 827

Glossary

(A-Arabic, B-Bangla, H-Hindi, M-Marathi, P-Persian, Turkish)

Achaar (H):	Pickle, Preserves.
Adalat-e- Diwani (P):	Civil Court.
Aimma (A):	Plural of Imam meaning a head or chief in religious matters whether he be the head of all Muslims as the Khalifa or the priest of a mosque or the leader in the prayers of a congregation.
Al-tamgha (T):	The Royal seal; a grant of land under the royal seal in perpetuity; Royal insignia; a diploma; a medal.
Amani (P):	Held in trust or deposit; applied especially to land held or work done under government supervision or control.
Amil (A):	An official; a revenue officer; a collector of revenue.
Amir (A):	A confidential; a trustee; a commissioner; a masticator; an officer appointed to take charge of an estate and collect the revenue or to investigate and report their amount.
Amir (P):	Head; Chief.
Amwal-o-ajnas (P):	Goods and provisions.
Anna (Ana) (H):	A copper coin; the sixteenth part of a rupee.
Asharfi (P):	A gold coin; a gold muhr.
Arzi (P):	A petition; representation; written statement.
Bahangi (H):	A pole with sling at either end supporting portable boxes or baskets for baggage carried over at one's soldier.
Bakhshi (P):	Pay Master General; Commander-in-Chief (the office of pay master being combined with that of General).
Bandagan-e- Aali (P):	A distinguished person.

Bandobast (P):	Arrangement; settlement of revenue to be paid by the zamindar or renter or farmer to the government or by the tenent to the zamindar.
Bandooq-e- Chaqmaqi (P):	Matchlock gun.
Barqandaz (P):	A matchlock man, commonly applied to an Indian armed with a sword and shield who acts as doorkeeper, watchman, guard or escort.
Chaudhuri (H):	The headman of a caste, guild profession or trade, the headman of a village, a holder of landed property classed with the zamindar or talluqadar, a title, an honorific form of address.
Chauki (H):	Security post.
Chauth (M&H):	Assessment equal to one fourth of the actual government collections demanded by the Marathas from certain chiefs of India who desired protection from their plunder.
Dafadar (H&P):	A police officer, Commander of a body of horse, head of a party of police, ledger keeper, a registrar, a revenue officer.
Darogha (P):	Superintedent, manager, inspector.
Darshan (*Darsana*)(H):	Visiting temple and seeing or reverencing idols.
Dastak-e-rahdari (P):	A passport, permit, license.
Dastgardan (P):	A loan without any voucher.
Deorho (H):	Threshold, parch, ante chamber, entrance door.
Dhor (M&G):	A man of low caste.
Dhur (*Dhoor*)(H):	A measure of land the 20th part of a biswa.
Dhura (H):	A boundary or boarder or limits of a village.
Faujdari (P):	Jurisdiction of a faujdar, duties and responsibility of a faujdar.
Ganda (H&B):	20th part of one anna, an aggregate of four cowries (kauris).
Gumashta (P):	A correspondent, superintendent, agent, representative, officers appointed by the zamindars to collect rent.
Haakim (P):	Administrator.
Haram (*Harem*) (A):	Forbidden, sacred, the sacred territory of Mecca, women's apartment.

Harkara (P): A messenger, courier, spy.

Haveli (P): A house of brick or stone, house, dwelling, habitation, mansion, the district or land attached to and in the vicinity of a town (the revenue of which were devoted to the support of the military garrison).

Hundi (H): A bill of exchange, money order, draft, cheque, bond.

Inam-al-tamgha (P): A grant of rent free land under royal seal.

Istamrar-e- theka (P): Perpetual contract, irrevocable contract.

Itr (B): Scent, perfume, fragrance.

Jagir-e-istamrari (P): Perpetual jagir, a perpetual assignment of land.

Jagirdar (P): The holder of a jagir.

Jamadar-e-topkhana (P): Head of artillery division.

Julus (P): Accession to the throne.

Kachehri (H): An office, a court.

Kaifiat (*Kafiyat*) (P&H): Statement, description, account, particulars.

Kharif (*Khareef*) (H): The season of autumn, the autumnal harvest.

Khata (H): A register, ledger, account book.

Khilat (A): A dress, a robe of honour with which princes or those in authority confer dignity on subjects, a present, a gift.

Kothi (H): Banking house, Bank, a mercantile house or firm, a factory, a treasury, a ware house, a house built of bricks or stones, mansion, dwelling, residence.

Kotwal (H): A police officer in charge of a kotwali (police station).

Kuroh (*Karoh*) (P): A measure of distance nearly equal to 2 miles (but varying in different parts of India), a kos.

Labada (P): A cloak for rain, a quilted cloak, wrapper, great coat.

Maafi-e-mahsulat (P): Exemption from taxes and duties.

Madad-e-maash (P): Grant of means of subsistence in general and also assignment of revenue for the support of learned and religious persons.

Maghrib (P): West.

Mahal (A):	Palace, house, street, square, court, ward, district, department, land and public fund producing a revenue to the government, real and landed estate.
Mahalsara (P):	The inner and female apartment.
Malguzari (P):	Land revenue, rent paid in money.
Masnad (A):	Seat of state or throne.
Mauza (P):	Village.
Mazarey (P):	Farmer, cultivator.
Misri (A&H):	Sugar candy.
Mufti (A):	Jurisconsul who notifies the decision of the law in or respecting case submitted to him, expounder of Islamic law.
Muhr (*Mohr*) (P):	A seal, seal ring, impression of a seal, a gold coin.
Munshi (H):	A writer, a secretary, applied by the Europeans usually to teachers or interpreters of Persian and Hindustani.
Murabba (H):	Preserves (sweets).
Mustajir (A):	A farmer, renter, one who holds land under a proprietor, also farmer of revenue appointed to make collections on the part of a zamindar.
Mu-tarashi (P):	Head shaving.
Mutasaddi (A):	A writer, a clerk, an accountant, an official.
Mutawassil (A):	To strive, to recommend oneself.
Naib (A):	A substitute, a deputy, a representative, a lieutenant, a viceroy.
Navishtadar (P):	Record keeper.
Nazim (P):	Governor, an administrator, the superior officer or governor of a province charged with the administration of criminal law and police.
Nazr (P):	Ceremonial present or gift generally from an inferior to a superior.
Nazr-e-dakhlai (P):	Nazr presented on the occasion of the arrival of a dignitary.
Nazr-o-nisar (P):	Presents offered to a superior from an inferior.
Nikah (A):	Marriage, legal marriage, matrimony.
Nizamat (A):	Office of a Nazim or provincial governor

	charged with the administration of criminal law and police.
Pargana (P&H):	Subdivision of a district, a tract of country comprising many villages.
Parwana-e-rahdari (P):	A permit for journey, a passport to travel.
Patta-e-qaul-o-qarar (P):	Deed of agreement.
Patwari (H):	A village accountant responsible to keep all papers connected with lands, rental demands and its collection.
Peshkash (P):	Offering or tribute paid to a superior man, a present to the ruling power on receiving an appointment or on the renewal of a grant, lease etc.
Peshwa (P):	A leader, head of a party, General of an army, the first executive officer among the Marathas.
Piada (*Piyadah*)(P):	One on foot, footman, foot soldier, peon.
Pindari (H&M):	Plunderer, a member of an organized association of mounted marauders and plunderers who from time to time issued from their villages and made distant excursions to commit depredation and bring home plunders.
Pitara (H):	A large basket generally of cane or wicker work covered with leather, box for clothes.
Qaladar (*Qiladar*)(P):	Governor of a fort, commandant of a garrison.
Qand (P):	Root of plant, Sweets.
Qanungo (P):	An officer whose duty is to register and expound the lows of the empire, an officer in each district acquainted with its customs, the nature of the tenure of the lands etc, registrar of a pargana or the hereditary registrar of landed property in a pargana, a superintendent of villager accounts.
Qasba (A):	A large village, a small township.
Qazi (A):	A judge, a muslim judge or magistrate who passes sentence in all cases of law, religious, moral, civil and criminal.
Qazi-al-Quzat (A):	The chief or supreme judge under the muslim rule.
Rahdari (P&H):	Toll or transit duty, road tax.

Risaladar (P): Commander of a troop of horsemen.

Roz-e-kalan (P): Christmas.

Rozinadar (P): A person receiving a daily allowance or pension for his religious dispositions.

Rubakar (P&A): Court proceedings.

Sanad (A): Anything on which one leans or trusts, a grant, a diploma, a charter, a patent, a document conveying to an individual emoluments, titles, privileges, officer's or government's right to revenue from a land etc. under the seal of the ruling authority.

Sardar (P): Headman, head, chief, commander, officer of rank, general, chief representative (of a community), president (of a committee) etc.

Sarishtadar (P): A keeper of records, a registrar, superintendent of a court of justice or collector office with the charge of the public records and official documents.

Sarkar (P): Government or the supreme administrative body of a country, tract of territory under muslim rule corresponding to a district or division under British rule, Indian servants who keeps account and disburses money for his employer.

Sarraf (P): A money changer, Banker, an official employed to ascertain value of different currencies.

Sawar (*Suwar*) (P): A cavalryman, horseman, rider, trooper.

Sazawal (P&H): A native revenue collector, land steward.

Silahdar (P&H): A soldier wearing armour, a horse soldier who provides his own horse and arms.

Subadar (*Subedar*) (P): Governor of a province, Indian infantry officer.

Tahsildar (P): A sub collector of revenue, an officer collecting revenue from zamindars.

Taliqa-e-naqd-o-jins (P): A list of moveable and immoveable articles or property.

Talluqa (P): A district, division of a province, estate of tract of proprietary land.

Talluqadar (P): One who holds a talluqa, land holder, possessor of an estate.

Tamassukat (plural of *Tamassuk*)(P): To hold fasts, an obligation, bonds, promissory notes, notes of hand, securities etc.

Than (H): A roll of cloth, a unit of measurement (of length).

Thana (H): A military or police post, a guard.

Tuman (P): Persian coin.

Turk-Sawar (P): Horseman.

Ummal (P): Revenue official.

Vilayat (*Wilayat*)(P&H): A foreign country (applied by the native Indians especially for England and Europe).

Wahabi (A): A follower of the doctrine of an Arab reformer of Muslims.

Wajh-e-Saliana (P): An annual grant or salary.

Wajuhat (plural of *Wajh*) (A): Salaries, emoluments.

Wakalat (P): The office of a wakil, attornyship.

Wali Ahad (A): Successor designate, a deputy, an heir apparent.

Wasiqa-e-maafi-e-mahsul (P): Certificate of exemption from taxes and duties.

Wazir (P): Minister, Advisor to the King.

Wazir-e-mamalik (P&A): Minister of the dominion, the title of the Nawwab Wazir of Awadh till 1819.

Yaddasht (P): Remembrance, recollection, a note, memorandum, memorial, a petition, a certificate, a reminder, a souvenir.

Zabanbandi (P): Verbal statement, witness.

Zamindar (P): Land lord, holder of land, landed proprietor, farmer.

Zar-e-tahsil (P): Amount of revenue or duties.

Index

(All references are to be serial numbers)